MULTICULTURAL EDUCATION SERIES

JAMES A. BANKS, *Series Editor*

Campus Uprisings: How Student Activists and Collegiate Leaders Resist Racism and Create Hope
TY-RON M. O. DOUGLAS, KMT G. SHOCKLEY, AND IVORY TOLDSON

Transformative Ethnic Studies in Schools: Curriculum, Pedagogy, and Research
CHRISTINE E. SLEETER AND MIGUEL ZAVALA

Why Race and Culture Matter in Schools: Closing the Achievement Gap in America's Classrooms, 2nd Edition
TYRONE C. HOWARD

Just Schools: Building Equitable Collaborations with Families and Communities
ANN M. ISHIMARU

Immigrant-Origin Students in Community College: Navigating Risk and Reward in Higher Education
CAROLA SUÁREZ-OROZCO AND OLIVIA OSEI-TWUMASI, EDS.

"We Dare Say Love": Supporting Achievement in the Educational Life of Black Boys
NA'ILAH SUAD NASIR, JARVIS R. GIVENS, AND CHRISTOPHER P. CHATMON, EDS.

Teaching What *Really* Happened: How to Avoid the Tyranny of Textbooks and Get Students Excited About *Doing* History, 2nd Edition
JAMES W. LOEWEN

Culturally Responsive Teaching: Theory, Research, and Practice, 3rd Edition
GENEVA GAY

Music, Education, and Diversity: Bridging Cultures and Communities
PATRICIA SHEHAN CAMPBELL

Reaching and Teaching Students in Poverty: Strategies for Erasing the Opportunity Gap, 2nd Edition
PAUL C. GORSKI

Deconstructing Race: Multicultural Education Beyond the Color-Bind
JABARI MAHIRI

Is Everyone Really Equal? An Introduction to Key Concepts in Social Justice Education, 2nd Edition
ÖZLEM SENSOY AND ROBIN DIANGELO

Teaching for Equity in Complex Times: Negotiating Standards in a High-Performing Bilingual School
JAMY STILLMAN AND LAUREN ANDERSON

Transforming Educational Pathways for Chicana/o Students: A Critical Race Feminista Praxis
DOLORES DELGADO BERNAL AND ENRIQUE ALEMÁN, JR.

Un-Standardizing Curriculum: Multicultural Teaching in the Standards-Based Classroom, 2nd Edition
CHRISTINE E. SLEETER AND JUDITH FLORES CARMONA

Global Migration, Diversity, and Civic Education: Improving Policy and Practice
JAMES A. BANKS, MARCELO SUÁREZ-OROZCO, AND MIRIAM BEN-PERETZ, EDS.

Reclaiming the Multicultural Roots of U.S. Curriculum: Communities of Color and Official Knowledge in Education
WAYNE AU, ANTHONY L. BROWN, AND DOLORES CALDERÓN

Human Rights and Schooling: An Ethical Framework for Teaching for Social Justice
AUDREY OSLER

We Can't Teach What We Don't Know: White Teachers, Multiracial Schools, 3rd Edition
GARY R. HOWARD

Teaching and Learning on the Verge: Democratic Education in Action
SHANTI ELLIOTT

Engaging the "Race Question": Accountability and Equity in U.S. Higher Education
ALICIA C. DOWD AND ESTELA MARA BENSIMON

Diversity and Education: A Critical Multicultural Approach
MICHAEL VAVRUS

First Freire: Early Writings in Social Justice Education
CARLOS ALBERTO TORRES

Mathematics for Equity: A Framework for Successful Practice
NA'ILAH SUAD NASIR, CARLOS CABANA, BARBARA SHREVE, ESTELLE WOODBURY, AND NICOLE LOUIE, EDS.

Race, Empire, and English Language Teaching: Creating Responsible and Ethical Anti-Racist Practice
SUHANTHIE MOTHA

Black Male(d): Peril and Promise in the Education of African American Males
TYRONE C. HOWARD

LGBTQ Youth and Education: Policies and Practices
CRIS MAYO

(continued)

MULTICULTURAL EDUCATION SERIES, *continued*

Race Frameworks:
A Multidimensional Theory of Racism and Education
ZEUS LEONARDO

Class Rules
PETER W. COOKSON JR.

Teachers Without Borders? The Hidden Consequences of
International Teachers in U.S. Schools
ALYSSA HADLEY DUNN

Streetsmart Schoolsmart
GILBERTO Q. CONCHAS AND JAMES DIEGO VIGIL

Americans by Heart
WILLIAM PÉREZ

Achieving Equity for Latino Students
FRANCES CONTRERAS

Literacy Achievement and Diversity
KATHRYN H. AU

Understanding English Language Variation
in U.S. Schools
ANNE H. CHARITY HUDLEY AND CHRISTINE MALLINSON

Latino Children Learning English
GUADALUPE VALDÉS, SARAH CAPITELLI, AND LAURA ALVAREZ

Asians in the Ivory Tower
ROBERT T. TERANISHI

Our Worlds in Our Words
MARY DILG

Diversity and Equity in Science Education
OKHEE LEE AND CORY A. BUXTON

Forbidden Language
PATRICIA GÁNDARA AND MEGAN HOPKINS, EDS.

The Light in Their Eyes, 10th Anniversary Edition
SONIA NIETO

The Flat World and Education
LINDA DARLING-HAMMOND

Diversity and the New Teacher
CATHERINE CORNBLETH

Frogs into Princes: Writings on School Reform
LARRY CUBAN

Educating Citizens in a Multicultural Society, 2nd Edition
JAMES A. BANKS

Culture, Literacy, and Learning
CAROL D. LEE

Facing Accountability in Education
CHRISTINE E. SLEETER, ED.

Talkin Black Talk
H. SAMY ALIM AND JOHN BAUGH, EDS.

Improving Access to Mathematics
NA'ILAH SUAD NASIR AND PAUL COBB, EDS.

"To Remain an Indian"
K. TSIANINA LOMAWAIMA AND TERESA L. MCCARTY

Education Research in the Public Interest
GLORIA LADSON-BILLINGS AND WILLIAM F. TATE, EDS.

Multicultural Strategies for Education and Social Change
ARNETHA F. BALL

Beyond the Big House
GLORIA LADSON-BILLINGS

Teaching and Learning in Two Languages
EUGENE E. GARCÍA

Improving Multicultural Education
CHERRY A. MCGEE BANKS

Education Programs for Improving Intergroup Relations
WALTER G. STEPHAN AND W. PAUL VOGT, EDS.

City Schools and the American Dream
PEDRO A. NOGUERA

Thriving in the Multicultural Classroom
MARY DILG

Educating Teachers for Diversity
JACQUELINE JORDAN IRVINE

Teaching Democracy
WALTER C. PARKER

The Making—and Remaking—of a Multiculturalist
CARLOS E. CORTÉS

Transforming the Multicultural Education
of Teachers
MICHAEL VAVRUS

Learning to Teach for Social Justice
LINDA DARLING-HAMMOND, JENNIFER FRENCH, AND
SILVIA PALOMA GARCIA-LOPEZ, EDS.

Culture, Difference, and Power, Revised Edition
CHRISTINE E. SLEETER

Learning and Not Learning English
GUADALUPE VALDÉS

The Children Are Watching
CARLOS E. CORTÉS

Multicultural Education, Transformative Knowledge,
and Action
JAMES A. BANKS, ED.

Campus Uprisings

How Student Activists and Collegiate Leaders Resist Racism and Create Hope

EDITED BY

Ty-Ron M. O. Douglas
Kmt G. Shockley
Ivory Toldson

Foreword by Shaun R. Harper
Afterword by Jerlando F. L. Jackson

TEACHERS COLLEGE PRESS

TEACHERS COLLEGE | COLUMBIA UNIVERSITY
NEW YORK AND LONDON

Published by Teachers College Press,® 1234 Amsterdam Avenue, New York, NY 10027

Copyright © 2020 by Teachers College, Columbia University

Cover image by Robin Clouet / iStock by Getty Images.

Library of Congress Cataloging-in-Publication Data

Names: Douglas, Ty-Ron M. O., 1979– editor.
Title: Campus uprisings : how student activists and collegiate leaders resist racism and create hope / edited by Ty-Ron M. O. Douglas, Kmt Shockley, Ivory Toldson; foreword by Shaun R. Harper; afterword by Jerlando F.L. Jackson.
Description: New York, NY : Teachers College Press, [2020] | Series: MCE series | Includes bibliographical references and index. | Summary: "*Campus Uprisings* captures the voices and spirit of student activists, faculty, administration, and staff as they protest the racial and social injustices that occurred in communities like Ferguson, Missouri, and elsewhere, and to demonstrate the power and value of principled non-violent activism to provoke change"—Provided by publisher.
Identifiers: LCCN 2019052231 | ISBN 9780807763667 (paperback) | ISBN 9780807763674 (hardcover) | ISBN 9780807778456 (ebook)
Subjects: LCSH: Student movements—United States. | Political activists—United States. | Anti-racism—United States.
Classification: LCC LA229 .C278 2020 | DDC 371.8/1—dc23
LC record available at https://lccn.loc.gov/2019052231

ISBN 978-0-8077-6366-7 (paper)
ISBN 978-0-8077-6367-4 (hardcover)
ISBN 978-0-8077-7845-6 (ebook)

Printed on acid-free paper
Manufactured in the United States of America

Contents

Series Foreword   *James A. Banks*   vii

Foreword   *Shaun R. Harper*   xiii

Campus Uprisings: An Introduction   *Ty-Ron M. O. Douglas,*
Kmt G. Shockley, and Ivory Toldson   xvii

PART I: RESISTANCE IN PWI AND HBCU CONTEXTS

1. **"We People Who Are Darker Than Blue": Black Studies
   and the Mizzou Movement**   3
   Stephanie Shonekan

2. **Black Students Matter: A History of Activism and Protest
   at HBCUs from 1920 to 1940**   14
   James E. Alford, Jr.

3. **Black on Black Love: Protesting to Be Heard at an HBCU**   38
   Kofi LeNiles, Barbara Boakye, and Kmt G. Shockley

PART II: RESISTANCE TO/THROUGH SYMBOLS, IMAGES, AND SOCIAL MEDIA

4. **"Some of Our Historical Stones Are Rough and
   Even Unpleasant to Look at. But They Are Ours . . .":
   Pushing Back Against the Lost Cause**   55
   Travis D. Boyce, Winsome M. Chunnu, and Brian Heilmeier

5. **Women's Watch: Race, Protest, and Campus Assault**   79
   Noelle W. Arnold, Lisa Bass, and Kelsey Morris

PART III: RESISTANCE BY/FOR ADMINISTRATORS, FACULTY, STAFF, AND STUDENTS

6. Complexifying the Narrative: Campus Activism and the Impact on Professionals of Color   97

   Jonathan A. McElderry and Stephanie Hernandez Rivera

7. Preparing for the Storm in Times of Peace: Strategies for Preparing Higher Education Presidents for Campus Racial Crises   116

   Mahauganee Shaw Bonds and Sydney Freeman Jr.

PART IV: VOICES FROM THE FIELD

8. Presidential Leadership in the Midst of a Storm: An Interview with Andrea Luxton, President of Andrews University, on Her Leadership in Response to the #ItIsTimeAU Uprising on Her Campus   143

   Ty-Ron M. O. Douglas, Dena Lane-Bonds, Sydney Freeman Jr., Lucy Douglas, and Brittany Fatoma

9. #ItIsTimeAU: A Conversation with Chaplain Michael A. Polite About Advocacy, America, and Engaging Activism with Andrews University Students   152

   Ty-Ron M. O. Douglas, Ransford Pinto, Noelle W. Arnold, Evan Willis, and Christine Woods

Afterword   *Jerlando F. L. Jackson*   160

About the Contributors   162

Index   165

Series Foreword

This informative and timely book gives a comprehensive overview of the origin, historical development, and current manifestations of protests and uprisings that have occurred in the past and that are still taking place on college and university campuses. The wide scope and range of the institutions that have experienced uprisings that are examined in this book are among its important contributions to the higher education literature on diversity. This book describes and examines campus protests and uprisings at historically Black institutions such as Howard and Fisk universities, as well as at historically White colleges and universities such as the University of Missouri, Yale, Harvard, Winthrop, and Clemson universities.

An illuminating and informative chapter in this book by James E. Alford, Jr. describes the history of activism and protest at historically Black colleges and universities (HBCUs) from 1920 to 1940. Alford provides a complex and searing description of how Black colleges were controlled by White administrators, boards, and philanthropies from their founding until decades later. Many of the professors at the HBCUs during their early decades were also White. Howard University was founded in 1867. Its first Black president, Mordecai Wyatt Johnson, was not appointed until 1926. Spelman College was founded in 1881; its first Black and first male president, Albert E. Manley, was appointed in 1953.

During the years in which the HBCUs were controlled by White administrators and boards, the goal of most of the campus protests was to make these campuses more authentically Black and sites of a liberal rather than an industrial education. However, protest and rebellions on the HBCU campuses did not end when their administrators and boards became predominantly Black; rather, most of the goals of the protests changed and targeted the authoritarian and rigid rules that dominated campus life on HBCU campuses during the first decades of Black control.

Protest and rebellions continue to take place on both HBCU and predominantly White campuses. The comprehensive case studies of campus protest and uprisings on specific campuses in this book are informative and engaging. The chapter by Kofi LeNiles, Barbara Boakye, and Kmt G. Shockley chronicles and examines a protest that occurred at Howard University in 2018, which became the longest student occupation in the history of the university. The authors describe the ways in which social media was a major factor in the success of the Howard University uprising as well as in all other university uprisings and protests since the rise of social media. The chapter by Travis D. Boyce, Winsome M. Chunnu, and Brian Heilmeier provides vivid and interesting descriptions of how student activists have protested buildings on college campuses that commemorate men who supported the Confederacy and slavery. Several of the selections in the book give detailed and informative descriptions of Black studies and protests that occurred at the University of Missouri in Columbia.

The major purpose of the Multicultural Education Series is to provide preservice educators, practicing educators, graduate students, scholars, and policymakers with an interrelated and comprehensive set of books that summarizes and analyzes important research, theory, and practice related to the education of ethnic, racial, cultural, and linguistic groups in the United States and the education of mainstream students about diversity. The dimensions of multicultural education, developed by Banks (2004) and described in the *Handbook of Research on Multicultural Education, The Routledge Companion to Multicultural Education* (Banks, 2009), and in the *Encyclopedia of Diversity in Education* (Banks, 2012), provide the conceptual framework for the development of the publications in the series. The dimensions are content integration, the knowledge construction process, prejudice reduction, equity pedagogy, and an empowering institutional culture and social structure. The books in the Multicultural Education Series provide research, theoretical, and practical knowledge about the behaviors and learning characteristics of students of color (Conchas & Vigil, 2012; Lee, 2007), language minority students (Gándara & Hopkins 2010; Valdés, 2001; Valdés, Capitelli, & Alvarez, 2011), low-income students (Cookson, 2013; Gorski, 2018), and other minoritized population groups, such as students who speak different varieties of English (Charity Hudley & Mallinson, 2011), and LGBTQ youth (Mayo, 2014).

A number of other books in the Multicultural Education Series describe problems related to diversity in higher education and ways in which it can be reformed. These books include *Engaging the "Race Question": Accountability and Equity in U.S. Higher Education* by Alicia C. Dowd and Estela Mara Bensimon (2015); *Race, Empire, and English Language Teaching: Creating Responsible and Ethical Anti-Racist Practice* by Suhanthie Motha (2014); *Achieving Equity for Latino Students: Expanding the Pathway to Higher Education Through Public Policy* by Frances Contreras (2011);

Americans by Heart: Undocumented Latino Students and the Promise of Higher Education by William Perez (2011); *Asians in the Ivory Tower: Dilemmas of Racial Inequality in American Higher Education* by Robert T. Teranishi (2010); and *Immigrant-Origin Students in Community College: Navigating Risk and Reward in Higher Education*, edited by Carola Suárez-Orozco and Olivia Osei-Twumasi (2019).

Campus uprisings and protests have played a major role in humanizing, deracializing, and creating more just and equitable communities on colleges and university campuses throughout the nation on both HBCU and historically White campuses. Most of the faculty of color that were hired at predominantly White universities in the late 1960s and early 1970s were hired in response to protest and campus uprisings (Turner & Myers, 2000). In 1969, one year after the Black Student Union occupied President Charles Odegaard's office at the University of Washington and demanded change, I was the first African American professor hired by the College of Education. The University of Washington administration responded to the student activism, in part, by beginning to hire Black faculty across disciplines, from education, social work, history, business, and art (Brown, 2018). Jacob Lawrence, the eminent artist, was recruited and joined the faculty of the School of Art in 1971. Like other colleges and universities during the late 1960s and early 1970s, the University of Washington also responded to student protests by establishing programs in Black Studies, Asian/Pacific Islander Studies, and Chicano/as Studies. David Llorens, a writer and an associate editor of *Ebony* magazine in Chicago, was recruited to direct the newly established Black Studies program.

Black students, other students of color, and their White allies are continuing to take action on college and universities campuses today to make campus life more racially and culturally responsive and sustaining by protesting campus buildings that commemorate the Confederacy, by supporting the Black Lives Matter Movement, and by opposing the victimization of Black people by the police. The actions that college and university students are taking to humanize and to make the institutions of higher education more just today are consistent with the actions that college and university students took to attack racism and discrimination during the civil rights movement of the 1960s and 1970s that are powerfully documented in *The Children*, David Halberstam's (1998) magisterial book. When a group of Black students sat down at the lunch counter reserved for Whites at a Woolworth store in Greensboro, North Carolina, on February 1, 1960, it was a decisive event that initiated the sit-in movement to dismantle racial segregation at restaurants throughout the South.

Although the "arch of the moral universe is long and might bend toward justice" (Smith, 2018),* justice is not actualized on college and university campuses or in society writ large until citizens take action that is guided by democratic values and a commitment to social justice. The action taken by student activists on college and university campuses epitomizes citizen participation that is essential to humanize our educational institutions as well as society in the troubled and polarizing times in which we live. I am indebted to Professors Douglas, Shockley, and Toldson for editing this collection of timely and informative essays that describe the ways in which college and university students are taking civic action to close the gap between the ideals that college and universities articulate about diversity and inclusion in public statements and declarations and the daily lives that students experience on campus.

—James A. Banks

NOTE

* This quote is often attributed to Martin Luther King Jr. However, most reference sources indicate that King adapted the statement from one made by Theodore Parker (1810–1860), who was a minister of the Unitarian church, a reformer, and an abolitionist.

REFERENCES

Banks, J. A. (2004). Multicultural education: Historical development, dimensions, and practice. In J. A. Banks & C. A. M. Banks (Eds.), *Handbook of research on multicultural education* (2nd ed., pp. 3–29). San Francisco, CA: Jossey-Bass.

Banks, J. A. (Ed.). (2009). *The Routledge international companion to multicultural education.* New York, NY, & London, UK: Routledge.

Banks, J. A. (2012). Multicultural education: Dimensions of. In J. A. Banks (Ed.), *Encyclopedia of diversity in education* (vol. 3, pp. 1538–1547). Thousand Oaks, CA: Sage Publications.

Brown, Q. R. (2018). Thanks, Professor Banks: 'The father of multicultural education' is retiring after 50 years at UW. Retrieved from magazine.washington.edu /feature/james-banks-uw-retires-multicultural-education/

Charity Hudley, A. H., & Mallinson, C. (2011). *Understanding language variation in U.S. schools.* New York, NY: Teachers College Press.

Conchas, G. Q., & Vigil, J. D. (2012). *Streetsmart schoolsmart: Urban poverty and the education of adolescent boys.* New York, NY: Teachers College Press.

Contreras, F. (2011). *Achieving equity for Latino students: Expanding the pathway to higher education through public policy.* New York, NY: Teachers College Press.

Cookson, P. W., Jr. (2013). *Class rules: Exposing inequality in American high schools*. New York, NY: Teachers College Press.

Dowd, A. C., & Bensimon, E. M. (2015). *Engaging the "race question:" Accountability and equity in U.S. higher education*. New York, NY: Teachers College Press.

Gándara, P., & Hopkins, M. (Eds.). (2010). *Forbidden language: English language learners and restrictive language policies*. New York, NY: Teachers College Press.

Gorski, P. C. (2018). *Reaching and teaching students in poverty: Strategies for erasing the opportunity gap* (2nd ed.). New York, NY: Teachers College Press.

Halberstam, D. (1998). *The children*. New York, NY: Random House.

Lee, C. D. (2007). *Culture, literacy, and learning: Taking bloom in the midst of the whirlwind*. New York, NY: Teachers College Press.

Mayo, C. (2014). *LGBTQ youth and education: Policies and practices*. New York, NY: Teachers College Press.

Motha, S. (2014). *Race, empire and English language teaching: Creating responsible and ethical anti-racist practice*. New York, NY: Teachers College Press.

Pérez, W. (2011). *Americans by heart: Undocumented Latino students and the promise of higher education*. New York, NY: Teachers College Press.

Smith, M. D. (2018). The truth about 'The arch of the moral universe.' *Huffpost*. Retrieved from www.huffpost.com/entry/opinion-smith-obama-king_n_5a5903e0e4b04f3c55a252a4

Suárez-Orozco, C., & Osei-Twumasi, O. (Eds.). (2019). *Immigrant-origin students in community college: Navigating risk and reward in higher education*. New York, NY: Teachers College Press.

Teranishi, R. T. (2010). *Asians in the ivory tower: Dilemmas of racial inequality in American higher education*. New York, NY: Teachers College Press.

Turner, C. S. V., & Myers, S. L., Jr. (2000). *Faculty of color in academe: Bittersweet success*. Boston, MA: Allyn & Bacon.

Valdés, G. (2001). *Learning and not learning English: Latino Students in American schools*. New York, NY: Teachers College Press.

Valdés, G., Capitelli, S., & Alvarez, L. (2011). *Latino children learning English: Steps in the journey*. New York, NY: Teachers College Press.

Foreword

I begin with the presentation of four facts. First, higher education institutions in the United States were not built for people of color. Instead, profits from slavery, as well as the actual labor of enslaved African people, were used to build many of our nation's early colleges and universities. Second, when Black collegians were afforded access to what Prisca Dorcas Mojica Rodriguez and Aireale J. Rodgers call "White-serving institutions" (WSIs), their entry was almost always met with opposition, violence, and isolation. The majority of campuses that the first Black students entered prior to 1970 had no Black faculty, no Black history, no Black culture, no Black anything. The third fact is that WSIs have excluded students of color far longer than they have included them in any meaningful or measurable way. Some institutions are more than 300 years old—for 200 or more of those years, they only admitted and graduated students who are White. Fourth, and perhaps most relevant to this important book, is that the most significant racial breakthroughs in the history of American higher education were born of student protests.

The Student Nonviolent Coordinating Committee (SNCC) and other activist groups led a wave of campus uprisings in the 1960s that began to disrupt the exclusive, often violent, nature of WSIs. The Black Student Union and a coalition of other student groups known as the Third World Liberation Front (TWLF) orchestrated sit-ins and other demonstrations at San Francisco State University; the outcome was the birth of Black Studies on that campus and gradually elsewhere across the country. Chicanx, Asian American, Pacific Islander, and Black students stood in solidarity as they demanded that the curriculum at the University of California–Berkeley include their cultural histories and lives. Culture centers that still stand at WSIs were on lists of demands that student activists presented to their campus leaders 3 to 4 decades prior. Also, throughout the 1960s, students on the campuses of historically Black colleges and universities (HBCUs) were protesting racism and social injustice in the larger society.

I am not so sure that WSIs and the rest of higher education realize how indebted we all are to student activists and their supporters. There would be significantly fewer students, faculty, and administrators of color had protesters not demanded it. On some campuses, there would still be none. There would be no ethnic studies or ethnic culture centers. And the mainstream curriculum would likely include only Eurocentric and White American cultural perspectives. These suppositions of mine are informed largely by contemporary realities. Although previous generations of courageous student agitators have fought for these advances, they still remain obviously unimportant to the overwhelming majority of trustees, administrators, and faculty members at many WSIs.

Truth is, most boards of trustees are entirely White; many others include just one or two people of color. Eighty-seven percent of college and university presidents are White. This number is even higher when chief executives from HBCUs, Hispanic-serving institutions, and community colleges (which enroll a disproportionately high share of students of color in U.S. higher education) are excluded. Nearly 80% percent of full-time faculty members are White. Again, this number is higher at WSIs. On some campuses, African American Studies majors, minors, and programs were recently elevated to academic departments, mostly as a result of campus uprisings during the 2015–2016 academic school year. This is commendable. But the reality on lots of other campuses is that ethnic studies remain on the periphery, with a pathetically small number of full-time faculty and too few institutional resources. Moreover, ethnic culture centers and multicultural centers are located in raggedy buildings on the outskirts of campus, in dark basements of old buildings, and in tiny office suites that are incapable of accommodating more than a dozen students of color at one time. These are among the shortcomings of WSIs that activists are protesting in the modern era.

In addition to structural and systemic reminders of their unimportance, contemporary college students of color are also resisting commonplace encounters with racism and racial stress on their campuses. Researchers in the centers I founded at the University of Pennsylvania and University of Southern California have conducted face-to-face interviews with more than 10,000 undergraduates in every geographic region of the United States. Participants in our campus racial climate studies, many of whom are students of color, recalled for us numerous examples of horrifying racial violence at WSIs. For instance, on all but one campus where we have done this research, at least one Black student had been called a nigger by a White peer, professor, or faculty member. At other institutions, students of color had been racially profiled by campus police officers. White people called the police on tuition-paying Black collegians because they presumed them to be criminal outsiders who had come to inflict violence on campus.

In 2019, many students of color continue to be the only persons from their racial and ethnic groups in most classes they take at WSIs. Too many of them have told us that their classmates and instructors make racially offensive remarks in class without consequence; they expect the lone student of color to speak on behalf of all people of color in class discussions; and they are surprised when the one Latina writes well or thoughtfully contributes. Furthermore, they assume the one Latino man is an undocumented American and the Black woman was only admitted because of affirmative action—hence, they therefore do not deserve to be there. Black men are commonly presumed to be student-athletes and are treated in accordance with the "dumb jock" stereotype. Asian American, Pacific Islander, Native American, and multiracial students experience extreme invisibility and erasure; few campuses take the time to understand what their needs, issues, experiences, and expectations are.

At this point, I have several hundred examples of racial problems and occurrences that compel college students of color and their supporters to demand institutional change. These examples are from my research, studies that other scholars have published over the past 60 years, and other sources. During the 2016, 2017, and 2018 academic school years, *Diverse Issues in Higher Education*, *Inside Higher Ed*, and *The Chronicle of Higher Education* published nearly 400 news stories about racial incidents on campuses across the country. Few of those situations and tragedies surprised me, as they are fully consistent with what I have been hearing for years in my interviews with students of color about their experiential realities at WSIs.

Because of their extraordinary contributions to racial progress in American higher education, I deeply respect and admire college student activists. But unfortunately, most campus administrators fear them. They want uprisings to quickly deflate and campuses to return to normal. What they do not realize is that "normal" is racist, exclusionary, offensive, and sometimes violent. It is not as clear to them as it is to me that students of color and their supporters are resisting everyday racism, while putting their bodies and academic lives on the line to improve WSIs for themselves and future generations. Campus leaders also routinely fail to realize how uprisings help actualize the rhetoric concerning equity, diversity, and inclusion espoused in presidential speeches, in admissions brochures, on university websites, and elsewhere. That is, activists help hold administrators and faculty members at WSIs accountable for becoming what they claim to be. These campus leaders rarely choose to acknowledge what I and several others know is true: WSIs will continually uphold White supremacy if frustrated students of color and others discontinue their activist efforts. For this reason, I will forever be a huge appreciator and proponent of campus uprisings. I am grateful to

Professors Douglas, Shockley, and Toldson, as well as their brilliant cast of authors, for producing this timely book on the topic. I have even greater appreciation for the members of SNCC, TWLF, and other activist groups, as well as those who have advanced the Black Power, Black Lives Matter, and me too movements at colleges and universities across the country. Uprisings they led made campuses better, more diverse, more inclusive, more responsive, and more accountable.

—Shaun R. Harper, PhD, University of Southern California

Campus Uprisings: An Introduction

Ty-Ron M. O. Douglas, Kmt G. Shockley, and Ivory Toldson

Education researcher Sylvia Hurtado (2009) explains that "Just as a campus that embraces diversity provides substantial positive benefits, a hostile or discriminatory climate has substantial negative consequences . . . [and] students who reported negative or hostile encounters with members of other racial groups scored lower on the majority of outcomes" (p. 562). In addition, one of the negative consequences of discriminatory and hostile campus environments is minority student dropout rates. A study of students at the University of Washington found that "campus climate is significantly related to the academic achievement of African American students, as represented by GPA" (Taylor, 2006, p. 17). For decades, the data and numerous researchers have argued for inclusive campus environments (Astin, 1993; Fleming, 1985; Fries-Britt, 2002; Tinto et al., 2000). There is evidence that suggests campuses are becoming more hostile. As campuses are becoming more diverse, xenophobic sentiments and racial tensions promulgate. In colleges and universities across the nation, Black students and other historically marginalized groups confront institutional racism and systemic biases in the form of racial harassment and intimidation, racist symbols—such as Confederate flags and monuments to slaveholders—and discrimination in hiring and admissions policies.

In the past year alone, there have been several racist incidents on campuses that have received national and local media attention. For example, racist language and symbols appeared on the Southern Illinois University–Edwardsville (SIUE) campus. One such incident at SIUE included a note on the door of a student's on-campus apartment that read "filthy nigger." A swastika was carved into a campus elevator, and the word *nigger* was written on the whiteboard outside of a Black student's dorm room door at Drake University. The word *nigger* was written on door nametags of Black students at the University of Michigan, and fighting broke out over the university's response to the incident. The phrase "nigger lives here" was written on the door of a student at Westfield State University. White students on the University of

Louisville campus received fliers encouraging them to join a White national-ist group. White supremacist fliers were also distributed around Stockton University advertising the "alt-right" movement. At Purdue University, fliers were posted that encouraged students to join the White nationalist group "Evropa." In addition, a White student at the University of Hartford wrote racist social media posts about and put her bodily fluids on foods and on the toothbrush of her Black roommate.

Those incidents and others add to the negative climate on campuses around the country. In that sense, the uprisings we are witnessing are not simply appearing from nowhere. There is a historical and present-day con-text that seems to have created the need for such uprisings. This text cap-tures the context and climate, and via the inclusion of Voices from the Field, it also captures the real voices of the people who are in leadership of the movement to stand up to racial injustice on college campuses. Hence, the purpose of this edited book is to explore the antecedents, prevalence, and consequences of racial tensions in higher education, and propose recom-mendations to create campus structures that are fair and inclusive to stu-dents of all races and social statuses. The intended audience for *Campus Uprisings* is university personnel, including faculty, staff, and administra-tors, students of higher education, and those concerned with the well-being of campus stakeholders as it relates to issues of diversity, equity, inclusion, activism, and campus uprisings (which are often an antecedent to commu-nity uprisings). The vision for *Campus Uprisings* is for this book to serve as a "go-to" resource to access the voices and expertise of scholars, practi-tioners, students, and administrators engaging in contemporary debates in education policy and practice related to campus uprisings. Specifically, this text will be the most accessible, contemporary primary resource on campus uprisings.

This book is written in an era of activism that has been punctuated and critically necessitated by 3 years of a Trump presidency; at a time when the NAACP has declared in unprecedented fashion a state advisory for Missouri warning Blacks against visiting the state; weeks after the fifth anniversary of the killing of Mike Brown in Ferguson, Missouri; 2 years after horrific but not surprising scenes in Charlottesville, Virginia, left no question about the presence and persistence of White supremacy on col-lege campuses and communities across this republic; moments after the 2019 National Football League (NFL) season concluded without Colin Kaepernick being included on a team roster as a consequence of his activism; and only months after *The Chronicle of Higher Education*'s major report declaring that "White Supremacist Groups Are Targeting College Campuses Like Never Before."

The chapters included here provide insight into the specifics of what is causing campus uprisings and how those groups affected are responding to the uprisings.

REFERENCES

Astin, A. (1993). *What matters in college? Four critical years revisited*. San Francisco, CA: Jossey-Bass.

Elkins, S. A., Braxton, J. M., & James, G. W. (2000). Tinto's separation and its influence on first-semester college student persistence. *Research in Higher Education, 41*(2), 251–268.

Fleming, J. (1985). *Blacks in college. A comparative study of students' success in Black and in White institutions*. San Francisco, CA: Jossey-Bass.

Fries-Britt, S. (2002). High-achieving Black collegians. *About Campus, 7*(3), 2–8.

Hurtado, S. (2009). Assessing higher education's advancement toward a new vision of society. *Diversity & Democracy, 12*(1), 1–3.

Taylor, J., & Machado, M. D. L. (2006). Higher education leadership and management: From conflict to interdependence through strategic planning. *Tertiary Education and Management, 12*(2), 137–160.

Tinto, V. (2000). Linking learning and leaving: Exploring the role of the college classroom in student departure. In J. M. Braxton (Ed.), *Reworking the student departure puzzle* (pp. 81–94). Nashville, TN: Vanderbilt University Press.

Part I

RESISTANCE IN PWI
AND HBCU CONTEXTS

"We People Who Are Darker Than Blue"

Black Studies and the Mizzou Movement

Stephanie Shonekan

One of my favorite song titles is Curtis Mayfield's "We People Who Are Darker Than Blue" (1970). It connotes the deep and unique physical beauty and painful struggle of Black people all around the world. The song itself is a journey from Africa to the Americas, fusing the hypnotic djembe drum beats of a West African past with the funky improvisational jazzy horns and keyboards of African American R&B. Mayfield includes spoken word and sung lyrics, stories and didactic lessons, varying the tempo and the dynamism, all resulting in an urgent call to Black folks to remain steadfast in the fight against systemic oppression and racism. Although the 21st-century #BlackLivesMatter generation has gravitated toward hip-hop to find an apt soundtrack for their modern movement, this Curtis Mayfield song could serve as the theme song for the movement's continuum.

This chapter is both a personal narrative and a critical analysis of the role of the field of Black studies in the era of the Black Lives Matter Movement, a time that includes hashtags such as #SayHerName, #ICantBreathe, and #DontShootHandsUp. Each of these serves as a concentrated point of concern for the enduring racism and social injustice that directly impacts Black people and other marginalized groups in the United States. I will use the case of the University of Missouri (Mizzou), where the movement generated another hashtag that made its way into the cultural fabric of our time and space. The #ConcernedStudent1950 hashtag has personal significance for me, as a faculty and chair of the Department of Black Studies at Mizzou. The aim of this piece is to tell a story about and to deliberate on the role of a Black Studies department on a predominantly White campus in a predominantly White Midwestern college town in times of struggle and unrest.

In the summer of 2015, I stepped up to become the chair of the Department of Black Studies at the University of Missouri. For the year leading up to my appointment, I had watched students, many of them in my classes, become more and more uncomfortable with the campus. When Michael Brown was shot and killed in St. Louis, just the year before on August 9, 2014, our students had returned to campus that fall confused and upset. They began to raise their voices, letting the campus know that they felt the systemic oppression that had led to the killing of yet another Black person. Simply put, they were mourning. These tensions had emerged on campus for decades, but in the most recent past, there had been a national model for protest strategies in the form of the Black Lives Matter Movement that emerged after Trayvon Martin was killed in 2012. Founded by Patrisse Cullors, Opal Tometi, and Alicia Garza, the movement provided a refuge for the frustrations and urgency of a generation. So, when Mike Brown was shot, our students had a peaceful but assertive way of channeling their energies. In addition, Eric Garner was choked to death in July 2014. The spirit of awareness, Black empowerment, and an insistence on social justice accompanied the students to campus in that fall of 2014. Toward the end of that semester, other tragic injustices had occurred, such as the unjust shooting of 12-year-old Tamir Rice on November 22, 2014.

As a faculty member, I was struck by our students' determination and resolve when they came into my classes. My colleagues and I shared stories about how our Black studies classes became spaces where our students could draw connections from the histories, theories, readings, and literary and artistic expressions to their realities in the moment. We encouraged them in our survey courses and seminars to engage with the context that led to the Black Lives Matter Movement. We challenged them to consider some important questions. For instance, in the "Introduction to Black Studies" class, what did Du Bois's conclusions in *The Souls of Black Folk* (1903/2003) tell us about the future of Black folks in the 20th century and beyond? Was the color line still a threat to the existence and health of the Black community? In a "Slavery and Freedom" history class, students could study the Haitian revolution and follow the trajectory of liberation movements in the diaspora as a way of understanding what they were experiencing in the second decade of the 21st century. In my own classes, such as my "Black Women in Music" class, we listened to the chilling lyrics of Billie Holiday's (1939) "Strange Fruit" and discussed how Michael Brown's body, left on the street for over 3 hours, represented a sort of modern-day strange fruit. In an educational leadership class taught by one of our Department of Black Studies affiliates, students learned about privilege and systemic racism.

Our Black studies courses continue to be uniquely positioned to help our students encounter the most difficult conversations about the reality of their lives. In addition, and in some ways just as importantly, the students who ventured into our classes who were not Black were offered a wealth of new knowledge about one side of American history and reality that they had never had, and a precious glimpse into the conversations that have been happening in this country for generations.

From its inception, Black studies as a field provided academia with the substance to fill a gaping void in higher education curriculum, one that Black students had pointed at in the 1960s. Other scholars have argued about the true beginnings of the field (Karenga, 1988; Stewart, 1984), but its presence as a program on campuses began in 1968 at San Francisco State University. One of the "fathers of the field," Maulana Karenga (2009) explains that the field has three major characteristics:

> (a) the primary rootedness of the discipline in the African American initiative and experience, (b) the Black Freedom Movement's indispensable and central role in providing the condition of the discipline's existence, and (c) the resultant and required emancipatory character and thrust of the discipline. (p. 43)

As a result, the classes we offer emerge from a field that allows our students to draw a thread between the 1960s and the 2000s. James Stewart (1984) reiterates this notion of the viability and distinct position of Black studies in academia. He insists that the "interdisciplinary nature" of the field, "the explicit linkage between scholarship and praxis," and "the history of Black Studies as a coherent intellectual enterprise [which began] with its violent birth in institutions of higher education in the late 1960s" makes it a unique field in academia, one that is different from other fields (pp. 296–297). Stewart's second point, linking scholarship and praxis, became the central impetus of our role in 2014–2016. Outside our classrooms, students began organizing silent processions, peaceful marches, sit-ins and die-ins, all of which had historical roots in the Black experience. These kinds of narratives are touched on and dwelled on in every Black studies class.

The tension on campus rose with each news story and topic trending on social media. The spring of 2015 brought news of the deaths of multiple Black women in custody or at the hands of the police, among them Meagan Hockaday in March 2015, Alexia Christian in April 2015, and Sandra Bland in July 2015. Our students, still reeling from the well-known cases in previous years, asked themselves and one another how this could still be going on over 50 years after the civil rights movement. Ultimately, they were also asking their community this same question. The tipping point arrived locally when the N-word was spat at various individuals and groups of students in the fall of 2015. This kicked off a series of responses from graduate students, who had already been challenging the way they had been treated by the administration, and coalitions of graduate and undergraduate students who wanted to know what the administration would do about the racism they encountered every day on campus. Student leaders at the forefront of these actions included student body president Payton Head, graduate student Danielle Walker, and a group of students who called themselves Concerned Student 1950, in honor of the year that the first Black student had been admitted at Mizzou. This latter group tried to get the attention of the president of the University of Missouri system, Tim Wolfe, by stopping his motorcade during the homecoming parade on October 10, 2015. His decision to ignore them communicated an unwillingness to engage with students on the matter of the racism that they and so many others were experiencing on campus.

By this time, I had taken over as chair of the department. I realized quickly that, as ever, the Department of Black Studies would be important in providing the intellectual backing for our campus to understand what was going on. Our annual Black studies fall conference was held in October 2015. We titled it "Black Life: Transdisciplinary and Intergenerational Conversations" and invited professors, staff, students, and community members onto panels to help us all deal with what was transpiring on our campus, in the United States, and around the world. Faculty and administrators, students and staff, and community members who had never attended a Black studies program arrived and participated in the discussions. We were the first academic space on campus that latched onto the difficult themes and invited folks in to grapple with them. (Our Black History Month calendar responded similarly the following February with relevant programming and other opportunities for engagement.)

Later that same month of October, Concerned Student 1950 arranged more marches, and then, in early November 2015, graduate student Jonathan Butler embarked on a hunger strike to demonstrate his commitment to the movement. He would not eat until the president and the chancellor stepped down. In an unexpected twist, the Mizzou football players decided to boycott practice until the situation was resolved. Black Studies faculty and affiliates quietly stepped in to try to support the students. The reason we did this was first based on the fact that most of us had at one time lived and learned on a campus like this, and as Black folks, we knew exactly how our students felt. Second, we were moved by the historical mission of the field, which, as Stewart (1984) explains, acts from the intersection of scholarship and action. Finally, our very own department had been established first as a program in the 1970s after students insisted that it was time. Those students were the reason we had jobs doing research and teaching in various areas of Black studies. Turning away from them was not an option. We could have stayed away from the movement and kept ourselves in our safe silos as most departments did. But our unique history would not allow that. The first lines of Curtis Mayfield's song explains it succinctly: "We people who are darker than blue/Are we gonna stand around this town/And let what others say come true?"

As I watched the administration flounder in its response to the students, I decided to write an open letter to the president and the chancellor, which was published in the school paper, *The Maneater*, on October 15, 2015:

Dear President Wolfe and Chancellor Loftin,

As a member of the Mizzou community and as Chair of the Department of Black Studies, it is necessary to acknowledge and amplify the great social justice work that our students are actively engaged in. For the past two years, they have organized and conducted marches, silent processions, sit-ins, study-ins, die-ins, town halls and discussions, all peaceful and all geared toward addressing national and local problems dealing with race and racism. I realize that as a Black Studies scholar, I am in a unique position to understand that these sorts of actions have been effective in shifting the way that people think about identity and culture in the United States. As a field, Black Studies was founded by this sort of agitation. In the 1950s and 1960s university administrators had to listen to these voices and they implemented new programs and concentrations on campuses all over the country. So it is important that we listen carefully to what our students are trying to tell us.

About a week ago, the United States lost a great civil rights activist, Grace Lee Boggs, a Chinese American who found great purpose in working to eradicate social inequalities and injustice. Her wisdom is relevant in so many ways to what we are going through here at Mizzou. According to Boggs, "You cannot change any society unless you take responsibility for it, unless you see yourself as belonging to it and responsible for changing it." The students who have tried to raise awareness to the racial climate on Mizzou's campus embody this challenge. They are taking responsibility for the society to which they aspire to belong. They are exerting mental and physical energy and time to drive change in this society. We should all do the same. As administrators, faculty, staff and students, we all inhabit and make up this unique space called the University of Missouri.

We live, work, learn, teach, do research, and ultimately, hope to grow as an intellectual community. When a part of our community is uncomfortable, we should all feel the weight of that burden to push for meaningful change.

If citizenship is to be measured by the amount of effort and dedication expended on making a society a more just and amenable space for all, then these students are the best citizens that Mizzou has to offer. The work that they are doing for all of us—across race, nationality, gender, and sexual orientation—should be commended and encouraged. And at the very least, it should be acknowledged for what it is: a valiant attempt to change our culture and our society for the better. If our students feel a need to march, protest, and raise awareness about their position on this campus and the need to address what they perceive to be a racist environment, our job is to listen, acknowledge, think, and design curriculum and programs that address these concerns so that ultimately, we can all inhabit a society for which we are proud.

Black Studies is a department that promotes and supports scholarship and critical thinking about global Black experiences, but it is also a resource for the rest of the campus as they contend with these important messages that our students are sending us.

Stephanie Shonekan, PhD
Chair, Department of Black Studies
Blackstudies.missouri.edu

It was important to put our department in context, to explain that we were committed to the same overall goals as our students—that is, to foster a welcoming campus for all of our students. As events became tenser, a group of Black Studies faculty and affiliates met with the Black student leaders and let them know that we were listening, we were watching, and quite simply, we were there. We also conveyed this in our classes. On November 8, at the height of the movement, we issued a statement that was signed by most of our faculty and posted on social media via Twitter and Facebook:

November 8, 2015

We, the Black faculty and staff as well as Black Studies affiliates, would like to express deep and sincere support for our students who are engaged in bringing awareness to institutionalized racism and its intersected forms of oppression at the University of Missouri. We are gravely concerned with our students' ability to succeed and thrive at this institution. As faculty and staff, we applaud our students' resilience as they work to challenge this oppressive environment. We appreciate the students' bravery and dedication, and anticipate that the administration, including the Board of Curators, will take immediate steps to address their concerns.

After this statement was released, we knew we were in the spotlight because our department began to get hateful calls and emails. Many of the faculty members who cosigned the statement, including myself, personally received threats and even items in the mail such as a box of diapers for the "crybaby" student protesters. Again, we did not have the luxury to do nothing. The legacy of scholars before us had taught us that by the very fact that we are positioned in the mainstream academy, our scholarship, teaching, and very physical presence all are radical acts of resistance to a dominant worldview. Also, the hateful racist response we were getting from the local community, all anonymous of course, confirmed that we were right to listen to and support our students. Racism was alive and well in our community.

On reading our statement and hearing about the responses we had received, a group of allies, both faculty and staff, reached out to support us. This grew our ranks and gave us a buffer against the vulnerability of standing alone. Allies also supported the students. One of them, Dr. Melissa Click, was fired for her actions at the camp where the students had been camping out. On the morning that the president and chancellor resigned, when the students needed some time away from the cameras, Dr. Click stepped in to shield the students from the press. It was her way of supporting the students. Her firing caught us all by surprise, and in our bewilderment, we seemed to retreat slightly. But Black studies, like all other Black liberation organizations, has always been at the forefront of supporting allies. I decided to write an op-ed to the local paper:

Sympathy, Empathy, and Action

Sympathy is nice. Empathy is nicer. But they are both inadequate for real change. They are feel-good emotions for the suppliers but they change nothing for those in need of real tangible support. I know we think very highly of ourselves when we sympathize or empathize with those who are struggling. The truth is that neither sympathy nor empathy require more than a sad shake of the head, an earnest shoulder shudder, a deep sigh, and maybe a few dollars in a basket. Bottom line, expending sympathy or empathy costs us very little. We do the "good deed", we pat ourselves on the back, and we return to our normal lives. The "good deed" rarely changes anything substantial.

It is when we advance from sympathy (that deep moving of the spirit) to empathy (putting ourselves in the shoes of others), and arrive at meaningful action that we can truly change the course of people's lives. Our 2016 MLK Day speaker, civil rights activist Diane Nash, would call that "agapic energy." On January 20, she spoke at our annual MLK celebration and described agapic energy as the kind of force that emerges from a love of people to drive the kind of action that moved mountains in the 1960s.

Since last week I have been thinking a lot about this in the light of the student activism on our Mizzou campus last fall. It was agapic energy that caused our Black students and their allies to raise awareness about the racial climate on campus and beyond. It was agapic energy that moved a group of faculty and staff to support these students. We wrote letters, signed statements, provided food and provisions, and tried to surround them with love and support. And it was agapic energy that caused my colleague Melissa Click to spend time at the campsite supporting the students. Nobody asked us to do it. Something moved deep in our spirits, moved us from sympathy to empathy to action.

I have always thought that when we get to a stage where twenty-first century racism is condemned with as much vehemence by White people as by people of color we will have crossed an important threshold. I know it is more difficult for people who do not experience Blackness every day to understand that existence. This is why we Black folks have spent time and energy explaining what that experience feels like. That is why our student activists pushed hard last year. That is why Melissa's actions should be examined with this threshold in mind.

Most of the reports on Melissa Click at the campsite have misrepresented her because they have omitted the context that put her in that place, at that time. None of the reports have captured her journey from sympathy to empathy to action. I did not know Melissa prior to November 2015. But she was one of few faculty and staff that spent time at the campsite. If you did not spend time there, you would not understand the deep resolve in the heart of that vibrant student movement to drive for change; you would not comprehend the tensions, uncertainties, emotions, and deep exhaustion in the midst of long dark and sometimes freezing nights.

On that fateful Monday morning, I was not at the campsite, or I may have been standing right next to Melissa, trying to protect our students who had reached a fragile state, having spent weeks carrying a heavy load for the rest of us. Melissa has apologized for her spontaneous actions that morning, and many of us understood what happened because we knew the full context. Most of the reports of Melissa's actions that day do not paint a complete or accurate picture. It is as if the larger movement has been eclipsed by that moment. While the media and others rush to judge her on her momentary interaction with two students, they ignore the corollary reality that she was also acting in support of a larger group of students and their mission.

In the final scene of John Singleton's *Boyz n the Hood* (1991), Ice Cube's character Doughboy watches grimly as the television newscaster reports on shootings and police action in Compton. He wonders where the help will come from and then concludes, "Either they don't know, don't show, or don't care about what's going on." This has too often been the way our society has acted in defense of people of color. It appears to me that Melissa Click did show up because she did care about what was happening. She stood up for our students; we should all stand up for her now.

So I stand firmly with Melissa Click. I may be biased because as a proud Mizzou faculty member, I hope that we all stand up for our students, that we all care that we are building classrooms and a research campus where all our students feel equal and safe. I may be biased because as a mother of three Black teenagers who could have needed protection in that camp that day, I would hope that there would be faculty and staff like Melissa Click who do more than sympathize and empathize from far. I would hope that they would feel that agapic energy, that force that is born of love and the push for social justice.

Thanks to our students, things are shifting. Many faculty and staff are moving beyond sympathy and empathy to adopt actions in their curriculum, in their programming, all with a unified purpose of achieving a better environment where diversity, inclusion and equity are true pillars of this land-grant campus. I am proud to be a member of a growing multi-racial collective of faculty and staff that have determined to work together to help our campus adjust to the charge from our students to become a better space for us all, where social justice is more than just an empty aspiration.

Before I took the position of chair in 2015, my colleagues and I had been engaged in conversations about the name of the department. We considered the other names that we might choose, since departments like ours have evolved to be called "African American Studies," "African and African Diaspora Studies," "Africana Studies," and so on. We thought, at the time, that it may be time to bring our department into the 21st century by changing our name to align with other departments like ours around the country. This wrestling with our name had been a national debate at the National Council for Black Studies conference in 2006. There was no resolution. According to Patricia Reid-Merritt (2009), at the session, "scholars and students were perplexed by the proliferation of various academic units and titles to describe the historical and contemporary experiences of African ascendant people in the Americas, Caribbean, and throughout the African Diaspora" (p. 78).

After the fall of 2015, we agreed that our own recent history had served to remind us of the legacy and power of the name "Black Studies." As our students had taught us, our world has not changed significantly in terms of its esteem for "we people who are darker than blue." If, as Reid-Merritt states (2009), Black Studies was created out of "the pride, and the fury, that was part of the Civil Rights and Black Power Movements" (p. 78), and if, as Karenga (2009) insists, the use of the term *Black Studies* reflects a "persistent preeminence . . . in informal and formal discourse" (p. 42), then we consider ourselves fortunate to be one of the few departments that call ourselves "Black Studies." In the fall of 2017, the theme of our Black Studies fall conference was "This Is Not Your Grandfather's Black Studies: Centering Pleasure and Anti-Respectability as Methodology." This will update our focus, bringing in the important aspect of intersectionality, which is at the forefront of scholarship around racism, sexism, and homophobia.

What we continue to strive for in this field, what we work to convey to every student who walks on our campus and into our classroom, is the knowledge and the hope that will help them think about and change their world. Our goal resonates well with the last lines of Mayfield's "We People Who Are Darker Than Blue": "I know we've come a long, long way/But let us not be so satisfied for tomorrow can be an even brighter day."

REFERENCES

Du Bois, W. E. B. (2003). *The souls of Black folk.* New York, NY: The Modern Library. (Original work published 1903)

Holiday, B. (1939). *Strange fruit* (Abel Meeropol, songwriter). New York, NY: Commodore Records.

Karenga, M. (1988). Black studies and the problematic of paradigm: The philosophical dimension. *Journal of Black Studies, 18*, 395–414.

Karenga, M. (2009). Names and notions of Black Studies: Issues of roots, range, and relevance. *Journal of Black Studies, 40*, 41–64.

Mayfield, C. (1970). We are the people who are darker than blue. *Curtis* [Album]. Chicago, IL: Curtom Records.

Reid-Merritt, P. (2009). Defining ourselves: Name calling in Black studies. *Journal of Black Studies, 40*, 77–90.

Shonekan, S. (2015, October 15). Our responsibility [Letter to the editor]. *The Maneater.*

Shonekan, S. (2016). Sympathy, empathy, and action [Letter to the editor]. *The Maneater.*

Stewart, J. B. (1984). The legacy of W.E.B. Du Bois for contemporary Black studies. *The Journal of Negro Education, 53*, 296–311.

CHAPTER 2

Black Students Matter

A History of Activism and Protest at HBCUs from 1920 to 1940

James E. Alford, Jr.

Considering what is currently happening across the nation regarding the Black Lives Matter Movement, it is important to reflect on similar undertakings that preceded such actions involving Black youth and social activism. Parallel to today's struggle for freedom and equality, during the 1920s and 1930s, Black students led a movement on Black campuses that mirrored what is currently playing out in social media and at various Black institutions across the nation. Alongside these young men and women of the early 20th century were alumni and the leading Black academic-activists of the period. As a result of their concerted efforts, historically Black colleges and universities (HBCUs) witnessed a dramatic change in the overall governance, structure, and administration at their institutions.

Black students challenged administrators and their notions of racial differences and inferiority on their campuses, which brought about institutional and administrative changes. These students were often silenced and subjugated by White administrators and boards of trustees at their institutions. What naturally occurred at HBCUs during this period was a mass movement of unrest that led to protest quite similar to what is currently happening today on Black campuses.

UNDERSTANDING THE CONTEXT

The significance of examining student activism and protest at HBCUs between 1920 and 1940 is to provide a social and historical context for better understanding how Black students influenced change and ushered in a new era of leadership and culture at their institutions. Prior to the

1920s, students at Black colleges and universities were nothing more than silent partners regarding the governance of their colleges and universities. This chapter examines the 20-year time period starting in 1920 and ending in 1940 because this period represents a turning point for most Black colleges and universities. There is an overwhelming amount of research involving the student movements of the 1960s, but very little scholarship has been produced on earlier student acts of resistance that took place at HBCUs during the first half of the 20th century. According to Aptheker (1969), starting in the 1920s, campus rebellions took place at the following HBCUs: Talladega, Fisk, Livingstone, Oakwood, Howard, Lincoln, Shaw, Hampton, St. Augustine, Knoxville, and Wilberforce. This chapter examines the various acts of resistance student activists demonstrated on their campuses and how they were able to transform social and political ideology surrounding racial tension at HBCUs.

During the 1920s and 1930s, Black colleges and universities were hotbeds of campus unrest. Students at HBCUs found their voice and banded together to integrate their institutions, address Jim Crow segregation, form student government associations, and create organizations that spoke directly to administrators to address student concerns. This research establishes a starting point in the history of student activism and protest at HBCUs. What these Black student leaders undertook during the first half of the 20th century laid the foundation for the civil rights movement of the 1960s and 1970s and led into what is currently happening regarding social justice and Black lives. At present, the topic of Black higher education has gained much traction as accreditation agencies, legislators, and various segments of the Black community battle over their legitimacy, sparking a new controversial question: Do Black Students Matter?

AMERICA DURING THE 1920s AND 1930s

The student rebellions that began in the 20th century stretched across the United States during a time of war and prosperity. World War I fueled the country with promises of hope and wealth as well as a new era of democracy both at home and abroad. The new century was further distinguished by several inventions of far-reaching proportions, unprecedented industrial growth, an increase in consumer demands, and the assurance that the United States was among the world's most powerful nations (Brinkley, 1993). As a result of these changes, a new generation of college students found their voice on campuses across the country and displayed streams of postwar consciousness that redefined the role of students forever in

American higher education. In many ways, the college youth of the 1920s were rebelling against the paternalistic structure at colleges and universities as well as the social norms that past generations had expected them to follow (Fass, 1977).

The 1920s saw student unrest on both White and Black college campuses. The period represented an era in the history of U.S. higher education when students rebelled against what historian Paula Fass (1977) called "old-fashioned authority." Education historians (Fass, 1977; Geiger, 2000; Rudolph, 1962; Thelin, 2004) have written extensively on this topic, but unfortunately, they have all but omitted the activities that occurred at Black colleges and universities at the start of the 20th century. Fass (1977), however, captures the mood of the nation by noting, "In the 1920s, youth appeared suddenly, dramatically, even menacingly on the social scene. Contemporaries quite rightly understood that their presence signaled a social transformation of major proportions and that they were a key to the many changes which had remade the society" (p. 6). Black and White student protesters shared a common belief that they should have more autonomy and freedom to govern themselves on their campuses. In many ways, these two racially different student populations shared similar ideas when it came to petitioning the administration for more student rights at their institutions. Student strikes and protest at White institutions involved issues such as drinking, smoking, living (residence halls) conditions, and sexual freedom. Many of the White colleges and universities that were involved in the student demonstrations, such as Harvard, Yale, Brown, Bryn Mawr, Temple, Amherst, and Lafayette, found it hard to control their student protesters and most often moved quickly to a compromise (Fass, 1977). Black students, however, were battling White administrators and faculty on their campuses for freedoms that their White counterparts were already enjoying at their institutions based on racial and cultural privileges. What differentiated Black students and White students was the color line that divided the nation. Black colleges were not exempt from the racially oppressive climate that was prevalent in every aspect of American life. Unlike Black churches and civic organizations, colleges were culturally unique in that they inherited and sometimes embraced a system of White control over Black lives.

At HBCUs, students were chiefly concerned with campus life and administrative issues that involved student government associations, Greek letter organizations, student representation on boards of trustees, and eventually, the call for Black leadership. Historian Maxine D. Jones (1985) suggests that "Student protest at Black colleges, however, was not necessarily a product of the Roaring Twenties. There had long been a pattern of resisting injustices on Black campuses" (p. 73). Long before the 1920s, there was a small group of Black students, alumni, and academic activists who publicly condemned the inferior conditions that were being imposed at Black institutions. Students at HBCUs capitalized on the idea that America's fight for democracy did not include them and used that ideology as their premises for rebelling. Black students firmly believed that freedom and equality were rights that should belong to all Americans citizens. Though the reason for protest or the overall mission of student activism on Black campuses might have differed from what occurred on White campuses, the 1920s ignited a mass movement of campus rebellions that changed the landscape of higher education at both Black and White institutions forever (Wolters, 1975).

The idea of fighting a war for democracy abroad and the reality of living in a nation that denied Black Americans those same inalienable rights and freedoms at home inspired a change in consciousness. The young men who left America's Black colleges and universities as soldiers during both World Wars I and II returned to their campuses frustrated and prepared to take up the mantle of protest along with those individuals who had already been transformed by the widespread effects of the New Negro Movement in America. Thrilled with the delights of a growing Black educated elite, and conscious of the war efforts abroad, many Black Americans embraced the idea of the New Negro Movement, recognized the importance of Black leadership, and adopted an unyielding intolerance for Whites controlling their schools (Wolters, 1975).

To fully understand the large-scale protest that occurred at historically Black colleges and universities during the first half of the 20th century, it is important to examine the history of campus activism that erupted across the nation (Wolters, 1975). At these institutions, Black students were concerned with four broad issues: (1) racism versus egalitarianism, (2) education for freedom versus education for manual labor, (3) Black student self-determination versus White administrative control, and (4) Black leadership versus White authoritarianism. The history of African American education in the United States points toward a unifying theme at Black institutions across the nation involving race pride, social freedom, and student involvement that led to turbulence on their campuses during the 1920s and 1930s. Black students took an activist approach in confronting their colleges' and universities' administrators to challenge notions of racial inferiority and for more student rights on campus (Anderson, 1988; Wolters, 1975). More importantly, they were fighting to dismantle what had become a longstanding practice of formalized Jim Crowism on their campuses as a means to integrate the faculty, staff, and administration.

ACADEMIC-ACTIVISTS: SUPPORT AND INSPIRATION
FROM OUTSIDE THE CAMPUS WALLS

The leading Black scholars of the period such as W.E.B. Du Bois, Kelly Miller, E. Franklin Frazier, Carter G. Woodson, Alain Locke, James Weldon Johnson, Langston Hughes, Countee Cullen, and Charles S. Johnson used their academic prowess to speak to the racial issues that characterized the first half of the 20th century. In addition to these men, Black women academic-activists such as Mary McCleod Bethune, Mary Church Terrell, Alice Dunbar Nelson, Sadie Tanner Mossell Alexander, Lucy Diggs Slowe, and Willa Beatrice Player were instrumental in their own right in fighting for change concerning the Black youth of the 1920s and 1930s. These academic-activists were responsible for building and shaping the social and political discourse on race as it pertained to African American education in the United States. They were the intellectual architects of the student movements and gave encouragement to student strikers to resist the oppressive climate that was ever-present on Black campuses. Students who did not resist were heavily criticized by these Black scholars: "Black college students came under public attack from Carter G. Woodson, Langston Hughes, W. E. B. Du Bois and other Black spokespersons and activists for their disinterest and distance from the pressing social issues facing the African American community" (Franklin, 2003, p. 7). Giving way to the mounting pressures put on them by these leading Black academic-activists, Black students began to mobilize on their campuses at the start of the 1920s to express their views on democracy and education. As students started their fight for change at their alma maters, it became clear to them that the leading Black academic-activists had already laid the foundation of opportunity for them to challenge White control and authoritarianism on Black campuses.

The two most outspoken of these Black scholars were Du Bois and Woodson. Du Bois led the charge for many students and alumni who opposed the Jim Crow conditions that existed on Black campuses. He was the chief motivator behind many of the student protests at HBCUs (Anderson, 1988; Franklin, 2003). Like many of his academic counterparts who used scholarly publications as a platform to address social injustices, Du Bois relied heavily on *The Crisis* magazine to voice his disdain for what was happening at Black schools. He also used his groundbreaking work *Black Reconstruction in America* (1935) to explain how the failure of post–Civil War relations ultimately led to Jim Crow laws in the United States. In addition to Du Bois's *Crisis* and *Black Reconstruction*, Carter G. Woodson's *The Journal of Negro History* and *The Mis-Education of the Negro* (1933) challenged Black intellectuals, students, and graduates of HBCUs to critically examine how education was being used by "whites who [had] educated them and shaped their minds as they would have them function" (p.14) in addition to reinforcing notions of Black inferiority at Black institutions.

These academic-activists were inspirational for Black students, alumni, and community leaders who had reached their breaking point when it came to White authoritarian control at Black colleges and universities. In part, Du Bois, Woodson, Bethune, Terrell, and others were responsible for sparking the ideas and laying the blueprint for protest and change at Black colleges and universities between 1920 and 1940. These Black academic-activists influenced students to demand more Black representation and autonomy on their campuses. Black students and alumni read their scholarly work, attended their public lectures, and found solace in their approach to addressing the country at a time of racial indifference (Drewry & Doermann, 2001; Wolters, 1975).

To shed further light on what was happening on and off Black campuses during the era of activism and protest at HBCUs, student rallies were held in various parts of the country; editorials were published in the leading Black magazines and newspapers such as *The Crisis*, *The Afro American*, and *The Chicago Defender*; and Black students found their voice and began to speak out publicly against White-controlled schools. In 1923, Countee Cullen, then a student at New York University, gave a speech to the League of Youth, an organization that primarily consisted of Black college students. He stated:

> Youth the world over [are] undergoing a spiritual and an intellectual awakening, [are] looking with new eyes at old customs and institutions, and [are] finding for [themselves] interpretations which [their] parents passed over. . . . The young American Negro is going in strong for education; he realizes its potentialities for combating bigotry and blindness . . . the main point to be considered here is that it is working a powerful group effect. . . . Then the New Negro is changing somewhat in his attitude toward the Deity. . . . There is such a thing as working out one's own soul's salvation. And that is what the New Negro intends to do. (quoted in Aptheker, 1969, p. 164)

Cullen's words defined a generation of frustrated and dissatisfied Black students who understood that the time had come for White Americans to accept the fact that they could no longer control Black lives or Black colleges. During this same period, academic activist E. Franklin Frazier petitioned for a "Negro University, for Negroes, by Negroes." He argued that "Spiritual and intellectual emancipation of the Negro awaits the building of a Negro university, supported by Negroes and directed by Negro educators, who have imbibed the best that civilization can offer; where his savants can add to human knowledge and promulgate those values which are to inspire and motivate Negroes as a culture group" (quoted in Aptheker, 1969, p. 165). Frazier was clear in his ideas and was openly criticizing the failed work of White-controlled "Negro institutions," which he believed did little to uplift Black students. Woodson (1933) goes on to argue that "If, after three generations the Negro colleges have not produced men qualified to administer their affairs, such an admission is an eloquent argument that they have failed ingloriously and should be immediately closed" (p. 20). Frazier and Woodson both make the case that Negro institutions founded by White people contributed greatly to the "mis-education" of the Negro in America and that the time had come for Black-controlled and -operated colleges and universities.

ACTIVISM AND PROTEST AT HBCUS:
1920–1940, A STRONG FOUNDATION

The idea of HBCUs was just as controversial at their founding as it is today concerning their merit in American higher education. The first Black institutions of higher learning were founded in the North as early as 1837, starting with the Institute for Colored Youth (Cheyney University of Pennsylvania) in Philadelphia. Within 20 years, two more institutions were established: Ashmun Institute (Lincoln University) in Chester County, Pennsylvania, and Wilberforce University in Wilberforce, Ohio. Following the Civil War, several other Black institutions opened throughout the South, thanks to the benevolent work of Northern missionaries, industrialists/philanthropists, and Black Southerners. These three groups sometimes worked together and sometimes worked contentiously apart when it came to organizing Black schools. Notable missionary societies such as the American Missionary Association, the Freedmen's Aid Society, and the American Baptist Home Mission Society were instrumental in establishing prominent HBCUs such as Fisk, Talladega, Spelman, Dillard, Morehouse, Hampton, Howard, and Atlanta (Anderson, 1988; Drewry & Doermann, 2001). These White missionary societies often came into conflict with wealthy White industrialists who were staunch proponents of vocational and manual education for Black people. As both groups pushed their own political, social, economic, and racial agendas, they often subjugated the Black people these institutions were created to serve. Black Southerners were quite vocal about and instrumental in establishing their own schools. Although challenged by not having access to resources comparable to those of the missionary societies and philanthropists, Black Americans were nonetheless determined to create their own schools. Examples of their extraordinary accomplishments included the founding of schools such as Wilberforce, Morris Brown, and Payne (Anderson, 1988).

The Black college youth of the 20th century, fueled by the Black academic elite, were determined to change the oppressive culture at their institutions. They did this in several ways: They asked for the "dismissal of conservative faculty members, disrupted lectures by invited guests, called for amnesty for protest participants, and demanded that the dean of students be a student advocate, not a hired arm of the administration" (Gasman, 2007, p. 122). The student strikes also consisted of students withdrawing from school, forming and joining radical student organizations, creating alliances with alumni groups, and petitioning their boards of trustees, among other things. Black students were simply responding to a broad range of phenomena that increasingly touched everyone within and outside of the college community. Although the protests that took place on Black campuses were aimed at dismantling the paternalistic and authoritarian leadership styles of the current White administration, it is important to note that as part of their efforts, Black students were also questioning social norms and making a case for democracy and education for all. Black students pressed for an administration and president who were respectful, responsive, and sympathetic to the increasingly tense situation that was taking place outside of and on Black campuses between 1920 and 1940.

Howard University, Fisk University, Hampton Institute, Talladega College, and Oakwood College represent some of the best examples of protest and activism at Black institutions between 1920 and 1940. At their founding, these schools were classified as private Black institutions whose mission was to uplift the race through education. For many private Black colleges, religion was a major part of the school's identity. Talladega, which was associated with the United Church of Christ, and Oakwood, which had been founded as the only Black Seventh-day Adventist school, had strong religious ties that greatly affected relationships between the school's Black stakeholders and White administrators. Howard, Fisk, and Hampton, having no religious affiliations, witnessed a slightly different conflict regarding manual education versus classical education—and at the heart of the matter was funding. Philanthropists were more willing to give large financial gifts to Black institutions such as Hampton and Tuskegee that implemented vocational and industrial programs as opposed to a more classical curriculum. This forced schools like Howard and Fisk to either compromise their academic programs and surrender to wealthy industrialists or weather their financial storms and remain true to their academic mission. The biased decision made by wealthy philanthropists to support one institution's mission over another was in direct conflict with the beliefs of many Black Southerners who adamantly opposed vocational education (Anderson & Moss, 1999). The student body at these institutions varied in size, class, and gender, but what they all had in common was a shared identity as Black students struggling to reconcile their educational opportunities on Black campuses managed and operated by White faculty and administrators. During the 1920s and 1930s, trustee boards, faculty, and staff at these institutions were majority White. "Because most early black colleges were founded by missionary groups and staffed by white Americans motivated by religious commitment, it is not surprising that these groups sought to maintain control over the administration of 'their' institutions and did so with the racial framework of the times" (Drewry & Doermann, 2001, p. 55).

RACISM VERSUS EQUALITARIANISM IN THE 1920s

Thanks to a new sense of race consciousness that spread throughout the country, in 1925 students at Howard University took issue with having to participate in what they described as "plantation behavior" when they were forced to sing spirituals during compulsory chapel services. The students brought their concerns before the administration and demanded that the university relax the rules. Students decided to refrain from any further singing of spirituals, and as a result of their actions, they were reprimanded by the university's administration, who claimed they were being insubordinate. One student recalled that it was more than just the singing; it was also the idea of having to attend compulsory chapel that eventually led to student unrest. Nonetheless, historian Rayford Logan (1969) contends: "The belief is still widely held that the strike by Howard University which began on May 7, 1925, was caused by resentment against the singing of spirituals in Chapel. Had this been true, it would have been a natural reaction on the part of 'The New Negro' against what he considered a reminder of the 'Plantation Traditions'" (pp. 220–221). President J. Stanley Durkee and his administration dismissed the students' concerns, and on May 7, Howard students began their strike by not only refusing to sing spirituals in chapel but also by staging sit-ins, refusing to attend class, blocking classroom doors to prohibit other students from entering, and organizing student-led speak-outs by the student council. Lastly, the student government association demanded control of all social activities involving student life and that there be student representation on the Academic Council (Dyson, 1941; Logan, 1969).

Like Howard University, Hampton Institute in Virginia had observed a long tradition of singing Negro spirituals as a part of mandatory chapel service. In October 1927, students at Hampton Institute, dissatisfied with the authoritative conditions on their campus, decided to challenge the administration's rigid rules by participating in a spontaneous demonstration. At the heart of the matter, students were demanding more participation in institutional governance as well as more rights and freedom on campus to govern themselves. Students refused to back down and allow the administration to dictate unfair policies to them, which they believed created "hat-in-hand and me-too-boss Negroes" (Student Strike File, 1927). The controversy began when students broke the longstanding tradition and refused to sing what they referred to as "plantation melodies." Students found musical arrangements such as "Swing Low, Sweet Chariot" and "Go Down, Moses" to be demeaning and redolent of the olden days of slavery in America. The catalyst for the student rebellions at Hampton may have been student stakeholders who felt "Negro spirituals" stood in direct contrast to the progressive changes being brought on by the New Negro Movement in America. The New Negro Movement represented a new way of thinking by Black people who refused to conform to and internalize Jim Crow segregation (Locke, 1925/1968). The singing of "slave spirituals/plantation songs" was a point of contention for many students at Hampton, just as the songs had been for students at several other Black colleges and universities during the 1920s (Wolters, 1975).

STUDENT SELF-DETERMINATION IN THE 1920s

At Talladega College in Talladega, Alabama, students declared that they were displeased with the paternalistic administration and their repressive rules. On numerous occasions at Talladega, students had tried to organize campus clubs and organizations that reflected their cultural interests. With each try, they were met with strong opposition (Jones & Richardson, 1990). One significant point of interest to Black college students of the 1920s was the founding of Black fraternities and sororities. Black Greek letter organizations were established on Black college campuses by 1907, and by the 1920s, they were beginning to make major contributions to the student movements at these institutions. Talladegans, like most other HBCU students, were impressed with the work and service that Black Greek letter organizations provided to and for Black communities. "Very important among these was Alpha Phi Alpha, which in the twenties . . . sponsored meetings in school auditoriums, on campuses, and with churches and Y's throughout the nation" (Aptheker, 1969, pp. 161–162). The work and service that Black Greek letter organizations provided to their community was steeped in race pride and racial uplift. Starting in 1919 at Talladega, students pleaded unsuccessfully with the trustees to allow fraternities on campus. Five years later, in 1924, a new group of student leaders petitioned trustees regarding the same issue. The board reluctantly voted to permit Alpha Phi Alpha and Omega Psi Phi fraternities to organize, and a year later, Alpha Kappa Alpha and Delta Sigma Theta sororities were chartered, but with well-defined limitations. The newly organized fraternities and sororities were permitted to exist at Talladega under strict guidelines set forth by an all-White board of trustees and administration. The board members claimed that they were concerned about "snobbery, Greek domination, and cliques" that would cause academic excellence to suffer (Jones & Richardson, 1990). One student contended, "Talladega has started the year with so very many donts and cants [sic], that we really often wonder whether we are attending one of America's leading colleges for Negroes or a reform school" (Jones & Richardson, 1990, p. 93). For students at Talladega, this battle meant more to them than merely establishing fraternities and sororities on their campus; they were pushing the administration to relax the rules on student governance and for the right to freely organize on campus.

The fight to establish fraternities and sororities on campus was just one incident among many by students at Talladega to effect change in student life at their institution. By 1926, when the student protests on campus actually began, the student body at Talladega had endured enough and was ready for a change in the administration and campus life. That same year, the student newspaper, the *Mule's Ear*, published a plea by the student body to the administration for more social freedoms. They gave the following reasons for implementing change on campus:

> First, we are already, because of our political subordination, robbed of the right to express our true political genius and to restrict us in college would throw us in the world unprepared for civic duties. 2nd, denying us the right to self expression we are also robbed of the facility of group solidarity and the invaluable lesson it teaches.
>
> Last, to restrict the natural tendencies of a group is uneducational, as well as harmful. (Jones & Richardson, 1990, pp. 91–92)

Black students seized the opportunity to confront administrators at their institutions concerning issues of autonomy, racial equality, and representation in institutional governance. They were armed with ideas of democracy and freedom, brought on by the political and social climate that was building both inside and outside their campus community. No longer did they want their institutions or themselves to be seen as projects of charity or as a community of people who needed saving from "unscrupulous moral behavior" as the White missionary teachers and philanthropists had viewed them in the past; instead, they wanted to be recognized as young adults who were well prepared to think for and manage themselves.

TOWARD GREATER STUDENT CONTROL

Perhaps the most widely known incident involving student protest and activism at HBCUs during the 1920s took place at Fisk University. On June 2, 1924, Dr. W.E.B. Du Bois returned home to his beloved Fisk for his daughter Yolande's graduation. His visit set in motion the framework for the next 3 decades of student activism at Fisk. During the commencement weekend, he was invited to speak for the first time since he had publicly criticized the university in 1908 for its movement toward industrial education. Du Bois took center stage at the annual alumni meeting and captured the attention of all in attendance with a message of rebellion and racial uplift. As published in *The Fisk Herald*, Du Bois (1924) began his speech by stating that "Fisk University had fallen on evil days; it had gotten money and lost the Spirit of Cravath, Spence, Bennet, Chase and Morgan," all of whom were founders and early supporters of the Fisk idea. At the heart of Du Bois's address was a public criticism of Fisk's board of trustees and President Fayette McKenzie. He condemned McKenzie for disciplinary policies and dress code restrictions; for suppressing the school's newspaper (the oldest student newspaper among Black colleges); for having "deliberately embraced a propaganda" that discredited Black achievement; for refusing to allow fraternities and sororities or a chapter of the NAACP to operate on campus; for taking the girls' Glee Club down a back alley at night to "sing in a basement to Southern white men while these men smoked, laughed and talked"; and finally, for entering into a "Corrupt Bargain" with philanthropists and the South for funding in return for control of Fisk. At the close of his remarks, he warned everyone who had a stake in Fisk that the "great institution must be rescued or it will die" (Du Bois, 1924). What angered Du Bois and his band of followers most was the way in which McKenzie and his administration treated students as well as their blatant disregard for Black lives and social freedoms at Fisk.

The compelling speech Du Bois delivered at the meeting struck a chord with student listeners. Outraged by the suppressive White board of trustees, faculty, and administration, Fisk's alumni became deeply concerned that a message of inferiority was being delivered to Black students at the university. According to Alumni Bulletins (1924), graduates of Fisk moved quickly to the side of student dissenters and lent their support in whatever way possible. During that same week, dissatisfied students voiced their concerns to visiting alumni and described conditions within the university that were less than desirable, particularly in relation to student life. Armed with convictions of their own, agitated students rallied around Du Bois's (1924) rebellious message of freedom and immediately began their attack on McKenzie and his unreasonable disciplinary policies.

At the start of the fall semester, student leaders made several attempts to appeal to university administrators regarding Fisk's disciplinary policies. Refusing to budge on the issue, McKenzie and his administration adamantly defended the rules by stating, "young Negroes were much more susceptible to sex differences than white folks" (Wolters, 1975, p. 37). Angry students considered McKenzie's statement insulting and demanded an audience with him and the board of trustees. Once again, Du Bois (1972) came to the aid of the student leaders, proclaiming:

> Discipline does not mean the abolition of all rights to student meetings and organizations except under personal faculty supervision; discipline does not call for refusal even to listen to respectful student's complaints; discipline does not demand the suppression of the student periodical, of the student athletic association and of practically every student activity. And, above all, discipline includes freedom. (p. 131)

The students who met with McKenzie regarding the disciplinary policies went even further, demanding that all departments and offices be integrated. They suggested that a Black understudy be assigned to each department head and that, if the president was to be White, then the dean should be Black. As in the past, President McKenzie refused to compromise or even consider the students' demands (McKenzie, 1924–1926, meeting minutes, 1924).

In November 1924, during the university's Founders' Day celebration, the board of trustees was on campus to announce a gift of a million-dollar endowment. As trustees arrived, students began to strike: "They rioted with tin pans and yells; they refused to attend classes and they demanded a hearing before the trustees" (Du Bois, 1972, p. 132). Seizing the moment, student leaders presented the board with a meeting request and petition to oust McKenzie, along with his paternalistic rules. A committee of seven student leaders succeeded in getting a hearing before the board and presented their desires for more student organizations, fewer compulsory exercises, and greater consideration of student opinion. Lasting nearly 10 days, the student strikes proved to be successful. The consensus of the board was that all the student demands be granted except for the dismissal of McKenzie, and finally, all the trustees, except McKenzie, voted for a student council, athletic association, and modification of dress codes. The idea to allow fraternities and sororities to organize on campus was not decided and was placed back in the hands of McKenzie (Du Bois, 1972). Although McKenzie managed to avoid being removed from office, it would not be long before he found himself back at the center of student controversy. Within the next year, McKenzie resigned from office.

EDUCATION FOR FREEDOM VERSUS EDUCATION FOR MANUAL LABOR IN THE 1930s

Just as Hampton, Howard, Talladega, and Fisk had grappled with student unrest during the mid- to late 1920s, Oakwood College, a small private Black Seventh-day Adventist institution in Huntsville, Alabama, experienced similar situations with its student body during the 1930s. Students at Oakwood "started complaining about the conditions at the school, calling it a 'plantation' because of the heavy work schedule, low student wages, and the inability to accumulate academic credits due to their workloads" (Fisher, 2003, p. 114). Disgruntled students offered the following statement to their General Conference (governing board) regarding the matter:

> We are tired of lying. In view of the fact that conditions at Oakwood Junior College are not favorable to mental, physical, and spiritual advancement, we the student body, are appealing to our interested brethren in the field for help. Too long, Oakwood has had to feel the brunt of despotic rules. Too long, we have been living under conditions entirely contrary to God's plan of operation for Christian institutions. (Fisher, 2003, p. 115)

The students at Oakwood not only challenged the institution on issues of paternalism, but they also tried to appeal to the church, which they felt had a moral obligation to uphold Christian principles, regardless of race. It was the consensus of the Seventh-day Adventist General Conference, the president of the school, and White church leaders that "coloreds could not supervise nor manage themselves" (Fisher, 2003, p. 116). This outraged students and moved them even closer to protest against the inherent racialized system that existed at Oakwood, which inferred that Black students did not need or deserve to be in control of their own lives. Upset with the oppressive conditions on campus, the General Conference, and the administration, angry students mobilized on the campus of Oakwood College. On October 8, 1931, they commenced to strike (Fisher, 2003).

Students held secret meetings, organized demonstrations around the campus flagpole, confronted administrators, and rallied the support of interested alumni. During the strikes, a committee known as the Excelsior Society formulated a plan calling for the "appointment of a competent African American as the college president, African American faculty members, as well as more emphasis on liberal arts education rather than vocational training" (Fisher, 2003, p. 114). Much of the students' discontent and frustration stemmed from their strong disapproval of Oakwood's president, J. A. Tucker. Student protesters devised a secret plan to oust him, which they called operation P.O.T. (Put Out Tucker). These activities set in motion a string of events that ultimately led to widespread campus unrest, causing Oakwood College to come face-to-face with what many HBCUs across the nation had already struggled with during the 1920s (Fisher, 2003).

For assistance with their strike plans, Oakwood students solicited the spiritual support of the Black Seventh-day Adventist clergy. Most notable were Elder Owen A. Troy Sr. and Elder George E. Peters, who were also alumni of Oakwood. Both Troy and Peters were in full support of the student movement and felt it was not only time for Oakwood to give students more autonomy on campus but also time for the institution to consider hiring African Americans for key campus positions. That same year, Troy wrote to the president of the General Conference for the Seventh-day Adventist Church, stating, "Oakwood needs building up and if we fail to bring in men [such as Arna Bontemps] who can do this, we cannot hope for the school to have the support that it should have" (Fisher, 2003, p. 114). Troy and Peters's involvement in the student protest marked a significant turn of events at Oakwood and substantiated the influence that alumni had in bringing about change at their alma maters.

During the course of campus unrest at Oakwood, Fisher (2003) contends that a campaign was waged against the institution as a result of the administration's paternalistic treatment of students as well as their "customs of separating the races" (p. 114). The protest at Oakwood ended in 1932 with both a victory and a defeat for student participants. At the close of the strikes, negotiations took place between the student protesters, the General Conference, and the president of the college. The victory was the immediate resignation of President Tucker. The defeat was that upon his departure from Oakwood, he urged the General Conference to expel five of the student strike leaders from the college. Despite Tucker's final demands, the campus protests were a success that brought much attention to the problems students were facing at Oakwood College (Fisher, 2003).

As White boards of trustees and presidents at Black colleges and universities asserted their power to make academic and structural changes, they were often met with outright defiance by Black students. What happened at Shaw in 1919 and 1931 is an example of how two White presidents resigned their office because of campus unrest. According to Wolters (1975), Charles Francis Meserve was forced to resign his post as president in 1919 by angry alumni and students after charges that "he had betrayed the race by closing Shaw's schools of medicine, pharmacy, and law" (p. 277). Shaw's board of trustees chose to ignore the fact that the outgoing White president was forced to resign by angry alumni and students over issues of racial dissidence and again in 1920 appointed another White president, Joseph Leishan Peacock. What followed this appointment was a decade of campus unrest: "Black protest continued at Shaw during the 1920s, and in 1931 Joseph Leishan Peacock, the last White president of the university, resigned after repeated complaints that he was not in sympathy with the Negro race and that the time had come for Blacks to assume leadership at Shaw" (Wolters, 1975, p. 277).

In 1934, the students at Fisk found themselves amid another string of protests. Ishmael Flory, a graduate student at the university, was the impetus behind the campus unrest that took place at Fisk exactly a decade later following the 1924 protests. This time, the fight was not an attack on paternalistic leadership but rather an assault on the moral conscience of Fisk University for instituting a practice of Jim Crow segregation on campus.

Ishmael Flory had received a fellowship in sociology to attend Fisk after graduating from the University of California–Berkeley with a bachelor's degree in economics. Upon his arrival at Fisk, Flory immediately became involved in controversial issues on and off campus. During his first month at the university, he participated in gathering witnesses for Fisk's president, Thomas Elsa Jones, in regard to a lynching that had taken place half a block away from the institution. In addition, he invited the entire student body, along with Professor E. Franklin Frazier, to a meeting on campus to discuss the inhumanity of lynching in America, particularly in the South. In December 1933, Flory, along with several other students, decided to organize a silent protest parade to bring attention to the lynching incident that had occurred near campus. The small group of students who gathered at the protest meeting received much of their advice on organizing the parade from Mrs. James Weldon Johnson, who spoke to them about the work that the NAACP had done concerning such issues. Even though President Jones had come to the meeting to subdue the students' emotions regarding the parade and the lynching incident, Flory (1934), as the chairman of the meeting, encouraged his fellow students to carry on with their agenda and have the parade.

The following day, an article appeared in the paper along with President Jones's photo, stating that he had arrived on campus just in time to stop the students from marching on the state capitol. Incensed student participants declared that Jones's statement was not true, claiming that they failed to march because of a lack of cooperation from city officials who denied them a parade permit. In an attempt to defuse the situation, Jones (1934) called the student leaders to his home to explain his opposition to a parade. Flory (1934) informed Jones that "the parade ought to be held because it would serve as a stimulus to students in other Negro colleges and to Negroes at large to see that Fisk students had taken a stand against lynching and had developed an attitude of attempting to do something about it." The two sides weren't able to come to an agreement regarding the matter, but Jones seemed to have won since no parade took place. Flory's involvement in the protests against the lynching incident caused university officials to pay close attention to him and the subtle commotion he was making on campus.

Shortly after the lynching protest, another incident occurred on campus when members of the Fisk community were imposed upon to accept segregated seating at a basketball game being held in the University Social Center. The center was a shared facility for the three Black universities in the area. The event was advertised in advance, indicating that segregated seating would be provided for White patrons. On the day of the game, Black citizens sat on one side of the center and Whites on the other. The problem occurred when the Black section became overcrowded while the White section had ample space to accommodate the overflow of Black guests. Aaron Allen, a chemistry instructor at Fisk, refused to abide by the segregated seating policy and found a seat among the White spectators. Dismayed by Allen's forwardness, the White crowd became irate, which nearly resulted in a fight. Allen told the White people in attendance that "if they did not like it, they could get their money back." He went on to tell the Black manager of the center that he was nothing more than a "sambo nigger" and that he was greatly disappointed in the way things had been handled (Jones, 1934). Following the incident, Charles S. Johnson, head of Fisk's Department of Social Sciences at the time, urged Flory and other students to take action and stir up sentiment that would end in some sort of boycott of the center. Flory tried to rally a protest regarding the incident but received very little student support. He observed that the university did very little to fight against Jim Crow and failed to take a firm stand either for or against the matter. He also noticed that "students attended jim crow theatres and jim crow affairs without seeming to realize the significance of the thing or to have any feeling of shame when they did so" (Flory, 1934, pp. 1–2).

In February 1934, Fisk's Jubilee Singers were invited to perform at the Loew's Theatre. The concert sparked controversy among Fisk students because it was well known throughout Nashville that Loew's enforced Jim Crow laws for any performances held there. Outraged that the university would commit to such an engagement, Lionel Florant, an undergraduate student from New York and former member of Fisk's concert choir, approached Flory about organizing a small group of Fisk students to protest the event. Florant had resigned from the concert choir because of performances held before Jim Crow audiences in the past, and Flory had already developed a reputation on campus as a student activist for racial equality. Together, the two students organized a protest that attempted to unravel Jim Crow segregation in Nashville and at Fisk University. The first protest they planned was a whispering campaign against the concert to arouse reactions from the administration. Their plan was successful. An Executive Committee at the university met on February 12, 1934, to investigate the students' concerns, but protest leaders felt that nothing was being done to stop the performance. A week later, the Educational Policy Committee decided that the university would move forward with the concert (Flory, 1934).

The following day, three male students—Florant and Flory, along with Howard Bennett—met with the director of the Jubilee Singers, Mrs. Myers, to express their concerns regarding Fisk students performing at a Jim Crow location. She reported their grievances to the dean of the university, who called a meeting with 13 faculty members. Twelve of these 13 members voted to cancel the engagement and said the university should take responsibility for any repercussions involving the matter. The 13th member, a White faculty member and the university comptroller Jesse F. Beals, disagreed with breaking the contract and insisted that the singers should make their appearance (Jones, 1934). The news of the faculty meeting never reached the students or the singers, and as a result, students organized a public meeting to voice their concerns the following day. After unsuccessfully soliciting the help of the Student Council president, who feared he might anger President Jones, student leaders garnered the support of the Denmark Vesey Forum to help bring the student body together. Within days of their meeting, protest organizers were able to present to the administration a petition with signatures of more than 100 students who objected to the Loew's performance (Flory, 1934).

After learning that the university had no plans to cancel the concert, Flory decided to take matters further and wrote to the Black press about what was happening. On February 17, 1934, one of the leading Black news-papers, *The Afro American*, published Flory's article, which ultimately led to his forced withdrawal from Fisk and an outbreak of student protest. Flory stated:

> I felt that if any group should stand out against jim crow, it should be the Negro Universities where some semblance of enlightenment is supposed to prevail. All of this information I published in the papers, linking the incident up with the time of 1924 when Dr. W. E. B. Du Bois in a memorable speech denounced jim crow as it was developing at Fisk, which speech ultimately led to the ousting of the former president, McKenzie. (Flory, 1934, p. 6)

The president of the university demanded that action be taken against Flory immediately regarding the newspaper article. President Jones met with student leaders and university deans to inform them that Flory's article mis-represented the university and was detrimental to the welfare of Fisk. A shocked Flory was surprised, since he had written articles in the past con-cerning the lynching and the basketball game incidents and had never been punished by the university. What made this particular submission different was the personal attack he made against Fisk's administration for accepting an invitation to have the renowned Fisk Jubilee Singers perform at a Jim Crow theater. Although Flory was forced to withdraw from the university, all the work he had done at Fisk to bring attention to racial segregation and injustice was not in vain. Furthermore, he was successful in preventing the concert from taking place (Flory, 1934).

An appeal was made before the Executive Committee to reinstate Flory, but they decided that, for the good of the university, the decision should stand and Flory should leave. On February 24, 1934, President Jones gave Flory the balance of his fellowship for $133.33 and requested that he leave Fisk immediately. When four female Fisk students interviewed the president regarding the situation and requested that he rescind his decision, Jones (1934) told them: "if the whole three hundred and sixty students wanted to air the University's dirty linen out on the front lawn, they would all go, too" (p. 7). On February 28, 1934, more than 25 students representing practically all the student organizations on the campus called the Executive Committee before them. Refusing to show up, the Executive Committee requested that President Jones inform the student body that "they were not on trial." Students accused Jones and his administration of being unfair and failing to take Jim Crow segregation matters at Fisk seriously (Jones, 1934). No one believed that Flory had been forced to withdraw because of the article he had written; it was clear to everyone involved that the university was avoiding a direct confrontation with the White South and its rigid segregation policies.

Immediately following the incident, Jones published an article in the *Fisk News* addressing the university's position on the matter: "The whole spirit of the administration at Fisk is one of democracy. No one individual controls the Fisk program. On the other hand, each unit as represented by the students, faculty, alumni, Board of Trustees, and the public which it serves, has a say in the running of Fisk University" (*Fisk News*, 1934). Jones went on to list his accolades, highlighting the work he had done to raise Fisk's academic standards and how he had placed the school on a solid financial foundation. Jones's article did not go over well with students and alumni, who were still convinced that Fisk was avoiding the issue of segregation. Rumors abounded that the university was trying to appease White donors on whom they depended for financial support. George Streator, a Fisk alumnus, former 1920s student protest leader, and managing editor of *The Crisis*, had this to say regarding President Jones's comments:

> You succeeded in convincing a lot of people about Flory—Firm in the belief that graduate schools cannot afford to be so picayunish, and further, that Fisk is just about what it has been for twenty years—just another institution for the training of Negro students in which the Negro student is trained to get along with the white South as it is now being run. Your speech to the students shows that you have not read carefully the history of McKenzie's failures. He too, boasted of his power to raise money. That is not the whole job of a Fisk president. (Streator, 1934)

Jones had done a great deal to place Fisk at the forefront of Black higher education. Although Jones and his administration's reputation were nothing like McKenzie's, this incident still placed suspicion about them in the minds of those, particularly students and alumni, who came to distrust White leadership at Black colleges and universities.

FORCES PREVENTING/IMPEDING STUDENT ACTIVISM

In large part, campus unrest ensued at HBCUs across the nation. Unfortunately, histories and research covering the student activism that occurred on Black campuses between 1920 and 1940 are limited. We can conclude that some type of activist conflict took place on a number of Black campuses, but little has been documented in individual school histories, so there is not much to draw from. Not every conflict that occurred at Black institutions took the form of organized student movements. Often, individual students stood alone in confronting administrators and trustees. Most frequently, these incidents were never documented or made public out of fear that such publicity might garner negative attention from the local and national community or from other dissatisfied students.

Moreover, students were reluctant to participate in strikes out of fear that they would be expelled, suspended, and sent home in disgrace. The circumstances for many students became even worse after they returned home to their parents. Black families had sacrificed a great deal of themselves and their financial resources to send their sons and daughters to college. These sacrifices turned into resentment as their children returned home from school facing suspension or expulsion. Du Bois (1927) described the situation: "They turn upon their own children like wild beasts, ready to beat them into submission" (p. 347). The Black students who participated in the student movements of the 1920s and 1930s jeopardized their education, their family reputation, and possibly their future.

What made the effort of change so difficult, aside from issues of racial oppression, was the fact that most schools were seeking to improve their institutions while at the same time holding on to financial contributions from vocationally oriented White philanthropists. In such a dichotomy, Black students were bound to lose in order to keep and satisfy wealthy White contributors. Du Bois argued, "It has gradually become a recognized rule of philanthropy that no Negro higher school can survive unless it pleases the White South. The South still wants these schools to train servants and docile cheap labor" (quoted in Aptheker, 1969, p. 157). Du Bois used his platform as leader of the NAACP, editor of *The Crisis* magazine, and proud Fisk alumnus to make his sentiments known. V. P. Franklin (2003) contends:

> Although W. E. B. Du Bois, through his blistering commentaries in *The Crisis* magazine, helped to stir up the rebellions, the protest at Fisk, Howard, Lincoln Universities and Hampton Institute represented efforts aimed at modernization of race relations on campus and a bid for intellectual and social independence on the part of students who openly challenged the traditional authorities. Student activism in the 1920s paved the way for larger reforms in the organizational structures and administrative practices in Black higher education. (pp. 105–106)

Du Bois did much to advance the protest efforts. Many students looked to him as a guide and mentor during campus unrest. Likewise, many White administrators and philanthropists also pointed to him as the chief agitator and saw him as solely responsible in many ways for fueling the unwelcomed protest on their campuses. They accused him of publicly bringing negative attention to the inequalities that White administrators fostered at Black institutions.

WHY STUDENTS MATTER

The students' petition for democracy on their campuses ultimately resulted in relaxed school policies and freedom on campus to engage in more social activities. Black college students, armed with social convictions and a shared philosophy of change, garnered widespread buy-in for their cause. Gasman (2007) contends, "The students, who believed that Black people ought to control their own educational institutions, translated their broad concerns about political nationalism into a desire to determine educational policies at Black colleges" (pp. 121–122). The catalyst for these institutional changes was Black students pushing White administrators into uncomfortable spaces on their campuses. These efforts caused a revolutionary shift in the culture and structure of these institutions, bringing about a much-needed awaking and cultural consciousness for everyone involved.

Black students shifted these institutions from racism to egalitarianism, from education for manual labor to education for freedom, from total administrative control to student self-determination, from White administrators to Black leadership. It can be argued that Black students were simply petitioning for social change and against paternalistic leadership, but what actually transpired was the unmasking of an oppressive White power structure that began to fall at the feet of Black students who used their collective voice to fight for their institutions. Because of the past generation of Black men and women who understood the power of protest and activism at HBCUs during the 1920s and 1930s, a new generation of Black students will continue in that same spirit of social justice and racial uplift on campuses today—which is why Black student activism matters at HBCUs.

REFERENCES

Anderson, E., & Moss, A. A. (1999). *Dangerous donations: Northern philanthropy and southern black education, 1902–1930*. Columbia, MO: University of Missouri Press.

Anderson, J. (1988). *The education of blacks in the South, 1890–1935*. Chapel Hill, NC: The University of North Carolina Press.

Aptheker, H. (1969, Spring). The Negro college student in the 1920s—years of preparation and protest: An introduction. *Science and Society*, 33(2).

Brinkley, A. (1993). *The unfinished nation: A concise history of the American people*. New York, NY: McGraw-Hill.

Drewry, H., & Doermann, H. (2001). *Stand and prosper: Private black colleges and their students*. Princeton, NJ: Princeton University Press.

Du Bois, W. E. B. (1924). Speech to alumni (commencement/alumni reunion). The John Hope and Aurelia E. Franklin Library at Fisk University Archival Collection.

Du Bois, W. E. B. (1935). *Black reconstruction in America*. New York, NY: Macmillan Publishing Company.

Du Bois, W. E. B. (1972). *The emerging thoughts of W. E. B Du Bois: Essays and editorials from the crisis*. New York, NY: Simon & Schuster.

Dyson, W. (1941). *Howard University: Capstone of Negro education, a history, 1867–1940*. Washington, DC: Howard University Press.

Fass, P. (1977). *The damned and the beautiful: American youth in the 1920s*. New York, NY: Oxford University Press.

Fisher, H. (2003). Oakwood college students' quest for social justice before and during the civil rights era. *The Journal of African American History*, 88(2), 110–125.

Fisk News. (1925–1947). Published by Fisk in the interest of alumni. The John Hope and Aurelia E. Franklin Library at Fisk University Archival Collection.

Flory, I. P. (1934). Student statement: Ishmael Flory Box. The John Hope and Aurelia E. Franklin Library at Fisk University Archival Collection.

Franklin, V. P. (2003, Spring). Introduction: African American student activism in the 20th century. *The Journal of African American History*, 88(2), 105–109.

Gasman, M. (2007). *Envisioning Black colleges: A history of the United Negro College Fund*. Baltimore, MD: Johns Hopkins University Press.

Geiger, R. (2000). *The American college in the 19th century*. Nashville, TN: Vanderbilt University Press.

Jones, M. D., (1985). Student unrest at Talladega College, 1887–1914. *The Journal of Negro History*, 70(3/4), 73–81.

Jones, M. D., & Richardson, J. (1990). *Talladega College: The first century*. Tuscaloosa, AL: The University of Alabama Press.

Jones, T. E. (1934). Thomas E. Jones collection. The John Hope and Aurelia E. Franklin Library at Fisk University Archival Collection.

Locke, A. (Ed.). (1968). *The new Negro*. New York, NY: Atheneum. (Original work published in 1925)

Logan, R. W. (1969). *Howard University: The first 100 years, 1867–1967*. New York, NY: New York University Press.

McKenzie, F. (1924–1926). Fayette McKenzie collection. The John Hope and Aurelia E. Franklin Library at Fisk University Archival Collection.

Rudolph, F. (1962). *The American college and university: A history*. New York, NY: Alfred A Knopf.

Streator, G. (1934). Letter to Thomas E. Jones. Thomas E. Jones collection. The John Hope and Aurelia E. Franklin Library at Fisk University Archival Collection (Box 34, Folder 20).

Student Strike File. (1927). The University Museum and Archives at Hampton University: The Fisk Herald (1924 & 1925). The John Hope and Aurelia E. Franklin Library at Fisk University Archival Collection.

Thelin, J. (2004). *A history of American higher education*. Baltimore, MD: Johns Hopkins University Press.

Wolters, R. (1975). *The new Negro on campus: Black college rebellions in the 1920s*. Princeton, NJ: Princeton University Press.

Woodson, C. G. (1916–1940). *The Journal of Negro History*. University of Chicago Press: The Association for the Study of Negro Life and History

Woodson, C. G. (1933). *The mis-education of the Negro*. Washington, DC: Associated Publishers.

CHAPTER 3

Black on Black Love

Protesting to Be Heard at an HBCU

Kofi LeNiles, Barbara Boakye, and Kmt G. Shockley

For decades, researchers have been reporting that students who attend historically Black colleges or universities (HBCUs) are more academically successful and experience more success in their careers. However, HBCUs often do not have the facilities and resources of predominantly White institutions (PWIs). This chapter focuses on the complexities of being a student at an HBCU and needing to protest the institution to pay more attention to student voices related to challenges within the institution. The chapter maps the strategies that students used to protest the challenges on campus, discusses the sacrifices students made to engage in prolonged protest, unveils the strategies that students used to bring attention to their cause, and captures the voices of student leaders as they employed tactics to pressure university administrations to meet their demands.

WHY WE MUST BE HEARD

College and university campuses were created in part to instill the skills and teach the processes needed for students' continued success in their chosen profession after postsecondary completion (Habermas, 1965). Habermas (1965) also suggests that postsecondary institutions were established to "transmit, interpret, and develop the cultural traditions of the society" and "forms the political consciousness of its students" (pp. 2–3). As college students develop their political consciousness on university campuses, some of them identify local and national issues that they feel must be addressed through protest. For example, in 2012, college and high school students across Quebec, Canada, staged a 6-month protest against the administration when school officials proposed a 75% increase in tuition (Spiegel, 2015). In another case, in 1992, students at Brown University took over the administration building, protesting against university admissions practices, until their eventual arrest ("Brown University students," 1992). These two incidents are representative of the types of issues that many university students have chosen to protest over the past 30 years. Much of the research conducted on university protests centers around students protesting for specific changes to personnel or administration policy; however, not a single body of work focuses on protests at historically Black colleges or universities in which students are demanding changes to university bylaws and increased student representation on the board of trustees. This chapter focuses on the student protest that occurred on Howard University's (Howard) campus during the spring 2018 semester. Specifically, we discuss students' protest strategies on campus, the sacrifices students made to engage in prolonged protest, strategies that students used to bring attention to their cause, and the voices of student leaders as they employed new age tactics to pressure the university administration to meet their demands.

On Thursday, March 29, 2018, Howard administrators were conducting business as usual when more than 100 students quickly and unexpectedly began filing into the lobby of the administrative building. Within minutes, students began chanting and playing music, disrupting all business in the building; it soon became apparent that the students had no intention to vacate the building. The phones in the offices of the university's president, provost, and police chief rang to inform the administration of the situation. However, thanks to Instagram, Twitter, Facebook, and Snapchat, people across the country already knew what Howard's administration was just learning: A student occupation had begun.

Ground Zero for the occupation was the building that contained the offices of the bursar, financial aid, student accounts, and the provost and the president. The occupation was organized and led by an on-campus student activist group named HUResist. HUResist gained popularity across campus and garnered national attention in September 2017, when its members continually interrupted an on-campus speech by former FBI director James Comey, wrote a caustic letter against the appointment of Comey as the Howard convocation keynote speaker and endowed chair in public policy for the 2017–2018 school year, and released a video mocking some of Comey's previous professional work. One of the first acts undertaken by HUResist members after taking over the building in March 2018 was to post the students' demands on posters hung outside the building. Outside the administration building, a crowd began to gather. Each person in the crowd read the demands quietly (see Figure 3.1). After approximately 2 minutes had

Figure 3.1. A Gathering of Students and Student Leaders Reviewing Information About the Student Protest

Photograph by coauthor Barbara Boakye

passed, the crowd began speaking to one another and pointing at the specific demand(s) that resonated with them personally. The continuous nods of approval affirmed that the nine demands were student-centered and worth the imminent battle with university officials. The nine demands posted were as follows:

1. We demand that Howard University provide adequate housing for all students under the age of 21 and extend the Fall 2018 housing deposit deadline to May 1.
2. We demand the immediate end to unsubstantiated tuition hikes and complete access to administrative salaries.
3. We demand that Howard University actively fight rape culture on campus to prevent sexual assault.
4. We demand that Howard University implement a grievance system to hold faculty and administrators accountable in their language and actions toward students with marginalized identities.
5. We demand that Howard University hire more counselors and implement an inclusive attendance policy that accounts for mental and emotional health issues.
6. We demand the immediate disarming of campus police officers and the formation of a Police Oversight Committee controlled by students, faculty, staff, and off-campus community representatives.
7. We demand that Howard University allocate more resources toward combating food insecurity and gentrification within the LeDroit-Shaw community.
8. We demand the immediate resignation of President Wayne A.I. Frederick and the Executive Committee of the Board of Trustees.
9. We demand that students have the power to democratically influence the decisions of the administration and the Board of Trustees by way of popular vote.

After posting the demands, the protesters went back inside the building and discussed the need for solidarity and organization. HUResist leadership held a meeting on the first night of the occupation to clarify to all protesting students that the occupation could potentially last for days or weeks. Within 24 hours, occupying students left and returned with air mattresses, futons, blankets, comforters, computers, stereos, and studying materials. What began with students disrupting university business ended in the longest student occupation in the history of Howard. Using social media, grassroots activism, alumni support, and their bodies, Howard students occupied the school's central administrative building for 9 consecutive days. Led by undergraduate student activists, protesters forced board members and university administrators to engage in conversations focused on changing the university's culture and bylaws.

Howard currently has approximately 10,000 students enrolled, and about 6,900 of these are undergraduates. While graduate students comprise a large percentage of Howard's student population, it is significant to note that this movement was led by undergraduate student activists. Throughout Howard's history, the university's students have been involved in national issues. Most notably, Howard Law School students played a significant role in the *Brown v. Board of Education* case, and more recently, Howard's School of Education graduate students and professors developed and implemented a national comprehensive urban superintendent academy focused on the enhancement of K–12 school administrators' political, intellectual, and financial competency so they are able to take a more dynamic approach in addressing the educational needs of students of color. Both of these actions taken by Howard graduate students were national in scope, while the actions taken by the undergraduate students during the protest were at the university level and were centered around improving the culture and administrative governing structure. This is significant because the protest led by the undergraduates in spring 2018 forced the board and other administrators to reinvest in the university's culture, which has proven to produce students who engage in activism at the national level.

THE UNIVERSITY

Howard was established in the 19th century and chartered as a private, nonprofit HBCU in the Mid-Atlantic region with a mission to provide high-quality education to Black students at the undergraduate, graduate, and professional levels. Howard has an enduring commitment to advance the education of underrepresented populations domestically and internationally. In 2018, the quality of Howard University undergraduate teaching ranked in the top 35 nationally, and Howard as a university ranked in the top 100 (*U.S News*, 2018). While Howard's reputation for academic rigor and quality are well recognized, the university's facilities are deteriorating, and in some cases, dilapidated. For example, in January 2018, the university postponed the start of the spring semester for more than a week due to burst pipes and collapsed ceilings across the campus (Goodwin, 2018). The building damage across campus included dormitories and historical learning halls.

The news of the unprecedented postponement of undergraduate and graduate courses and damaged buildings sparked a clarion call among students for systemic change across the university. Students following the lead of HUResist challenged the school's board and administration to explain why maintenance across the campus had been delayed or ignored for so many years. Moreover, students expressed their lack of faith in the university's leadership and stressed the need for Howard to make drastic changes to the university's Board of Trustees, president, and bylaws.

FOLLOW ME OR TWEET ME:
#STUDENTDEMANDSANDPROTESTSTRATEGIES

Garnering alumni support was a key strategy used by the protesters. On April 2, 2018, the local Fox News affiliate ran a story entitled "Alumni, Students Take Sides as Howard University Protest Draws on" (Coffin, 2018). The story highlighted the lack of consensus among students and alumni regarding the protest. While some alumni supported the protest, others felt it brought negative attention to the university and that student protesters should use other methods, such as petitions and open letters, to share their grievances with university officials. Although division existed among alumni, those who supported the protest sent food and water and offered legal advice. HUResist student leaders spoke and worked with alumni to better understand how to leverage the occupation strategically to obtain their demands. For example, the Howard University bylaws are a legal document; hence, to make any changes would require an understanding of the law and the legal process. Protest leaders understood their limitations regarding such matters and worked with experts in the field daily to create talking points for negotiation before meeting with members from the Board of Trustees or other university officials. As the protesters were increasing their knowledge of the university's inner workings, the #TakeBackHU campaign trended on social media.

#TakeBackHU was the social media hashtag used by Howard students and alumni to voice their support of the protest, and in many cases, their personal experiences with Howard. While alumni tweeted comments such as "♥ Howard, back in my day I remember twisting my ankle countless times on campus potholes & financial aid was ALWAYS late . . . changes are needed #TakeBackHU" and "I graduated #HU 17 years ago, how do current students have the SAME complaints I had when I was there. This is a shame #TakeBackHU," student activists met with local and national media to express their resolve and commitment to continue the occupation. For example, students shared their "why." Your "why" is the reason you are protesting. For some students, their why was that they were one tuition hike away from not being able to afford the cost of attending Howard, and for others, it was that they felt this was a moment in time when students could work together to correct some of the negative aspects of campus culture. Throughout the occupied building, students used strategies such as sharing their why to connect with and support one another.

CREATING A UNIFIED VOICE

Once the administration building was occupied, protesters gathered together and determined the direction of the protest. Initially, to find group direction, they held a large brainstorming session. During this session, protest members divided into small groups, of 20 or fewer and freely shared their initial ideas and demands. These ideas included the nine demands posted on the front doors; however, the students' conversation also included general thoughts on how to improve Howard. Armed with clarity of thought regarding their demands, the students continued to engage in dialogue about the best strategies to use to ensure the success of their protest.

STANDING IN THE VOID: OUR COLLECTIVE VOICE

Student protesters determined that there was more at stake than the original nine listed demands identified. Using the groups created during the brainstorming session, they ranked the most important demands and asked for counsel from alumni and graduate students, finding that they needed to be unified in dismantling the established bylaws. Although the original nine demands were warranted, the groups found that the demands involved changes that did not attack the policies leading to lack of student voice. During a nightly meeting with protesters, HUResist leaders discussed the negotiations between student leaders and members of the Board of Trustees and informed students of progress made. In these meetings, HUResist student leaders also conducted information sessions, explaining university policy and how it influenced student experience at Howard overall. HUResist and the voluntary alumni who offered legal advice walked students through university policy and helped the students understand the intent and impact of the discussed policies. HUResist members explained, "We want students to first understand the policy so they can understand why it needs to change." The political and organizational information students exchanged created a situation in which the protest became an information-rich environment. Participants expressed that the information they learned at the protest facilitated an immediate personal change, specifically in the role of activism and social justice.

As one voice, student protesters used collaborative efforts to pare down the demands. Instead of the original nine demands, HUResist protesters no longer required the removal of the university president. Unlike the cheerleader protests at Kennesaw State in 2017 (Roll, 2017) and the racially driven protests at the University of Missouri in 2015 (Douglas & Shockley, 2017; Seltzer, 2018) and Ithaca University in 2016 (Svrluga, 2016) calling for the resignation of their university presidents, HUResist and student protesters realized that a concentrated effort to change board policy provided a more effective solution to student demands. After evaluating other student protests that led to university president removal, HUResist and student protesters altered their demands and asked that each Howard president, regardless of who holds the office, be evaluated by students, faculty, and board members yearly. Before the protest campaign, Howard university presidents had been evaluated only once per decade during their tenure. Student protesters not only understood the importance of reshaping the presidential evaluation process, they also saw the need to reshape the bylaws that govern the Howard University Board of Trustees. First on the students' list was Section 2 of the bylaws (Howard University, 2018). Last amended in October 2018, Section 2 stated:

SECTION 2: Membership of the Board of Trustees

The number of Trustees, shall be up to 35, unless otherwise specified by recommendation of the Governance Committee, for a specific period, and by the majority vote of the full Board. Of such number, three shall be designated as Alumni Trustees, two as Faculty Trustees, and two as Student Trustees. The President of the University shall be designated a Trustee by virtue of incumbency in that Office. In addition to the 35 Trustees described in foregoing provisions of this Section 2, the number of Emeriti Trustees and Honorary Trustees designated pursuant to Section 6 of this Article I shall be established from time-to-time by the Trustees and shall not be counted against the limitation of 35 contained in this Section 2. (Howard University, 2018, p. 1)

The bylaw mentioned above limited student representation by allowing only two students to sit on the board at any given time. Students protesting at Howard were not solely pushing for more representation on the board, but also entreating board members for more transparency in decisionmaking at the board level. Students specifically challenged Section 7b (23–25) of the Board of Trustees bylaws, which stated:

all deliberations conducted during an executive session shall be considered confidential and may not be disclosed outside of the meeting, except as may be authorized by these Bylaws or as otherwise directed by the Chair on the Board of Trustees. (p.11)

Students felt the combination of both bylaws above emphasized the board's desire to limit student voice and maintain the status quo.

DIVERSITY IN BLACKNESS: HONORING OUR REASONS

Strangely enough, the protest was a manifestation of student voice via a grassroots movement that began earlier in the 2017–2018 academic year. HUResist created a student survey to get a better understanding of how students felt about their experience at Howard. The informational survey addressed to all students was conducted via GroupMe, text message, word of mouth, and email. HUResist organizers gathered the data received from the survey and used the information to shape a protest. Buoyed by the survey and contacts made through it, the activist organization spread the word across campus, organizing a student-led protest at the flagpole. Thanks to the wide-reaching survey, the contact list of HU students was vast and varied, and included every significant president from each of the university's major student groups. According to research (Fisher, 2018), student protests generally include a common thread or a particular subsection of the general student body. For example, Fisher (2018) notes that in most protests, organizers "exclud[e] input from anyone outside their group" (p. 25). Unlike such protests, the incidents at Howard included representation from all sectors of the school's population. The protesters included freshmen, sophomores, juniors, and seniors—representation from all undergraduate classes. There were students from each of the undergraduate schools: the college of arts and sciences, the school of engineering and architecture, the school of education, the school of business, and school of allied health and sciences. Through the student contact list, HUResist was able to reach more than just undergraduate students. Graduate and professional students created a network of shifts in order to offer tutorials and academic assistance to all students (see Figure 3.2). These shifts covered most of the major subject areas and disciplines, with organizers hoping to empower students without hindering their academic progress. The alumni supplied academic assistance, funds for food, legal direction, transportation, and mentorship to protest leaders and participants.

Again, the protest was a multifaceted subsection of the university campus. Nowhere was this more prominent than inside the administration building, where student groups and organizations sectioned off each of the four floors as safe havens, acknowledging the differing subsections of various student groups. We discuss the four floors in greater detail in the next section.

THE DIFFERENT FLOORS

During the administration building takeover, students organized as a unified group, under one roof. This unified group addressed university officials through the informal election of spokespersons, including student organization presidents. However, this unity did not suppress student interest or individuality, and the protesters worked to showcase this. The administration building was sectioned into four main areas, denoted by each of the four floors of the building.

The first level of the administration building, which consisted of the foyer, acted as the main gathering area. The glass-enclosed entrance acted as a security checkpoint to verify that only active Howard students were allowed inside the building. Many of the students in this initial inspection area acted as the first line of defense and dedicated a few hours each day. The foyer was heavy-laden with chairs and self-appointed security personnel. This section featured the common meeting area, the food distribution zones, and

Figure 3.2. Graduate students offering tutoring services and additional support to undergraduates

Photograph by Connor Benskin

small community gathering sections for group announcements, votes, and discussions.

The basement acted as an artist's commune for different types of arts. Students were given the freedom to write, recite poetry, and create visual art documenting their time protesting.

The second level served multiple purposes. In its original iteration, HUResist participants designated it as the LGBTQ+ floor in order to give those students the freedom to be safe in their space. Shortly after the occupation, student protesters democratically voted to turn this floor into a women-only floor. Because of the nature of the policy change, they found that even though the LGBTQ+ students felt safe in their space, the female population needed more protection. During the occupation, although no female students were harmed, organizers and participants wanted to make sure that women felt comfortable and did not have to avoid situations in which they felt physically vulnerable.

Lastly, the third floor was designated as the quiet area. Day and night, students kept this floor in near silence for those who needed to sleep or do homework. Participants respected the area by policing themselves and encouraging one another to attend class, complete their assignments, and get some rest.

Students chose to allocate specific floors of the building to different purposes to encourage individual growth and offset any possible trauma triggers. Once again, students used communication and their own voices to accomplish their unified goals while remaining aware of individual students' personal needs.

WE WILL VACATE, BUT WE MAY RETURN

After a little more than a weeklong occupation, HUResist and all protest participants released the building to administrators. They agreed to this after the following list was presented and accepted by the school's Board of Trustees:

1. An overhaul of the school's sexual assault policy
2. Howard University will create a food bank to service students and the surrounding community.
3. University police weapons policy will be reviewed.
4. Students will have a voice in selecting the student ombudsperson, who will be a graduate student, will report to the vice president for student affairs and is expected to attend the Board Student Life and Affairs Committee meetings to make reports.

5. Subject to approval, the university "stakeholders will engage with the student body, to provide a forum to convey concerns regarding all aspects of student life to the Board as needed."
6. The Board agrees to establish a task force, co-chaired by a student, with representation from the Howard student body and Howard administration to review existing grievance mechanisms at the University, and best practices at other universities, and establishing a grievance system that holds faculty, administrators and students accountable in their language and actions towards anyone in the Howard community (Romo, 2018).

HUResist occupied the administration building for a total of 9 days, halting business as usual. Administration and student services were forced to remain outside of the building until protest-appointed leaders and board members reached an agreement. The HUResist team gathered consensus from participants and dismantled the protest, releasing the administration building back to the university (see Figure 3.3).

Figure 3.3. A Gathering of News Reporters Before the Agreement Is Announced

Photograph taken by Ashley Gray

RESILIENCE PAYS OFF

Using both innovative protest methods (such as social media, student surveys, and alumni voices and expertise) and inclusive academic counterspaces, protesters forced the university to create structural shifts at the board level and cultural shifts universitywide. Academic counterspaces foster learning to nurture a supportive environment wherein an individual's experiences are validated and viewed as essential knowledge (Solórzano & Villalpando, 1998; Solórzano & Yosso, 2002). The development of specific floors to acknowledge the identities of marginalized occupants represents the creation of such counterspaces. The acknowledgment of diversity among student protesters resulted in a unified voice and a sustained protest.

Policy implications resulting from the protest cannot only be understood by the immediate results. The mass mobilization of students to commandeer the administrative building and the methods used to introduce student-to-student education on university policy showed students' willingness to use the measures necessary to be heard by the university administration. Moving forward, Howard's administration and policymakers must be proactive and create structural shifts to increase student voice and representation. If not, Howard may experience similar protests again in the near future.

REFERENCES

Brown University students protest admissions policy. (1992, April 23). *The New York Times*, 18A.

Coffin, C. (2018, April 2). Alumni, students take sides as Howard University protest draws on. Retrieved from www.fox5dc.com/news/howard-university-student-sit-in-protest-continues-into-day-5-officials-agree-to-1-of-9-demands

Douglas, T. M. O., & Shockley, K. G. (2017). Truths, triumphs and testaments of hope when campus and community voices rise. *Journal of Negro Education. 86*(3): 199–203.

Fisher, M. (2018). Still fighting the good fight: An analysis of student activism and institutional response. *Public Relations Review, 44*(1), 22–27. doi.org/10.1016/j.pubrev.2017.11.005

Goodwin, J. (2018, December 21). Howard University stricken with damages; A test of resilience. Retrieved from thehilltoponline.com/2018/01/21/howard-university-stricken-with-damages-a-test-of-resilience/

Habermas, J. (1965). *Toward a rational society: Student protest, science, and politics.* Cambridge, UK: Polity Press.

Howard University. (2018). *The Howard University bylaws of the Board of Trustees.* Washington, DC: Author.

Open Meetings Act. (n.d.). Retrieved from www.open-dc.gov/open-meetings-act

Roll, N. (2017, December 15). Culture was casualty. Retrieved from www.inside highered.com/news/2017/12/15/following-cheerleader-protest-inquiry-kennesaw -state-president-resigns

Romo, V. (2018, April 7). 9-day student protest at Howard University ends with a deal. Retrieved from www.npr.org/sections/thetwo-way/2018/04/06/600401378 /9-day-student-protest-at-howard-university-ends-with-a-deal

Seltzer, N. (2018, September 12). Missouri 3 years: Lessons learned, protests still reso-nate. Retrieved from www.insidehighered.com/news/2018/09/12/administrators -students-and-activists-take-stock-three-years-after-2015-missouri

Solórzano, D. G., & Villalpando, O. (1998). Critical race theory, marginality, and the experience of students of color in higher education. In C. A. Torres & T. R. Mitchell (Eds.), *Sociology of education: Emerging perspectives* (pp. 211–224). Albany, NY: SUNY Press.

Solórzano, D. G., & Yosso, T. J. (2002). Critical race methodology: Counter-storytelling as an analytical framework for education research. *Qualitative In-quiry, 8*(1), 23–44.

Spiegel, J. (2015). *Rêve général illimité?* The role of creative protest in transforming the dynamics of space and time during the 2012 Quebec student strike. *Anti-pode, 47*(3), 770–791. doi: 10.1111/anti.12133

Svrluga, S. (2016, January 14). Ithaca college president resigns after protests over race issues. Retrieved from www.washingtonpost.com/news/grade-point/wp /2016/01/14/ithaca-college-president-resigns-after-protests-over-race-issues /?noredirect=on&utm_term=.b37dadf9d84f

Part II

RESISTANCE TO/THROUGH SYMBOLS, IMAGES, AND SOCIAL MEDIA

"Some of Our Historical Stones Are Rough and Even Unpleasant to Look at. But They Are Ours . . ."

Pushing Back Against the Lost Cause

Travis D. Boyce, Winsome M. Chunnu, and Brian Heilmeier

"Some of our historical stones are rough and even unpleasant to look at.
But they are ours. . . ."

—David Wilkins, Clemson University Board of Trustees (Cary, 2015b)

"Public monuments do not arise as if by natural law to celebrate the deserving; they are built by people with sufficient power to marshal (or impose) public consent for their erection."

—Kirk Savage (1994, pp. 135–136)

ROUGH HISTORICAL STONES

On February 11, 2017, Yale University President Peter Salovey announced that the highly problematic (John C.) Calhoun (residential) College would be renamed Hopper College beginning in the 2017–2018 academic year. The new name is in honor of a Yale alumna: computer scientist and Rear Admiral Grace Murray Hopper (1906–1992). In comparison, Calhoun's legacy is embedded in slavery and White supremacy (Peters, 2017). It's true that Calhoun graduated from Yale and served as the vice president of the United States from 1825 to 1832. But for decades, students, faculty, and staff have protested to remove Calhoun's name from the residential college building. Nevertheless, it took a national tragedy for Yale University officials to reopen the conversation regarding the renaming of Calhoun College.

In June 2015, White supremacist Dylann Roof entered the historically Black "Mother" Emmanuel African Methodist Episcopal (AME) Church in Charleston, South Carolina, and murdered nine African American parishioners (including its pastor) during a Wednesday night Bible study (Boyce & Chunnu Brayda, 2015). At the time, South Carolina's governor was Nikki Haley (now former ambassador to the United Nations under the Donald Trump administration). Haley called for the removal of the Confederate battle flag on the statehouse grounds when it became clear that Roof was a White supremacist, posed in photos with the Confederate battle flag, and longed for the Old South and apartheid regimes (Diamond & Bash, 2015). It's noteworthy to mention that Roof even visited Confederate monuments throughout the state prior to committing the horrendous murders (Boyce & Chunnu Brayda, 2015). In the college president's welcome address to the freshman class, President Salovey cited the Charleston church massacre as a catalyst for the university to consider renaming Calhoun College (Roach, 2015). This recent name change to Hopper College is a victory, part of a trend where student activism has led colleges and universities to change their building names, monuments, or mascots, thus acknowledging or overwriting their racist past (Bever, 2011; Hofmann, 2005; Ruff, 2016).

Attention (in terms of oppressive structures on college campuses) has now shifted to the state of South Carolina, the home of Calhoun (1782–1850) and also, coincidentally, U.S. Senator Benjamin "Pitchfork" Tillman (1847–1918). On the campuses of both Clemson and Winthrop universities, prominent buildings are named in honor of Tillman. There has been a mass movement on both campuses calling for the removal of Tillman's name because he was a segregationist, White nationalist, and proponent of lynching during the late 19th and early 20th centuries (Cary, 2017; *Ben Tillman: Memories of an Agrarian Racist*, 2001). Unfortunately, there is nothing either state-supported institution can do about renaming a building. According to South Carolina's Heritage Act, "any street, park, or plaque named for a historical figure in the state cannot be renamed without a two-thirds vote from the state's General Assembly" (cited in Brooks, 2017). Moreover, the Clemson University Board of Trustees, in early 2015, declined to rename Tillman Hall. The then board chairman David Wilkins (former U.S. ambassador to Canada) offered the following explanation:

> Every great institution is built by imperfect craftsmen. Stone by stone they add to the foundation so that over many, many generations, we get a variety of stones. And so it is with Clemson. Some of our historical stones are rough and even unpleasant to look at. But they are ours and denying them as part of our

history does not make them any less so. For that reason, we will not change the name of our historical buildings.

Part of knowledge is to know and understand history so you learn from it. Clemson is a strong, diverse university in which all of us can be proud. That is today's and tomorrow's reality and that is where all our energy is focused. To that end, the Board recognizes there is more work to be done. (Cary, 2015b)

Wilkins's statement in defense of preserving the Tillman Hall name is problematic, as Tillman Hall is a tangible and racialized structure that has been erected and honored in a revisionist historical perspective. However, the retaining of the name at Clemson and Winthrop is an opportunity for both university communities and, indeed, the larger society to rethink the rhetoric of the Lost Cause ideology and contextualize the legacy of Tillman as well the maintenance of oppressive structures on campuses throughout the country. Therefore, it is a responsibility of colleges and universities that elect to maintain these structures to provide a full truth of their "historical stones."

This chapter uses the Lost Cause ideology as the conceptual framework to understand how students facilitate online activism regarding the removal of oppressive structures within the systems (Clemson and Winthrop universities) of which they are a part. This chapter will first provide a historical account of student activism as a backdrop for understanding how student activism has evolved, concluding with a deeper examination of how current generations of students incorporate social media into their activism. Universities rely on structures and social interactions to function. Students, therefore, develop emotional attachments to their institutions through interactions with peers, faculty, and staff. There are pervasive structures and traditions present at most universities that allow students to develop emotional attachments to the history on which their university was founded. When the majority of students support this history, that support alienates students who are trying to change to that history. The Lost Cause ideology can provide the framework to best understand the institutional factors at Clemson and Winthrop universities and in particular student activism around dismantling oppressive structures. The chapter concludes with a discussion about the implications of maintaining these structures.

EARLY CAMPUS ACTIVISM

The Yale Calhoun College controversy is not the genesis of student activism. Campus activism in the United States is as old as campuses themselves. In the early days of many higher educational institutions, students complained about food and living conditions on campus. When their concerns were not heeded by the administration, students became more forceful in expressing their discontent. The earliest documentation of a university's response to student activism is 1638, when Harvard students were punished after they protested the bad cooking by the house master's wife (Dickey, 2016). At Harvard alone there were eight separate "rebellions" (student protests) between 1766 and 1834 (Ireland, 2012). These protests included the Bad Butter Rebellion of 1766, the Teatime Tiff in 1775, the Bread and Butter Rebellion in 1805, and the Rotten Cabbage Rebellion in 1807 (Meloni, 2016). Many of the rebellions on early campuses were sparked because of the constant tension between the students and the administration. After a student protest, the administration would impose harsher punishments for violations (Geiger, 2014). After the Revolutionary War, students felt a "disenchantment for college authority" and had a "hunger for liberty" (Ireland, 2012, para. 18).

Throughout the 18th and 19th centuries, the majority of the student protests were focused on internal campus issues. Broadhurst (2014) states, "Although students fought for greater control over the curriculum and against what they perceived as poor faculty, the most frequent attacks were levied against what were viewed as disciplinary injustices by the administration or unpopular campus doctrines" (p. 4). This feeling continued through much of the early part of the 19th century. The latter half of the 19th century was relatively calm on college campuses. Much of this calm can be attributed to the work that students did to gain more of a social outlet on campuses. Between 1820 and 1860, students started Greek letter organizations, literary magazines, and various sporting events (Ellsworth & Burns, 1970). These outlets were welcome distractions from their studies and provided students with an opportunity to engage in constructive activities on their campus. By 1900, students had established student governments on many campuses. The establishment of these student governments engaged students outside of the classroom and allowed for the creation of new student organizations focusing on various causes. These organizations and their causes would be the driving force of protests starting in the 1900s.

SHIFTING PRIORITIES, SOCIALISM, AND POLITICAL ACTIVISM

The 20th century saw a shift in the issues that students protested. Up until this point, most of the issues students had concerned themselves with were internal campus struggles. An example of an internal campus struggle was the creation of new student organizations, such as the Intercollegiate Socialist Society (ISS), focused on the needs of not only students, but also of the general public. The ISS focused on the needs of the working-class citizens and helped spread the idea of socialism as a political party (Broadhurst, 2014). Specifically, before World War I, individual ISS chapters and other campus groups worked to keep military establishments off campus. Students challenged the idea of Reserve Officer Training Corps (ROTC) programs being set up on their campuses. Over time, however, much of the socialism rhetoric generated by the ISS had fizzled out on campuses. Students were not completely quiet, though; they turned their focus toward ending the censorship that plagued student newspapers. They also tried to obtain more of a voice in university governance (Broadhurst, 2014). Altbach (1979) summed up the 1920s this way: "Without question, the twenties was a period of general campus apathy" (p. 611). That would all change during the 1930s.

NATIONWIDE MOVEMENTS: STUDENT CONGRESS AGAINST WAR (PEARL HARBOR TO PATRIOTISM)

During the 1930s, campuses saw their largest uprisings to date. Students began to start not only organizations on their own campuses, but also nationwide movements. In December 1932, there was a Student Congress Against War convention held in Chicago. This convention helped spread the peace movement to colleges across the country. Multiple national walkouts and peace strikes kept the movement alive. This was the first time students turned their attention to international matters, as the rise of fascism in Europe changed the role that the United States was playing in the world (Altbach, 1979).

Though these movements grew only modestly through the early part of the 1930s, the groups saw huge growth in the latter part of the decade. Two smaller organizations, the Student League for Industrial Democracy and the National Student League, merged in 1935 to form the American Student Union. This organization was a unified group for socialists, communists, and liberals that held numerous events through rest of the decade and up until the start of World War II, when all activism came to a halt.

Following Pearl Harbor, a patriotic feeling rose over most of the country, including college campuses. The peace movement that had dominated the 1930s was silenced, as students shifted to patriotic rallies. Following World War II and into the 1950s, the previously popular communist movement was reversed. Anticommunist sentiment was the catalyst for much of the activism (Broadhurst, 2014). The 1950s also saw court cases and movements against the separate-but-equal doctrine. These cases would lay the groundwork for the most active years for campus protests: the 1960s.

ACTIVISM FOR CIVIL RIGHTS, FREE SPEECH, AND PEACE

The 1960s ushered in three major political movements on college campuses: the civil rights movement, the free speech movement, and the antiwar movement. These movements were championed by a rapidly growing enrollment of college students. This influx of students fueled campus activism.

The Civil Rights Movement

Although student activism, particularly on the campuses of historically Black colleges and universities, has been ongoing and most notably prominent since the 1930s, the common narrative of origin is the student sit-in movement during the 1960s. On February 1, 1960, four African American students from North Carolina Agricultural and Technical (A&T) College went for lunch at a Woolworth store and were refused service. The students went back each day, progressively being joined by more students, both Black and White. This movement spread quickly across the country, and within 10 days, there were sit-ins happening throughout five different states (Oppenheimer, 1985). Student organizations popped up to help organize and plan these protests. In 1960, Students for a Democratic Society (SDS) started, followed by the Student Nonviolent Coordinating Committee (SNCC). These groups helped plan and organize many of the protests that took place in the early 1960s, many of which occurred off campus.

In the South, students from various colleges and members of the community banded together to form organizations that furthered the civil rights cause. In Jackson, the capital of Mississippi, students from Tougaloo College hosted a sit-in at the White-only municipal library. The nine students who staged the protest were arrested and jailed. Students from nearby Jackson State University then hosted a sit-in in support of the nine students arrested (Wallenstein, 2008). The two schools supported each other throughout the 1960s, and together they worked to further the civil rights movement.

The University of California–Berkeley experienced protest in the 1960s like it had not seen before. In *The Report of the President's Commission on Campus Unrest*, completed in 1970, the events at Berkeley were described this way: "The autumn of 1964 defined an authentic political invention new and complex mixture of issues, tactics, emotions, and setting that became the prototype for student protest throughout the decade. Nothing quite like it had ever before appeared in America, and it is with the nature and evolution of this long-lived invention, in all its variations, that this Commission is concerned" (President's Commission on Campus Unrest, pp. 22–23).

The Free Speech Movement

The free speech movement (FSM) at Berkeley organized a large, 2-day sit-in at the administration building. This sit-in ended when the governor brought in police to make hundreds of arrests. There were also numerous charges of police brutality from the protesters. While the governor's move might have ended that sit-in, ultimately it backfired, as the number of participants in the movement grew exponentially after the mass arrests. What followed was an unprecedented strike against the university (Unrest, 1970). The FSM at Berkeley had essentially achieved its goals, as the university's rules were changed to favor free speech. Berkeley had changed how protesting was done; the president's own commission said, "What happened at Berkeley had altered the character of American student activism in a fundamental way" (Unrest, 1970, p. 24). Students started using the Berkeley tactics across the country to further their cause. And one cause that was on everyone's mind throughout 1960s was Vietnam.

The Antiwar Movement

Peace movements against the Vietnam War increased dramatically throughout the 1960s. "What began as a core of only a few thousand ardent activists advocating for peace in 1960 transformed into a massive movement that could summon hundreds of thousands of supporters by the decade's end" (Broadhurst, 2014, pp. 9–10). The U.S. draft for soldiers particularly struck the student body and caused mass activism across the country (Altbach, 1979). Students were angry with the political system and felt that the war was the culmination of the government's failures. Universities felt the brunt, as most students connected their university with the government, and therefore attacked that system. Harsh responses to campus activism often incited more activism and made more students willing to join the cause.

1970s, 1980s, 1990s: Apathy, Divestment, and Identity

The 1970s brought a sense of apathy to college campuses once again. Altbach (1979) said of the 1970s: "The seventies, with considerable justification, has been called a period of apathy on the American campus. Virtually all of the political organizations which flourished during the sixties have disappeared, and few new groups have taken their place" (pp. 615–616). Many of the issues that students fought for were becoming realities. There was also a shift in the way students made their voices heard. In the 1970s, student lobby groups were formed at both state and national levels. These groups made sure that students' concerns were taken seriously and allowed them to voice their opinions without having to stage large riots (Altbach & Cohen, 1990).

The 1980s brought a hybrid of the early 1960s and the 1970s. This decade saw a continuation of the 1970s, with students working through government to make change, but also an uptick in peaceful campus protest. The issue that inspired these tactics was the divestment and anti-apartheid movement. The 1990s saw the same tactics that students had employed in the 1980s, but the topics had, once again, changed. Most students of the 1990s were protesting for social issues, such as rights of immigrants, better protections for students of color and LGBTQ+ students, overall increase in accessibility to education, and many other ideas (Broadhurst, 2014).

Technology, Black Lives Matter, and 2000s

In 2016, UCLA's annual CIRP (Cooperative Institutional Research Program) report showed that 8.5% of the more than 140,000 students surveyed believed they had a "very good chance" of participating in a protest while at college (Eagan et al., 2015). This is the highest percent that has ever been recorded since the report started 50 years ago. This number almost doubles, to 16%, when just Black students answer. Many campuses have seen this activism around racial issues on their campuses recently. Unfortunately, much of this activism is spawned out of racial incidents, either on campus or nationally (Jaschik, 2016). At Eastern Michigan University, for example, students took to the field after a football game to protest the spray-painting of KKK on the wall of a campus building (Folsom, 2016). At the University of Mississippi, students held a sit-in to demand a reaction from the university about a racist message that a student tweeted (Jaschik, 2016). College athletics has also seen an increase in students protesting the national anthem, following Colin Kaepernick's example. Football players at the University of Michigan, Michigan State, and the University of Nebraska–Lincoln have either "taken a knee" or raised their fist in protest (Jaschik, 2016). While campus activism in the form of protests, sit-ins, or marches can be very powerful, the reach of social media has made digital connection a critical tool for activists.

Wong (2015) notes that campus protests against racism, bigotry, and other forms of discrimination are happening frequently. She states, "Students at the University of Chicago hosted an event last November to raise awareness about institutional intolerance." All over the country, students held

"Hands Up, Don't Shoot" protests. Students also protested the killing of Mike Brown and Trayvon Martin. We concurrently witnessed the rise of the Black Lives Matter Movement, which started with a tweet in response to the George Zimmerman verdict. Aided by social media, the movement has taken root on college campuses all over the United States. Wong (2015) also notes that demonstrations used hashtags to mobilize. She points out that "most of the recent student uprisings during the fall of 2014 focused on racism and police violence. Many of hashtags that were used in 2014 around racism and police violence are still in use presently."

Although hashtags are relatively new for campus activism, the Internet is not new in helping activists. Starting in the 1990s, activists began to use emails to organize protests. Specifically, in 1999, organizers of the World Trade Organization (WTO) protests in Seattle used email to inform protesters where to be and when (Sliwinski, 2016). However, activism through social media did not hit its stride until 2011 in the wake of Arab Spring. Protesters used social media to organize protests and denounce leaders. Since then, most activist movements have developed a hashtag, with the most popular being #BlackLivesMatter. These hashtags allow participation not only from people in the protest but people around the country. On social media such as Twitter, the words after the # symbol are searchable, to link users to others who share their interest. In this way, hashtags can give a voice to the voiceless and create an equal playing field for protesters against authority (Khan-Ibarra, 2014). Social media have impacted the ways students and the general public have engaged in protest. Protesters raise awareness through this type of digital "activism." As noted by Scott Jaschik (2015), founding editor of *Inside Higher Education*, "In the age of the internet, when a student who might not have known Benjamin Tillman's history can quickly learn it—as well as see protests taking place elsewhere—activism is likely to spread, they said. Many students applauded when Bree Newsome opted not to wait for South Carolina lawmakers to make a decision on the Confederate flag, and instead climbed up the flagpole and took it down."

THE LOST CAUSE AND THE COLLEGIATE IDEA: CONFEDERATE SYMBOLS ON COLLEGE CAMPUSES AND STUDENT RESISTANCE

Social media continue to play an important role in generating awareness around oppressive monuments on college campuses. However, in order to grasp the ideology surrounding the challenges at Clemson and Winthrop universities, it is important to understand the role that ideology played in the erection of these monuments and in the naming of buildings. From 1880 to 1910, there was a social-political movement/ideology that dominated the American South: the Lost Cause. As Cynthia Mills (2003) notes in her co-edited volume titled *Monuments to the Lost Cause: Women, Art, and the Landscapes of the Southern Memory*, the Lost Cause movement, in essence, was a "restoration of respect" for White southerners (Mills, 2003, p. xvii). The Lost Cause ideology was fundamentally grounded in a revisionist historical perspective; slavery was a benevolent institution, and there was no shame in the Confederacy losing the American Civil War, as they fought for a noble cause (Mills, 2003). Moreover, the Lost Cause narrative also supported the ideals of redemption and patriotism, White racial reconciliation, and White supremacy (Emberton, 2013; Loewen, 1999). Furthermore, as the Lost Cause ideology honored the past, it also looked to the future under popular colloquial sayings such as "The South Shall Rise Again!" (Martinez & Harris, 2000, p. 145). Some of the most notable achievements during this period were the construction of monuments honoring the Confederacy throughout the country (Levinson, 1998).

As Mills (2003) notes, the federal government during the postwar era excluded the Confederacy in the construction of memorials to those who fought as part of the American Civil Confederate veteran groups. But more significantly, White women's civic organizations such as the United Daughters of the Confederacy (UDC) were instrumental in the fundraising and building of Confederate monuments. With the Reconstruction era over and the American South on the verge of fully disenfranchising African Americans, the construction of Confederate monuments helped in two ways: (1) to reinforce the Lost Cause ideology, and (2) interestingly, as James Loewen (1999) indicates, to reconcile White Americans, both Northerners and Southerners, through the lens of patriotism.

In cities across the American South (major, midsized, and small), one can find statues, building names, and other forms of memorials dedicated to the ideologies of the Lost Cause. In Richmond, Virginia, for example, former Confederate President Jefferson Davis and Generals Robert E. Lee, Thomas "Stonewall" Jackson, and J.E.B. Stuart are depicted as heroes and patriots and are memorialized on the famous Monument Avenue (Wilson, 2003). Furthermore, downtown Fort Mill, South Carolina, has a spot called Confederate Park, where there is a dedication to the "faithful slaves" who remained loyal to the Confederate cause during the war (Loewen, 1999, p. 253). This memorial grossly misrepresents African American who were enslaved and their full acceptance of the Confederate cause. It praises the benevolent institution of slavery (Loewen, 1999).

Collegiate Idea: Sports Teams, Greek Life, Mascots

Some images, monuments, and memories are situated within the framework of what historian J. Douglas Toma refers to as the *collegiate idea*: "the combination of community and campus culture associated with the traditional American small college (as cited in White, 2010, p. 471). For example, a university's alma mater, fight songs, sports teams, Greek life, mascots, building names, monuments, and other nonacademic features and/or traditions are essential to shaping the identity of a university (White, 2010). This essential quality is important to note because some students are ardent supporters of retaining oppressive structures.

College fraternities in the southern United States were at the helm of bringing the Lost Cause ideology to life on campuses. Their activities were part of the larger massive resistance movement against integration throughout the American South. In the wake of the 1948 presidential election in which the states' rights (Dixiecrats) third party emerged, fraternities such as Kappa Alpha Order on the campus of the University of Mississippi memorialized the Lost Cause. They "lauded its southern heritage, worshipped Confederate war veterans, and shrouded much of its festivity in Old South memorabilia" (James, 2008, p. 70). At the University of North Carolina–Chapel Hill, fraternity members appeared in its university yearbook, *Yackety-Yack,* donning Confederate uniforms and performing marches and formations in front of Silent Sam, the university's Confederate memorial. Furthermore, fraternities and sororities during the late 1940s and 1960s staged blackface minstrel shows.

The appropriation of the Lost Cause ideology extended beyond Greek and social club life, as it was deeply embedded into other aspects of college life. By 1950, the University of Mississippi held its first annual Dixie Week (James, 2008). On the campus of the University of Virginia, Navy ROTC cadets waved Confederate flags in celebration of the end of World War II (Nehls, 2002). During the 1962–1963 football season, the University of Florida's (UFL's) varsity football team donned Confederate flag emblems both on their jerseys and helmets as a matter of "Southern honor" (White, 2010, p. 471). Moreover, the UFL marching band played "Dixie" and displayed Confederate flags at the games as its team ran on the field prior to the opening kickoff (White, 2010). The aesthetics of the Lost Cause ideology, such as the Confederate flag, songs, and monuments, were described by White (2010) as "extensions of the collegiate ideal projected by a segregated university" (p. 474). As predominantly White institutions desegregated, students of color and their supporters protested for the removal and renaming of the oppressive structures. One of the names considered oppressive was Tillman Hall on the campuses of both Winthrop and Clemson.

#TILLMANHALL: THE ROLE OF SOCIAL MEDIA IN BRINGING CLEMSON AND WINTHROP TO LIFE

For student protesters and their supporters on the campuses of Winthrop and Clemson universities, the name Benjamin Tillman is a sign that these educational institutions and, frighteningly, the state of South Carolina directly and/or indirectly supports "a symbol of hatred, prejudice, and white supremacy" (Kimball, 2016). This "support" is seen by protesters as within the backdrop of the rise and legitimacy of the alternative right, White nationalism, and ultimately, the election of Donald J. Trump as this nation's 45th president.

Tillman was born into a large, slave-owning family in 1847 in Edgefield County, South Carolina. His perception of the world reflected the antebellum South's White, misogynistic, and racist culture. A series of unfortunate circumstances plagued the Tillman men prior to and immediately after the American Civil War. Tillman had to mature quickly and assume a great deal of personal and financial responsibility. Tillman lost his father at a young age, as well as his older brothers due to the Mexican-American War and the Civil War, which left him, at about 20 years old, as the head of the household (Kantrowitz, 2000; *"Pitchfork" Ben Tillman: The Most Lionized Figure in South Carolina History*, 2007/2008).

With the institution of slavery outlawed, Tillman became notorious for treating his emancipated African American workers as if they were slaves, forcing them to sign oppressive contracts that kept them in a figurative state of slavery and whipping those who challenged his authority. Having redeemed the family fortune and expanded his family's land, Tillman emerged as the largest landowner in Edgefield County in postwar South Carolina. Nevertheless, Tillman, like many White southerners, didn't like the newly emancipated African Americans' rise to political, social, and economic prosperity as a result of the federal government's Reconstruction policies. The Reconstruction era, in effect, shaped Tillman's future political career and legacy (*Ben Tillman: Memories of an Agrarian Racist*, 2001).

Under the banner of redemption, Tillman, like many of his fellow White Southerners, campaigned against the Reconstruction policies through the use of violence. In 1876, for example, he went with White vigilantes and attacked and murdered members of an all-Black militia group in the now-defunct town of Hamburg, South Carolina. The Hamburg massacre proved to be one of the decisive incidents of racial violence that subsequently led to overturning the Reconstruction era in South Carolina (Emberton, 2013; Kantrowitz, 2000). Framing himself as a populist and the champion of the White working poor, Tillman enjoyed a long political career from 1885 until his death in 1918. Tillman served in South Carolina's state legislature, served two terms (1890–1894) as South Carolina's governor, and spent the rest of his life as a member of the U.S. Senate (1895–1918) (Kantrowitz, 2000). During his time in political office, he tried to disenfranchise African Americans by supporting new legislation and rewriting the state constitution in 1895. He openly bragged about racial violence he had committed. He incited violence and advocated against African American education. He once stated that there was "no good in the education of black children. When you educate a Negro you educate a candidate for the penitentiary or spoil a good field hand" (cited in *Ben Tillman: Memories of an Agrarian Racist*, 2001, p. 49).

Holding true to his populist rhetoric and service to South Carolina's White working class, Tillman supported legislation and funding for the establishment of Winthrop University (an industrial and normal school for White women in 1886) and Clemson University (an agricultural college for White men in 1889) (Kantrowitz, 2000). Ironically, Tillman's accession to political power was timely. His rise and tenure in political office (1880s–1910s) coincided with the Lost Cause movement, which consequently resulted in the construction of thousands of Confederate monuments across the country.

Today, technology can facilitate social change. In an age where social media have become a common way to communicate, movement tags such as #BlackLivesMatter, #ConcernedStudent1950, and other slogans have helped create dialogue, organize, and facilitate student activism on college campuses. #TillmanHall and other such hashtags, accompanied by traditional forms of protests on the campuses of Clemson and Winthrop, have proven effective in addressing oppressive structures as well as structural racism on college campuses.

Clemson: Race, Resistance, and Campus Uprisings in the Information Age (Organized Within the Context of 21st-Century Technology)

What energized people against Tillman's name on the building? Certainly there had been concern historically regarding the maintenance of the name "Tillman" Hall on both the Clemson and Winthrop campuses. But then people started seeing change elsewhere—the subsequent removals, renaming, and/or contextualizing of oppressive structures on college campuses (such as the Confederate Memorial and the re-creation of its mascot at the University of Mississippi). Successes elsewhere energized those people opposed to the name of Tillman Hall. The biggest and most influential among the student voices came in the form of a poem that proved to be the catalyst for the push to remove the name in recent years. In 2014, Dr. A. D. Carson (then a PhD candidate at Clemson and currently a professor of hip-hop studies at the University of Virginia) uploaded a poem titled "See the Stripes" on YouTube. Carson's (2014) poem critiqued the institution's troubled racial history (including Tillman). He further made a plea to the university to offer a thorough history of the institution. To date, his video has been viewed over 23,000 times with a robust commentary that is overwhelmingly positive and supportive. The following semester, the faculty senate introduced a resolution to rename the place, a move that was counterprotested by Clemson students who wished to preserve the name Tillman Hall, under #SaveTillman (Cary, 2015a). In the wake of the Charleston shooting, the past presidents of the faculty senate published open letters on Clemson's website, calling for the renaming of Tillman Hall (Cary, 2015c). Within this period, the Board of Trustees declined to rename the hall; nevertheless, the resistance persisted.

A year later, a task force convened and submitted a report on February 5, 2016, that requested the university to tell a full, complete history of the institution to the public. This history was to include, but not be limited to, the contextualization of the biographies of its founders (including Tillman) and other prominent people associated with the institution. The task force recommended that the institution introduce a course on the history of Clemson. Another idea was the creation of social media accounts dedicated to sharing the history of the institution with the public (Wilkins et al., 2016). Getting recommendations from the task force was a start. Clemson committed to creating historical markers with the intention of acknowledging the institution's racist past (Barnett, 2016). Nevertheless, Tillman's name on the building remains intact, inaction that symbolically maintained the Lost Cause ideology. Student protesting and racial incidents on campus have increased.

Racist threats toward African American students were made on the now-defunct social media app Yik Yak. Most notably, in April 2016, rotten bananas (a racist iconography) were found hanging on an African American commemorative banner. Although there had been student protests prior to this date regarding the Tillman name, this banner incident energized the movement (there was a sit-in at Sikes Hall, Clemson's administration building), seeking not just the renaming of Tillman Hall, but more importantly, that structural racism at Clemson be addressed. On April 13, 2016, students organized what would be a 9-day sit-in protest through the use of social media platforms under hashtags such as #BeingBlackatClemson and #SikesSitIn. It is noteworthy to mention that on the second day of the peaceful sit-in, five students (including A. D. Carson), dubbed the #Clemson5, were arrested on charges of trespassing. Moreover, the administration threatened to revoke the charters of the Zeta Phi Beta and Delta Phi Lambda sororities if they elected to host their new member probate shows at the site of the sit-ins. Protesters were threatened with suspension and expulsion. Nevertheless, faculty, staff, students, and alumni took to social media (Facebook and Twitter) to organize, provide updates, and offer words of encouragement and solidarity. Protesters used social media to reinforce their purpose.

For example, Clemson University graduate student Abbie Beadle (@AbbBeadl) tweeted, "Having names of buildings such as Tillman & Strom Thurmond Institute sends the message that . . . the University values white supremacists over the emotional safety of their students" (Beadle, 2016a, 2016b). Cristina Perez (@CristinaPerez11) tweeted a brief commentary followed by a link to Clemson University English professor Jonathan Beecher Field's article "Yes, We Have No (Time For) Bananas," which was published in the university's student-run newspaper, *The Tiger* (Perez, 2016). In essence, Professor Field conveyed to readers that Black student anger was not the result of a singular racist act, but rather, was the culmination of years of structural racism at the university (which included the maintenance of the name Tillman Hall) and at the national/international level. Instead of condemning the protesters for what appeared to be a trivial prank, Field encouraged White students to be empathetic and look at the big picture when it comes to American history and institutionalized racism (Field, 2016).

Clemson University student Dustin Clark's (@dus10clark) (2016) tweet reinforces Perez's. While posting encouraging comments regarding the sit-ins, he also posted two juxtaposed photos of the desegregation of Clemson University in 1963 and its student body's reaction to the #SikesSitIn of 2016, noting that things have not really changed. The social media posts connected to #SikesSitIn did not just come from Clemson University student voices, but also from faculty, staff, and most notably members of university communities across the country. Students and staff at Duke University, using the hashtag #DismantleDukePlantation, stood in solidarity and held similar protests on their own campus (Duke Students & Workers in Solidarity, 2016).

During the 9-day sit-in, Clemson President Jim Clements held a series of meetings and discussions surrounding the students' concerns (in an amicable strategy to end the protests), a strategy that subsequently led the development of an "accountability checks timeline" by the administration to address student concerns. Students protesters, in general, were somewhat skeptical, as there was a lack of discussion surrounding Tillman Hall. A. D. Carson was quoted in *The Tiger*, questioning the sincerity of President Clements and the administration. Carson stated, "We're not hearing anything different than what was said previous to being out here" (quoted in Campbell, 2016). Other students were quoted in the paper, noting their skepticism with the administration. Moreover, an individual (presumably a Clemson University student) using the twitter handle @BenHyder tweeted that President Clement essentially deflected the Tillman issue in his email to the campus community upon the suspension of the sit-in. In the wake of the banner incident and protests, the administration accommodated some of the ideas from the protesters, such as diversity training and doubling the size of the minority faculty by 2025. However, the name Tillman Hall remains intact (Logue, 2016).

Winthrop—Race Resistance and Campus Uprisings in the Information Age (Traditional and Underground)

Students at Winthrop similarly protested the controversial Tillman Hall on their campus. Their protest, in comparison, appeared to be organic and reactionary. Nevertheless, their intentions were the same. At Winthrop, the administrative building was originally named Main Building, but it was renamed Tillman Hall in 1962 (Douglas, 2014). Coincidentally, the South Carolina state legislature voted to place the Confederate battle flag on top of the statehouse dome a year prior, in 1961, as a symbol of massive resistance against the desegregation of public schools (Worland, 2015), showing a trend of renewed interest in the Lost Cause ideology in response to the civil rights movement.

Coinciding with the timeliness of Dr. Carson's poem, former Winthrop students Michael Fortune and Richard Davis demanded that the Board of Trustees rename Tillman Hall. The board cited the Heritage Act, which virtually made it impossible for the board to change the name (Douglas, 2014). Nevertheless, students persisted and challenged the administration with notable recent protests during the fall semester of 2016. An organization called the Association of Artists for Change hung 18 stockings filled with dirt outside of Tillman Hall to deface Tillman's legacy. According to the group, the stockings represented the 18 lynching victims during Tillman's tenure (1890–1894) as governor of South Carolina (Collins, 2016).

Initially mistaken for a racist prank, this incident reenergized the students' efforts to rename Tillman Hall at Winthrop. Students, faculty, and staff immediately organized and protested not only for the removal of Tillman's name but also for the end of police brutality against communities of color, which is the essence of the #BlackLivesMatter movement (Thackham, 2016). Although it appears that Winthrop students did not fully use social media to organize this protest, if one does a #TillmanHall search, one will find issues and topics related to the Tillman Hall protest at Winthrop reported by media outlets as some of the top searches, as opposed to those related to the Clemson protest. Members of the Winthrop University faculty and administration—most notably Provost Dr. Debra Boyd—explained that there is little they can do in terms of offering immediate change. Protests may resume, and #TillmanHall could be what students rally around.

IS IT WORTH PROTESTING OR IS IT A LOST CAUSE?

In April 2016, Clemson University broke ground on a historical marker. This marker, many people say, is intended to express the institution's acknowledgment of its racist past. The university has since hired a chief diversity officer and has increased diversity and inclusion training. Nevertheless, the institution has yet to respond to calls to rename the controversial and symbolic legacy of the Lost Cause movement, the building called Tillman Hall.

The removal and/or renaming of monuments that embody the Lost Cause ideology continues to be in the news. In New Orleans, Louisiana, for example, after decades of protest, the city council and its mayor have removed a monument (first erected in 1891) commemorating "the Battle of Liberty Place." During this event, which occurred in 1874 , the paramilitary White League engaged in a violent confrontation with the intent of overthrowing Radical Republican rule and restoring White supremacy in the state (Levinson, 1998). Such violence in New Orleans and other places was meant to reaffirm White rule in the American South (Emberton, 2013).

The Confederate monuments controversy has even made its way into presidential politics. In August 2017, members of the so-called Alt Right (largely composed of neo-Nazi and other White Supremacist groups) convened a "Unite the Right" rally in Charlottesville, Virginia, to protest the removal of the Robert E. Lee statue. Despite the violence, racist rhetoric, and intimidation perpetuated by supporters of the Unite to Right rally as well as the subsequent horrific murder committed by a neo-Nazi against a counterprotester, President Trump used the Confederate monument controversy as a political weapon and effectively supported the neo-Nazis and the preservation of the Confederate monuments.

There are about 1,500 Confederate-related sites around the country. Most are located in the South, but there are also some sites in the North.

According to Graham (2016), "Six states include elements of Confederate flags in their official flags today. There are nine official state Confederate holidays. And as SPLC [Southern Poverty Law Center] notes, there's also the especially weird case of the 10 forts and military bases named for heroes of a cause that sought to defeat the U.S. military and killed tens of thousands of its soldiers. At the heat of the renaming push last summer, the Department of Defense was asked whether it was considering changing those names. A Pentagon spokesman said it was not."

The pervasive narrative is that these buildings, flags, and monuments represent Southern pride and accomplishments. In that viewpoint, this purge represents an elimination of Confederate artifacts. Some say removing them does not remove them from the history of the United States, and hiding them does not hide the ideology. Others argue that removing these statues and flags is sanitizing history. After World War II, the United States played a role in the removal of Nazi monuments and symbols. More recently, the U.S. Army assisted in the demolition of the statue of Saddam Hussein. Therefore, while these objections are worth articulating, it must be emphasized that they focus predominantly on an ideology within a larger social context, within a historical time frame. Furthermore, the majority of these arguments function as a post hoc rationalization or justification for hatred. These difficulties and ambiguities raise fundamental questions about the aims of those people perpetuating the Lost Cause ideology. This ideology generates considerable anxiety among college students, who are fighting for their place in the grand American narrative. To think that this ideology will be overcome simply by application of conscious rationality is essentially unthinking.

The advent of social media has significantly increased the glare on this issue. But this glare has also increasingly revealed the issue's complexity. Legal scholars Richard Delgado and Jean Stefancic (2004) note: "Tangible symbols have a quality that words—at least of the spoken variety—do not: They are enduring. Words disappear as soon as they are spoken. They may resonate in the mind of the victim, causing him or her to recall them over and over again. But a flag, monument, or a sports logo is always there to remind members of the group it spotlights of its unsolicited message" (p. 142). In the viewpoint of student protesters and their supporters on the campuses of Winthrop and Clemson University, the memory of the racist Benjamin Tillman is institutionally honored and sustained through government action. Additionally, there is the question of who is being empowered and under what circumstances.

The application of the "tear down/do not tear down the monuments" rhetoric is one-dimensional because it ignores the source of the issue. Central to deconstructing this binary is an understanding of the social, political, and economic functions of these artifacts. What are the social circumstances and ideology that surround the monument? What can be done now on campus? There is probably not one singular action that can solve the problem. Instead, there may be a combination of strategies that universities can employ. Because several campuses have removed statues and renamed buildings, those actions remain options. However, on the campus of the University of North Carolina–Chapel Hill, a student offered a suggestion to not remove the controversial Silent Sam, but rather to construct a counternarrative statue (Rubin, 2001). As another possibility, Slattery (2006) recommends a "diversity plaza," showcasing the contributions of people of color to Texas A&M and the University of Texas.

The University of Mississippi displayed its commitment to Lost Cause ideology and White supremacy when it erected a monument dedicated to the cause in 1906. In the report *A Brief Historical Contextualization of the Confederate Monument at the University of Mississippi,* faculty members from the history department recommended that a statement be placed next to the monument. We support the proposed revision to the wording on the plaque because it illuminates the fallacy of the often-accepted notions of the Lost Cause Movement that were used to justify White supremacy:

> Following the disfranchisement of black voters, the United Daughters of the Confederacy and similar organizations seized prominent public sites for monuments to Confederate soldiers. While memorializing the service and loss of southern troops, these monuments endorsed Lost Cause ideology, which justified Confederate defeat as a moral victory, insisted that slavery was not the cause of the Civil War, proclaimed Reconstruction a failed experiment in racial equality, and reaffirmed white southern nationalism. In 1906, the University of Mississippi welcomed white residents of Oxford and Lafayette County to dedication ceremonies for this monument, placed at the entrance to the campus. The monument's legacy as a symbol of racial exclusion continued through the century, especially during Dixie Week celebrations that began in 1950, and in 1962 when it served as a rallying point for opponents of integration. Although this monument commemorates local Confederate soldiers who died, today it reminds us of the distance traveled since the Civil War—that the Confederacy's defeat meant freedom for millions of southerners, that the war's end inaugurated constitutional amendments promising national citizenship and equal protection of the laws regardless of race, and that the University takes from its divisive past increased devotion to all who seek truth, knowledge, and wisdom (Neff, Roll, & Twitty, 2016, p. 11).

Nevertheless, the current sociopolitical and sociocultural issues relating to physical structures as well as organizational structures of oppression at universities are well documented. As noted earlier, the contention surrounding the vandalism of these sites has drawn attention to the reality that universities have accepted and sometimes celebrated images that are rooted in the oppression and marginalization of many Black students, faculty, and staff. Therefore, it is important to understand the historical roots of student activism as an agent of change on university campuses as well as how Lost Cause ideology can constrain/limit social change involving racist activities, organizations, and monuments at colleges and universities. As suggested previously, we can reinterpret them, talk about them, and teach about them. However, we cannot pretend that our institutions are not inextricably tied to human slavery and the oppression of Black people. Eliminating the symbolism of the Confederacy from public property does not eliminate the questions it represents from the collective historical consciousness. We hope our universities will play a significant role in rethinking the Lost Cause ideology. These statutes have never been acceptable to Black people. The removal of those statues is not just about present-day Blacks; it ought to be about those Blacks and others who fought on the Union side, so that, as President Lincoln stated, our "nation can have a new birth of freedom." Black people in the South did not fight and win so that monuments of their oppressors could be put up all over the South.

REFERENCES

Altbach, P. G. (1979). From revolution to apathy: American student activism in the 1970s. *Higher Education, 8*(6), 609–626.

Altbach, P. G., & Cohen, R. (1990). American student activism: The post-sixties transformation. *The Journal of Higher Education, 61*(1), 32–49. doi.org/10.2307/1982033

Barnett, R. (2016, April 13). Clemson students protest racism on campus. *The Greenville News*. Retrieved from www.greenvilleonline.com/story/news/local/pickens-county/2016/04/13/clemson-students-protest-racism-campus/82989312/

Beadle, A. (2016a, April 20). "Having names of buildings such as Tillman & Strom Thurmond Institute sends the message that . . ." #SikesSitIn [Tweet]. Retrieved from twitter.com/AbbBeadl/status/7229258716995 05152

Beadle, A. (2016b, April 20). ". . . The University values white supremacist over the emotional safety of their students." Clemson Peer Dialogue Facilitator #SikesSitIn [Tweet]. Retrieved from twitter.com/AbbBeadl/status/7229264675255 25504

Ben Tillman: Memories of an agrarian racist. (2001). *The Journal of Blacks in Higher Education,* (32), 48–49. doi:10.2307/2678766

Bever, M. (2011). Fuzzy memories: College mascots and the struggle to find appropriate legacies of the Civil War. *Journal of Sport History, 38*(3), 447–463. Retrieved from www.jstor.org/stable/10.5406/jsporthistory.38.3.447

Boyce, T., & Chunnu Brayda, W. (2015). In the words of the "Last Rhodesian": Dylann Roof and South Carolina's long tradition of white supremacy, racial rhetoric of fear, and vigilantism. *Present Tense, 5*(2). Retrieved from www .presenttensejournal.org/volume-5/the-last-rhodesian/

Broadhurst, C. J. (2014). Campus activism in the 21st century: A historical framing. *New Directions for Higher Education, 2014*(167), 3–15. Retrieved from doi .org/10.1002/he.20101

Brooks, R. (2017, February 17). Renaming university buildings with racist name-sakes is an uphill battle. *USA Today College*. Retrieved from college.usatoday .com/2017/02/14/renaming-university-buildings-with-racist-namesakes-is-an-uphill-battle/

Campbell, J. L. (2016, April 18). #SikesSitIn: Six day. *The Tiger*. Retrieved from www.thetigernews.com/news/sikessitin-six-days later/article_47277f0c-0519 -11e6-9137-7be75b8b6084.html

Carson, A. D. (2014, August 17). See the stripes [Clemson University]: A poem by A. D. Carson [Video File]. *YouTube*. Retrieved from www.youtube.com/watch ?v=tl1cSgbnZTo

Cary, N. (2015a, January 16). Clemson students plan protest to save Tillman Hall. *The Greenville News*. Retrieved from www.greenvilleonline.com/story/news/educat ion/2015/02/11/clemson-rename-tillman-hall-board- chair-says/23238993/

Cary, N. (2015b, February 11). Clemson won't rename Tillman Hall, board chair says. *The Greenville News*. Retrieved from www.greenvilleonline.com/story/news /education/2015/02/11/clemson-rename-tillman-hall-board-chair-says/23238993/

Cary, N. (2015c, July 2). Clemson won't rename Tillman Hall, board chair says. *The Greenville News*. Retrieved from www.greenvilleonline.com/story/news/educat ion/2015/02/11/clemson-rename-tillman-hall-board- chair-says/23238993/

Cary, N. (2015d, July 2). Renewed calls to rename Clemson's Tillman Hall. *The Greenville News*. Retrieved from www.greenvilleonline.com/story/news/educat ion/2015/07/02/renewed-calls-rename-clemsons- tillman-hall/29621879/

Cary, N. (2017, February 14). Yale's Calhoun College change renews calls about Clemson's Tillman Hall. *The Greenville News*. Retrieved from www .greenvilleonline.com/story/news/education/2017/02/14/clemson-tillman -hall-yale-calhoun-college/97869230/

Clark, D. (2016, April 16). We have come so far, but still have a long way to go. Proud of the students involved with the #SikesSitin #Clemson [Tweet]. Re-trieved from twitter.com/dus10clark/status/721403385576984576

Collins, J. (2016, November 14). Artists hang black nylons to protest post-Civil War racist. *The Associated Press*. Retrieved from apnews.com/c3183bae02d944d29 a10829e795aec0d/black-stockings-left-hanging-trees-sc-university

Delgado, R., & Stefancic, J. (2004). *Understanding words that wound*. Boulder, CO: Westview Press.

Diamond, J., & Bash, D. (2015, June 24). Nikki Haley calls for removal of Confed-erate flag from capitol grounds. *CNN*. Retrieved from www.cnn.com/2015/06 /22/politics/nikki-haley-confederate-flag-south-carolina-press-conference/

Dickey, J. (2016). The revolution on America's campuses. *Time*. Retrieved from time
.com/4347099/college-campus-protests/

Douglas, A. (2014, October 30). Winthrop board: SC law prevents changing Tillman Hall name. *The State*. Retrieved from www.thestate.com/news/local
/article1390650 5.html

Duke Students & Workers in Solidarity. (2016, April 22). A love letter to student
organizers at Clemson University. *Facebook*. Retrieved from m.facebook.com
/dukestudentsworkersinsolidarity/posts/898548213607134:0

Eagan, K., Stolzenberg, E. B., Ramirez, J. J., Aragon, M. C., Suchard, M. R., & Hurtado, S. (2015). *The American freshman: National norms fall 2015*. Los Angeles,
CA: Higher Education Research Institute. Retrieved from assets.documentcloud
.org/documents/2710405/The-American-Freshman-National-Norms-Fall-2015
.pdf

Ellsworth, F., & Burns, M. (1970). *Student activism in American higher education*.
Washington, DC: American College Personnel Association.

Emberton, C. (2013). *Beyond redemption: Race, violence, and the American South
after the Civil War*. Chicago, IL: The University of Chicago Press.

Field, J. B. (2016, April 11). Yes, we have no (time for) bananas. *The Tiger*. Retrieved from www.thetigernews.com/letters_to_editor/yes-we-have-no-time-for
-bananas/article_af9bfe96-0032-11e6-b590-ff3779e322b5.html

Folsom, B. (2016, September 27). Eastern Michigan issues punishments to 4 who
protested racist graffiti. *Detroit Free Press*. Retrieved from www.freep.com
/story/news/local/michigan/2016/11/30/eastern-michigan-issues-punishments-4
-who-protested-racist-graffiti/94676138/

Geiger, R. (2014). *The history of American higher education: Learning and culture
from the founding to World War II*. Princeton, NJ: Princeton University Press.

Graham, D. (2016, April 26). The Stubborn Persistence of Confederate Monuments.
The Atlantic. Retrieved from www.theatlantic.com/politics/archive/2016/04/the
-stubborn-Persistence-of-confederate-monuments/479741

Hofmann, S. (2005). The elimination of indigenous mascots, logos, and nick-
names: Organizing on college campuses. *American Indian Quarterly*, 29(1/2),
156–177.

Hyder, B. (2016, April 21). The Clements email is fascinating. Such a weird de-
flection of the Tillman issue #sikessitin [tweet]. Retrieved from twitter.com
/BenHyder/status/723260592346173441

Ireland, C. (2012, April 19). Harvard's long-ago student risings. Retrieved from
news.harvard.edu/gazette/story/2012/04/harvards-long-ago-student-risings/

James, A. (2008). Political parties: College social fraternities, manhood, and the defense of southern traditionalism, 1945–1960. In T. Watts (Ed.), *White masculin-
ity in the recent South* (pp. 63–85). Baton Rouge, LA: Louisiana State University
Press.

Jaschik, S. (2016, September 26). Epidemic of racist incidents. Retrieved from www
.insidehighered.com/news/2016/09/26/campuses-see-flurry-racist-incidents-and
-protests-against-racism

Jaschik, S. (2015, July 8). Vandalism or protest? *Inside Higher Ed*. Retrieved from www.insidehighered.com/news/2015/07/08/what-should-educators-make-spray-painting-campus-statues-and-symbols-old-south

Kantrowitz, S. (2000). *Ben Tillman and the reconstruction of white supremacy*. Chapel Hill, NC: The University of North Carolina Press.

Khan-Ibarra, S. (2014, November 13). The case for social media and hashtag activism. Retrieved from www.huffingtonpost.com/sabina-khanibarra/the-case-for-social-media_b_6149974.html

Kimball, T. (2016, September 26). Tillman Hall protest begins, ends peacefully at Winthrop. *The Charlotte Observer*. Retrieved from www.charlotteobserver.com/news/special-reports/charlotte-shooting- protests/article104801971.html

Levinson, S. (1998). *Written in stone: Public monuments in changing societies*. Durham, NC, & London, UK: Duke University Press.

Loewen, J. (1999). *Lies across America: What our historic sites get wrong*. New York, NY: Simon & Schuster.

Logue, J. (2016, April 25). Clemson students end lengthy sit-in. *Inside Higher Education*. Retrieved from www.insidehighered.com/news/2016/04/25/clemson-students-end-lengthy-sit

Martinez, J. M., & Harris, R. M. (2000). Graves, worms, and epitaphs: Confederate monuments in the southern landscape. In J. M. Martinez, W. D. Richardson, & R. McNinch-Su (Eds.), *Confederate symbols in the contemporary south* (pp. 130–194). Gainesville, FL: University of Florida Press.

Meloni, B. (2016). The history of food and dining at Harvard: Food fights. Retrieved from guides.library.harvard.edu/c.php?g=310694& p=2072617

Mills, C. (2003). Introduction. In C. Mills & P. H. Simpson (Eds.), *Monuments to the Lost Cause: Women, art, and the landscapes of the southern memory* (pp. xv–xxx). Knoxville, TN: The University of Tennessee Press.

Neff, J., Roll, J., & Twitty, A. (2016). *A brief historical contextualization of the Confederate monument at the University of Mississippi*. Retrieved from history.olemiss.edu/wp-content/uploads/sites/6/2017/08/A-Brief-Historical-Contextulzation-of-the-Confederate-Monument-at-the-University-of-Mississippi.pdf

Nehls, C. C. (2002). Flag-waving wahoos. Confederate symbols at the University of Virginia, 1941–1951. *The Virginia Magazine of History and Biography, 110*(4), 461–488.

Oppenheimer, M. (1985). The movement—A 25-year retrospective. *Monthly Review, 36*. Retrieved from www.questia.com/magazine/1G1-3621923/the-movement-a-25-year-retrospective

Perez, C. (2016, April 19). I'm so tired of folks belittling whats happening at the #SikesSitin. It's not just about bananas. #EducateYourself [tweet]. Retrieved from twitter.com/CristinaPerez11/status/722457810886332416

Peters, M. (2017, February 11). Yale renames Calhoun College over namesake's ties to slavery and white supremacy. *National Public Radio*. Retrieved from www.npr.org/sections/ thetwoway/2017/02/11/514747243/yale-renames-calhoun-college-over-namesakes-ties-to-slavery- and-white-supremacy

"Pitchfork" Ben Tillman: The most lionized figure in South Carolina history. (2007/2008). *The Journal of Blacks in Higher Education, (58)*, 38–39.

President's Commission on Campus Unrest. (1970). *The report of the President's Commission on campus unrest, including special reports: The killings at Jackson State, the Kent State tragedy.* New York, NY: Ayer Co. Pub.

Roach, R. (2015, September 9). Yale begins "conversation" on Calhoun College name. *Diverse Issues in Higher Education.* Retrieved from diverseeducation .com/article/77715/

Rubin, L. (2001). Of statuary, symbolism, and Sam. *Callaloo, 24*(1), 160–161.

Ruff, C. (2016, March 23). In explaining confederate symbols, colleges struggle to summarize history. *The Chronicle of Higher Education.* Retrieved from chronicle.com/article/In-ExplainingConfederate/235802?key=2cmlHiG21ND jnX87IjQa5bcFzq4o9g5GkqZg1aNtBgZZa0ljQlRGTkltZENkclJzS19EWllu TlppNVpOZWhYc XN3Q0JYc3ZzOE9J

Savage, K. (1994). The politics of memory: Black emancipation and the Civil War monument. In John R. Gills (Ed.), *Commemorations: The Politics of National Identity* (pp. 127–149). Princeton, NJ: Princeton University Press.

Slattery, P. (2006). Deconstructing racism one statue at a time: Visual culture wars at Texas A&M University and the University of Texas at Austin. *Visual Arts Research, 32*(2), 28–31.

Sliwinski, M. (2016, January 21). The evolution of activism: From the streets to social media. Retrieved from lawstreetmedia.com/issues/politics/evolution -activism-streets-social-media/

Thackham, D. (2016, September 28.). Tillman Hall protest begins, ends peacefully at Winthrop. *The Charlotte Observer.* Retrieved from www.charlotteobserver .com/news/special-reports/charlotte-shooting protests/article104801971.html

Wallenstein, P. (2008). *Higher education and the civil rights movement: White supremacy, black Southerners, and college campuses.* Gainesville, FL: University Press of Florida.

White, D. (2010). From desegregation to integration: Race, football, and "Dixie" at the University of Florida. *The Florida Historical Quarterly, 88*(4), 469–496.

Wilkins, D., Dukes, D., Lynn, L., Peeler, B., Wilkerson, K., McKissick, S., & Wood, A. (2016, February 5). *Recommendations from the Task Force on the History of Clemson to the Board of Trustees.* Clemson, SC: Clemson University.

Wilson, R. G. (2003). Monument Avenue, Richmond: A unique American boulevard. In C. Mills & P. H. Simpson (Eds.), *Monuments to the Lost Cause: Women, art, and the landscapes of southern memory* (pp. 100–115). Knoxville, TN: The University of Tennessee Press.

Wong, A. (2015). The renaissance of student activism. *The Atlantic.* Retrieved from www.theatlantic.com/education/archive/2015/05/the-renaissance-of-student -activism/393749/

Worland, J. (2015, June 22). This is why South Carolina raised the Confederate flag in the first place. *Time.* Retrieved from time.com/3930464/south-carolina -confederate-flag-1962/

CHAPTER 5

Women's Watch

Race, Protest, and Campus Assault

Noelle W. Arnold, Lisa Bass, and Kelsey Morris

In September 2016, more than 1,000 Berea College students, faculty, and staff members organized a protest as a response to incidents of campus sexual assault (CSA) and the college's response to those incidents. Student and sexual assault survivor Shanita Jackson, then 19, was "at the forefront of the protest" (Alfonso, 2016), and she spoke about the need to speak out: "Surviving sexual assault is not an easy task. It is not staying dormant. It is not settling for less. Survival is the refusal to be silent. Survival is calling out every system, every institution, every college, every perpetrator and holding them accountable."

The power in Shanita's survival was the protest that came afterward. More importantly, the use of the visual in the form of social media, protest signage, and other visualities created a space for agency in the midst of tragedy. Visualities go hand in hand with the creation of modern societies with new information and communication technologies. There is not only an increasing quantity of visual language but also important aspects in its use. Scholars of the visual claim that these re/presentations are "iconic" (Fellman, 1995), and agentic.

Visualities are central to the creation, preservation, and mediation of meaning (Kress & van Leeuwen, 2001). However, the specific performativity of visuals and visual discourse operates differently from mere text and holds generous potential.

This chapter seeks to examine visualities, as well as the role they play in protest. We particularly examine these phenomena by focusing on CSA and Black women. The rationale for this is multifold. First, we foreground Black women because they are left out of the overarching movement. Second, statistics and text alone rarely complete the mission of protest without the poignancy of collective discourse, persuasion, and emotiveness needed to empower a movement. Collins (2004) emphasizes that images, compared to verbal text, offer a more vivid and emotionally interesting persuasive case.

The power of the visual offers stark expression and persuasive potential (Aaron, 2007; Pollock, 2006). Third, visualities shine a light on sociocultural and institutional complexities within which Black women CSA survivors operate and make meaning.

While we provide statistics regarding CSA in the background, our focus is not on these numbers but on the *operative, performative,* and *appropriative* power of the visual in protest, particularly for Black women CSA survivors. We focus on the shared impacts among distinct CSA events of Black women, and what visualities and the protest they represent signify to each other and the larger society.

The meanings of visualities are tied to the contexts in which they are used. They also represent visual embodiments of social discourse and practice. Such visual demonstrations give power not only in their form but also through their content (Meyer, Höllerer, Jancsary & van Leeuwen, 2013). Thus, this chapter does not include traditional sections (literature review, framework, and so on). Instead, we provide literature and discursive exploration in the "context" of each visuality presented in this chapter. This provides a "grounded"[1] exploration of visualities, protest, and CSA as they relate to Black women.

THE PERVASIVENESS OF SEXUAL VIOLENCE

Sexual violence on campus is pervasive. Sexual assault has been described as assault of a sexual nature through physical force, violence, or incapacitation (Cantor et al., 2015). A 2015 report prepared for the Association of American Universities indicated that 11.2% of all students experience rape or sexual assault through physical force, violence, or incapacitation. For undergraduate students, 23.1% of females and 5.4% of males experience rape or sexual assault (Cantor et al., 2015).

Research has indicated that among female students, the rate of rape and sexual assault is reported as marginally higher for Whites, at 6.7 per 1,000 women, with Black women experiencing a rate of 6.4 per 1,000 and Hispanic women experiencing a rate of 4.5 per 1,000 (Sinozich & Langton, 2014). It is important to note that Black women comprised a much higher percentage of physically forced victims (23%) than any other victimization type on college campuses (Krebs, Lindquist, Berzofsky, Shook-Sa, & Peterson, 2016).

Compounding these disturbing statistics is the fact that only 20% of female student victims, aged 18–24, report their assault. Even when females are nonstudents, only 32% of those of the same age do make a report. However, groups and individuals are "reporting" in other ways, such as through activism and protest. Student activism has become more vocal than ever, creating a context of solidarity and support from the university community, and encouraging college members to act against gender violence (Vidu, Schubert, Muñoz, & Duque 2014). In fact, college students have been speaking out about CSA experiences, and this has led to a wave of activism, powering real change and influencing the national conversation. For example, these activists have experienced major victories, including a task force set up by President Barack Obama, the "It's on Us" White House campaign to prevent sexual violence, several bills in Congress,[2] a slew of state-level committees,[3] and continued government hearings about rape on campus.[4]

PROTEST AND VISUALITIES

Student-led justice and rights movements have increased and gained attention in national media (Anderson & Svrluga, 2015; Zimmerman, 2016). In response to CSA, students contribute regularly to organizing Take Back the Night rallies and events during Sexual Assault Awareness Month on campuses. In addition, student-led movements, such as Know Your IX (2016), End Rape on Campus (2016), and Survivors Eradicating Rape Culture (2016), highlight protest efforts to redress and ameliorate sexual assault, empower peers to dismantle norms around CSA, and hold institutions accountable for incomplete and inadequate responses to CSA. "Local grassroots activism, federal legislation, a nationwide campaign, and endless media attention have made sexual assault on college and university campuses a hot-button issue" (Feenstra, 2015, p. 33). Protest movements make clear when a college or university is not adequately responding to CSA. Journalist Emanuella Grinberg wrote a 2014 article detailing the stories of four activists' efforts to end CSA. The article describes "students taking matters into their own hands, filing complaints en masse and speaking out publicly" (para. 8). The article highlights the importance of the activists collaborating with other larger networks such as Know Your IX.

There are productive affinities between visual analysis and activist practices. Those who study protest and activism look for iconic images from certain social movements—labor movements, free speech movements, student movements, and so forth. Visual documentation can serve to galvanize protest but also provide understanding for the current and the next generation, like turning a mattress into a symbol of protest as one Columbia University student did. For her senior thesis, Emma Sulkowicz conducted a work of endurance performance art called "Carry That Weight" to protest the fact that her attacker remained at the institution. For an entire academic year, she carried a mattress wherever she went on campus—including to her graduation ceremony.

The idea of photography and visual memes—units of culture passed between people who make it their own as they go—being used for social movements is not new (Kessler & Schafer 2009). Visual media have influenced policy and called attention to social conditions across the various spaces. What visual and embodied protest has managed to do better than words is to foreground "the thing that matters most . . . the truth. The frustrating truth" (Hamill, 2013).

Let us note up front that the purpose of this chapter is not to pit Black survivors against other survivors or lessen all women's CSA experiences. Rather, this chapter examines how CSA is engaged on campus by examining the experiences of Black women. Very few studies foreground women of color and CSA. This chapter focuses on visual narratives and how they influence and impact structures on behalf of women of color. Examining and analyzing these narratives gives us a better understanding of how Black CSA survivors and their allies are building unique awareness surrounding CSA. The driving thesis of this chapter is that visualities promote voice, agency, and response to shifting campus culture in the age of information and social media. Visual protest assists in the fight against CSA in response to Black women being decentered in the movement. In addition, the chapter discusses how women of color have been "talking back" and "taking back" by reappropriating their images, pictures, and narratives to protest and advocate for social change (Witherspoon, 2008).

"Individuals act as agents of change, advocating against campus sexual assault and transforming campus norms about consent, prevention, support for survivors, and institutional response" (Krause, Miedema, Woofter, & Yount. 2017, p. 211). Researchers of CSA have largely ignored protest and advocacy movements in gaining a robust understanding of sexual assault. Those who mobilize and act within the "front lines" can provide new insights on this complex issue.

VISUAL METHODS

In particular, we approached visual as narrative and narrative as visual. In this case, images are treated as "telling a story" (by analyzing certain discursive elements in and of the image), and storytelling serves as image making (creating and normalizing "mind pictures" of taken-for-granted understandings). Narrative texts can be any type of text where a person relates a story in a particular medium, such as in words, imagery, sound, movement, or any combination of these (Bal, 1997; Bruner, 1990; Polkinghorne, 1988).

Images we studied included more than 200 newspaper photographs, screenshots of TV news coverage and websites, and image representations such as cartoons, caricatures, advertisements, mappings. Images were web and archival researched, and only public domain images qualifying for Fair Use policy were utilized as indicated in Section 107 of the U.S. Copyright Act, which states:

> The fair use of a copyrighted work, including such use by reproduction in copies or phono records or by any other means specified by that section, for purposes such as criticism, comment, news reporting, teaching (including multiple copies for classroom use), scholarship, or research, is not an infringement of copyright.

Historically, fields such as anthropology and sociology have examined images to evoke two types of response: physical and emotive. The former deals with analysis of technical aspects of the images such as framing, exposure, and an analysis of the image itself. However, the images here have been examined for deeper information of representation, discourse, experience, history, and subjectivity. Visual analysis helps detect and decode the hierarchies and differences it naturalizes (Fyfe & Law, 1988).

In particular, we referenced Rose's (2007) three-pronged approach to visual analysis: technological, compositional, and contextual. In other words, we looked at how the image is made, including the medium and modalities, as well as composition, or the content, color, and spatial organization. However, we focused mostly on the contextual because these imaged narratives function within specific contexts and spaces. By doing so, we were able to examine the social or situational relations, institutions, and practices that surrounded an image.

Audiences, or the "lookers," will always bring their own interpretations. We became convinced that the important idea in our analysis was not necessarily how the images looked, but what the images do and with what other representations they act in conjunction (Armstrong, 1998). "It is very unusual to encounter an image unaccompanied by any text at all whether spoken or written" (Wollen, 1972, p. 118). Therefore, spatial arrangements, captions, interview transcripts, broadcast transcripts, and other printed material served to triangulate our data both in source and in methodology (Angen, 2000) and provide confirmability and credibility (Lincoln & Guba, 1985). Sturken and Cartwright (2001) argue that the image itself is as important as how it is seen by the spectator who looks in particular ways. However, as illustrated in this chapter, ways of seeing do not occur in a vacuum. They are always mediated and mobilized by the ideologies and goals of the images and the image-maker and how images re/produce understandings.

WHAT WE LEARNED

Certain ideas about protest are "evoked/invoked" (Bauman & Briggs, 2003) in these images by preexistent sociocultural forms of interpretation. Each photograph was first coded for content. Longer memos were written to bring theoretical ideas to the photographs (Keats, 2009). Thoughts about associated theories were notated, which, in turn, informed codes and memos in an iterative, back-and-forth movement. Memos were used to document the conceptual ideas developing as data were assigned to codes. In thematizing, frequencies were noted and concepts were applied.

The Protest Is in the Picture

What counts as activism or protest? And what counts as evidence of them? There is indeed protest in the picture. In other words, the very act of documenting campus issues is a way to illuminate oppression and marginalization, considering that many of these injustices remain silent. Documenting and preserving any struggle becomes a way to bring the struggle out from the shadows in hopes that the offense shrinks from the light and is rendered incapable. The visual becomes a means of "intervention, meant to focus attention on a vital matter, to disrupt business as usual, if only briefly, or even, possibly, to effect change" (Bryan-Wilson, González & Willsdon, 2016, p. 6).

The term *visual* may seem to add more weight to protest that is public, seen, and photographed. However, the visual narrative perspective grants primacy to text or other forms of protest documentation. Is protest always public or can protest be private? Can there be INvisible protest? "Activism takes on specific, and sometimes surprising, visual forms that are not always aligned with or recognizable by pre-defined frameworks" (Bryan-Wilson, González & Willsdon, 2016, p. 7).

As noted, survivors often employ visual images or photographs to share their experiences and protest. A survivor named Jasmine from Arizona State University posed for a poster for KnowyourIX.org that stated, "I protested because my school refused to investigate reports of harassment, which it's required to do by law." Two Black women, Victoria and Melanie, who are survivors of CSA not only recounted their CSA experiences for a Buzzfeedstory, they bravely posed for a photograph that is featured prominently at the start of the article.[5] The portrait challenges the cultural frames that continue to influence reactions to women of color who assert claims of sexual assault in the modern era (Brake, 2017). Women of color contend with issues related to patriarchy, but they also experience a disproportionate level of victim blaming and shaming (Brake, 2017). For example, Jasmine's campus officials did not investigate her CSA complaint, and the investigation of Victoria and Melanie's complaints concluded there was no rape and that the victim was complicit in her CSA, respectively.

Race and gender intersect when examining the treatment of complainants. Women of color are often invisible when they are complainants. "The rape myths that undermine survivors' credibility and narratives of harm are not just gendered but also racialized, and they are especially pernicious in delegitimizing the experiences of women of color" (Brake, 2017, p. 138). The racial and sexual stereotypes that may derail survivors of color's claims of CSA are traceable to the inheritance of slavery, in which African American women were viewed as promiscuous (West, 1995). These myths "deny or minimize victim injury or blame the victims for their own victimization" (Carmody & Washington, 2001, p. 424).

Women of color are less likely to report sexual assault out of fears of being stereotyped or not believed (Donovan, 2007). There remains a double standard for Black female CSA survivors. It contributes to every stage in the reporting process, from pre-rape, through the actual occurrence, to post-rape (Burnett et al., 2009). This factors most prevalently in unacknowledgment and mislabeling of CSA. For instance, unacknowledged rape experiences can be caused by misidentifying or labeling by the victim herself due to how campus policies or procedures frame CSA (Fedina, Holmes & Backes, 2016; Littleton, Rhatigan, & Axsom, 2007; Wilson & Miller, 2016). Inchoate definitions and subjective application of policy (who is believed or who receives a response) cause unsound statistics on CSA. This is compounded for women of color survivors, who are already subject to increased stigma, and this certainly hinders understanding of the gender-raced (Witherspoon, 2008) complexities of CSA.

In spite of these problematic responses to CSA, our research found that visualities serve as quasi-reporting even when there has not been a formal complaint. Victims of CSA utilize the media to play a critical role in illuminating the truth for people. The media are able to place a particular incident in a broader context to ensure appropriate responses and services for victims, accountability and treatment for those who abuse others, and prevention strategies of organizations and communities.

#Hashtag

While protest may be *visible*, it is not always readily apparent in its *intensity*. We found that the contemporary use of the hashtag gets past the boundaries of the visual and integrates text to reinforce seriousness, pervasiveness, and force of a problem. This integration is all at once private (from one's own milieu) and public in its invitation for others to share, respond, and contest.

The hashtag (#) Say Her Name has become a rallying cry to high-light other forms of racist violence. Specifically, this campaign was used in response to police violence against Black women, such as in the cases of Sandra Bland, Rekia Boyd, Alesia Thomas, and Shantel Davis. These four Black women were killed in police custody. A powerful visual representation of these tragedies could be seen on a large banner displaying their faces, names, and #sayhername that was hung at a 2015 Milwaukee music festival (www.flickr.com/photos/40969298@N05/19490926964). The hashtag has also been featured on protest signage, such as one poster displayed at the National Day of Action that featured the hashtage alongside the words "BLACK WOMEN WILL NOT BE SILENCED."

Although the hashtag did not originate as a protest against CSA specifically, #sayhername has become a rallying phrase to highlight other forms of racist violence. On campuses, the White racial frame (WRF) (Feagin, 2013) is the "norm," whereby students of color are often represented according to predetermined heuristics in these institutions (Iverson, 2007). The WRF consciously and unconsciously denies blackness and brownness and serves to preserve certain social privileges. In addition it provides "a psychological cover for unencumbered fashioning of certain cultural notions of difference" (Watson, 2013, pp. 130–131). In particular, race-ing (foregrounding race) and hashtagging protest makes a case that CSA "encompass more than just perpetrators and victims" (Burnett et al., 2009, p. 468). In reality, CSA is psychologically, sociologically, and situationally located with the culture of campus and society.

In social media, the intensity or potency of an issue can sometimes fade due to its evolving milieu. We found that the hashtag serves as a continued reminder (and one that can be revisited as often as one likes) to maintain momentum and mobilization around a particular issue. Reappropriating and reusing hashtags can preserve the issue and the moment in history and unite all in interpreting and unmasking future issues.

On the the African American Policy Forum's (AAPF) page on CSA, they advise allies to "use the hashtags #HerDreamDeferred and #SayHerName to connect with us on twitter to share your story, uplift others and respond to the discussion with questions or thoughts" (aapf.org/sexual-assault-hbcus/). The page urges those who have experienced CSA to share their own experiences or others using hashtags. This form of protest invites the audience to connect to an issue personally, which often is the impetus for social action and advocacy (Weitz, 2002). In the world of social media, hashtags have become a call to action, if only to add one's voice to the stream publicly or privately.

One of the issues involved in CSA is the failure to agree on "what counts" as CSA (Schwartz & Leggett, 1999). Sexual assault estimates vary widely, namely because there are varying definitions of what actually constitutes sexual assault. Sexual victimization on college campus have been defined as physically forced or forcible rape, incapacitated rape, sexual coercion, and unwanted sexual contact (Fisher, Cullen, & Turner, 2000; Kilpatrick, Resnick, Ruggiero, Conoscenti, & McCauley, 2007; Krebs, Lindquist, & Barrick, 2010; Krebs, Lindquist, Warner, Fisher, & Martin, 2009). In a CSA report commissioned by the U.S. Department of Justice (Krebs, Lindquist, Warner, Fisher, & Martin, 2007), the authors framed CSA as a public health issue, citing the physical and psychological impacts of CSA. This investigation was undertaken specifically to document the prevalence of distinct types of sexual assault among university women. However, this same report discussed whether "drugs or alcohol were involved as well as the context, consequences, and reporting of distinct types of sexual assault" (p. viii). In addition, the report offered several CSA classifications defined by the "certainty" of victims or voluntarily-ness. This made the report somewhat counterintuitive. These classifications may actually make it easier for certain states and campuses to introduce "requirements" that place an undue burden on Black female victims, such as conditions of promptness (in reporting), credibility (of the complainant), and corroboration (of the event) (Treiman, 1981). For example, Texas requires corroboration when there is a lack of prompt reporting (Schafran, 2015). New York requires corroboration when a complainant's mental incapacity supports nonconsent. Ohio requires corroboration for the crime of sexual imposition.

THE RACIAL FRAME OF CSA

Myths surrounding CSA are often "unquestioned and unconscious" (Schein, 1992, p. 239). These myths form a visual yet hidden racial frame that is all the more powerful because it is visible but unseen. In the case of campuses, this frame exists in observable and encrypted visual norms, values, and practices. For instance, campus policies complicate CSA with inchoate requirements and procedures. Fedina, Holmes, and Backes (2016), in a report for U.S. Department of Justice urge universities to rethink current approaches and practices: "Universities should start with a detailed understanding of their students' needs when addressing sexual assault. Instead of a one-size-fits-all approach, schools should tailor programs . . ."

Moreover, when universities highlight the issue of CSA, they decenter the role race plays in CSA. In statistics, infographics, posters, and other material on campuses, race is a silent factor in information sharing, educative and awareness programming, and policy development. In this case, the use of only White women in visual campaigns further silences CSA for women of color. Moreover, Wooten (2017) found that race-neutral language in policies comanages this silence and undermines the experiences of women of color.

Individuals might re/interpret *institutional* visual culture surrounding CSA as deraced and/or universal in its scope and consequence. In reality, research has shown that race can have a strong impact on the daily experience of college students, and the experiences of ethnic/racial minority students within a predominantly White institution are distinctly different from those of their counterparts (Jones, Castellanos, & Cole, 2002; Suarez-Balcazar, Orellana-Damacela, Portillo, Rowan, & Andrews-Guillen, 2003). Moreover, survivors of color are often "left out" of CSA protest movements by a failure to address unique racial and cultural factors, which differentiates the experience and aftermath (Women of Color Network, 2006). In addition to dealing with CSA, a woman of color is forced to survive within institutions where myths associated with her sexual assault experience abound, and she is misunderstood and unsupported (Women of Color Network, 2006).

Students of color and their allies utilize visualities that counter colorblind tendencies and promote not only uniqueness but also intersectionality that counternarrates the homogeneity in concerns of CSA. Campuses may be un/intentionally oppressive, but perpetuate inequitable conditions (McIntosh, 2005; Tutwiler, 2016). When institutions are entrenched in attitudes, structures, and institutional practices that operate around those who are White, students of color are marginalized both overtly as well as inconspicuously. Whitewashing serves as a subtle act of racism or racist discourse and may invite racial microaggressions and reinforce entrenched racial frames (Ford, 2015; Smith, 2004).

Victims of sexual assault often fail to report their incidents because they fear they will either be blamed or not believed. Because of this, victim Kamilah Willingham, who posted a photo of herself on Twitter holding a sign that says, "We Believe You," shared her story. The photo showed the CSA survivor and Harvard graduate after a campus committee deemed her CSA complaint as lacking in foundation. Around this time, a group of students, who called themselves the Harvard "Harassment/Assault Legal Team" (2015), denounced the lack of acknowledgment of the racial bind in CSA:

> Women of color are at the greatest risk for sexual violence. . . . According to the results of the recent Harvard campus survey, women of color are victims of nonconsensual sexual touching involving physical force or incapacitation at the highest rates: 7% of American Indian & Alaska Native graduate-school women, 6.7% of Asian graduate-school women, and 5.7% of Black graduate-school women, compared with 5.1% of white graduate-school women. (para. 5)

Despite the rejection of the conditional requirements in most formal state law, some colleges and universities still apply new iterations of these conditions for CSA in the name of procedural redress or reporting structures. This represents tension among Title IX, the federal statute prohibiting sex-based discrimination at educational institutions receiving federal funding (1972, 20 U.S.C. §1681), campus procedure, and other legislation concerning CSA.[6] Institutions are cautioned that sexual violence and harassment are forms of sex-based discrimination that institutions must address. However, as we see in Kamiliah's case, this is not always the case.

"TALKING AND TAKING BACK"

This exploration of visualities highlights that visual media are a persuasive form of protest and can influence cultural change. The visual promotes voice, agency, and response to shifting campus culture in the age of information and social media. Visual media and visual protests assist in the fight against CSA in response to Black women being decentered in the movement. More importantly, women of color have been "talking back" and "taking back," reappropriating their images, pictures, and narratives to protest and advocate for social change (Denard, 1998). "Narratives can provide . . . access . . . to the values that we want to uncover and examine for their re-appropriative potential in the contemporary" (Denard, 1998, p. 92). Women of color demand reciprocity through visualities to sustain constant reflection and re/interpretation of events to advance their cause.

Consequently, re/appropriation, and reciprocity also acknowledge and coordinate others' standpoints, issues, and identities in eradicating oppression. Black women protest, interrogate, and activate momentum in their quest to achieve justice for Black women while also demanding justice for all oppressed and marginalized peoples (Floyd-Thomas, 2006b). "Human equality is categorical, absolute, and unconditional, and universally applicable" (Townes, 1993, p. 138).

Visualities allow women of color to protest and to live their lives in ways that allow for construction of new narratives and agencies to be appropriated by future generations. To develop protest leaders, Black visualities do not promote solitary leader development. They promote "more adaptive, relational, and interactive models of protest" (Fluker, 1998, p. 11) such as those we see in hash-tagging and culturally responsive interventions (Katz & Moore, 2013). Rather than viewing CSA experiences as natural (thus opening the door for stereotypes and misappropriations), Black women can visually "construct who they are and how they want to be known" (Riessman & Quinney, p. 394).

Lastly, Black women's visual narratives invite an *assault criticism approach* to CSA that interrogates assumptions about race, women, and assault. One must have a basic attitude of respect and dignity toward the individual—her stories and her interpretations—to bridge empathy. In addition, research utilizing this assault criticism approach should have the "insider's" epistemic voice to explore, examine, and reveal linkages between CSA and the dynamics of race, ethnicity, class, gender, and other human diversities. Protest work is an "intentional and concomitant invitation for others to participate in solidarity with and on behalf of Black women" (Floyd-Thomas, 2006a, p. 250).

Visual studies in protest make visible not just the results of our actions (through an article, a photo, or a video, for example) but also the systems of marginalization, power, and practice that activism is often aiming to address and influence. Visuality causes us to reexamine our own systems, or redraw our cognitive maps, to better understand the structures and systems in which we all operate (Chalabi, 2016).

NOTES

1. See grounded theory.

2. See H.R.5972—Campus Sexual Assault Whistleblower Protection Act of 2016; H.R.2680—HALT Campus Sexual Violence Act; Campus Sexual Violence Elimination (Campus SaVE) Act.

3. See Harnisch & Lebioda, 2016. Top 10 higher education state policy issues for 2016. American Association of State Colleges and Universities Policy Brief; Lebioda, 2015. State Policy Proposals to Combat Campus Sexual Assault. American Association of State Colleges and Universities Policy Brief.

4. See Health, Labor, and Pensions, U.S. Senate Committee hearings, July 29, 2015.

5. See www.buzzfeed.com/anitabadejo/where-is-that-narrative?utm_term=.rgwe WPwe8#.jbk6ZKL6x

6. See Clery Act (1990), the Campus Sexual Assault Victims' Bill of Rights (1992), the Revised Sexual Harassment Guidance from U.S. Department of Education (2001), and the Violence Against Women Reauthorization Act (2013).

REFERENCES

Aaron, M. (2007). *Spectatorship: The power of looking on*. London, England: Wallflower Press.

Anderson, N., & Svrluga, S. (2015, December 25). Sweetbriar College to close because of financial challenges. *The Washington Post*. Retrieved from www

.washingtonpost.com/news/grade-point/wp/2015/12/25/2015-a-year-of-tumult
-on-college-campuses/?utm_term=.c3bb45078e13

Angen, M. J. (2000). Evaluating interpretive inquiry: Reviewing the validity debate
and opening the dialogue. *Qualitative health research, 10*(3), 378–395. dx.doi
.org/10.1177/104973230001000308

Armstrong, G. (1998). *Football hooligans: Knowing the score.* Oxford, UK: Berg.

Bal, M. (1997). *Narratology: Introduction to the theory of narrative.* Toronto, Canada: University of Toronto Press.

Bauman, R., & Briggs, C. (2003). *Voices of modernity.* Cambridge, UK: Cambridge
University Press.

Brake, D. L. (2017). Fighting the rape culture wars through the preponderance of
the evidence standard. *Montana Law Review, 78,* 109.

Bruner, J. S. (1990). *Acts of meaning.* Cambridge, MA: Harvard University Press.

Bryan-Wilson, J., González, J., & Willsdon, D. (2016). Editors' introduction:
Themed issue on visual activism. *Journal of Visual Culture, 15*(1), 5–23.

Burnett, A., Mattern, J. L., Herakova, L. L., Kahl Jr., D. H., Tobola, C., & Born-
sen, S. E. (2009). Communicating/muting date rape: A co-cultural theoretical
analysis of communication factors related to rape culture on a college campus.
Journal of Applied Communication Research, 37(4), 465–485.

Cantor, D., Fisher, B., Chibnall, S., Townsend, R., Lee, H., Bruce, C., & Thomas,
G. (2015). *Report on the AAU campus climate survey on sexual assault and
sexual misconduct.* Retrieved from www.aau.edu/sites/default/files/%40%20
Files/Climate%20Survey/AAU_Campus_Climate_Survey_12_14_15.pdf

Carmody, D. C., & Washington, L. M. (2001). Rape myth acceptance among college
women: The impact of race and prior victimization. *Journal of Interpersonal
Violence, 16*(5), 424–436.

Chalabi, D. (2016). What is visual activism? *Journal of Visual Culture, 15*(1),
32–34.

Collins, P. H. (2004). *Black sexual politics: African Americans, gender, and the new
racism.* New York, NY: Routledge.

Donovan, A. R. (2007). To blame or not to blame: Influences of target race and observer sex on rape blame attribution. *Journal of Interpersonal Violence, 22*(6),
722–736.

Feagin, J. R. (2006). *Systematic racism.* New York, NY: CRC Press.

Feagin, J. R. (2013). *The White racial frame: Centuries of racial framing and counter-
framing.* New York, NY: Routledge.

Fedina, L., Holmes, J. L., & Backes, B. L. (2018). Campus sexual assault: A systematic review of prevalence research from 2000 to 2015. *Trauma, Violence, &
Abuse, 19*(1), 76–93.

Feenstra, A. E. (2015). Campus responses to sexual assault: An analysis of best and
worst administrative practices at large, public, research universities (Doctoral
dissertation). University of Nevada, Reno.

Fellman, M. (1995). *Citizen Sherman: A life of William Tecumseh Sherman.* New
York, NY: Random House.

Fisher, B., Cullen, F., & Turner, M. (2000). *The sexual victimization of college women*. Retrieved from www.ncjrs.gov/pdffiles1/nij/182369.pdf

Floyd-Thomas, S. M. (Ed.). (2006a). *Deeper shades of purple: Womanism in religion and society*. New York, NY: New York University Press.

Floyd-Thomas, S. M. (2006b). *Mining the motherlode: Methods in womanist ethics*. Cleveland, OH: The Pilgrim Press.

Fluker, W. E. (Ed.). (1998). *The stones that the builders rejected: The development of ethical leadership from the black church tradition*. Harrisburg, PA: Trinity Press International.

Ford, D. R. (2015). *Life in schools: An introduction to critical pedagogy in the foundations of education*. Boulder, CO, & London, UK: Paradigm Publishers.

Fyfe, G., & Law, J., (1988). *Picturing power: Visual depiction and social relations*. London, UK: Routledge.

Grinberg, E. (2014, February 12). Ending rape on campus: Activism takes several forms. *CNN*. Retrieved from www.cnn.com/2014/02/09/living/campus-sexual -violence-students-schools/

Hamill, A. (2013). *Learning ICT in the arts*. New York, NY: Routledge.

"Harassment/Assault Legal Team." (2015, November 15). Letter to the editor. *Harvard Law Record*.

House, W. (2017). The second report of the White House task force to protect students from sexual assault. Retrieved from www.whitehouse.gov/sites/whitehouse .gov/files/images/Documents/1.4,17

Iverson, S. V. (2007). Camouflaging power and privilege: A critical race analysis of university diversity policies. *Educational Administration Quarterly, 43*(5), 586–611. doi: 10.1177/0013161x07307794

Jones, L., Castellanos, J., & Cole, D. (2002). Examining the ethnic minority student experience at predominantly White institutions: A case study. *Journal of Hispanic Higher Education, 1*(1), 19–39.

Katz, J., & Moore, J. (2013). Bystander education training for campus sexual assault prevention: an initial meta-analysis. *Violence and Victims, 28*(6), 1054–1067.

Keats, P. (2009). Multiple text analysis in narrative research: visual, written, and spoken stories of experience. *Qualitative Research 9*(2), 181–195.

Kessler, F., & Schäfer, M. T. (2009). Navigating YouTube: Constituting a hybrid information management system. In P. Snickars & P. Vonderau (Eds.), *The YouTube reader* (pp. 275–291). Diva-portal.org

Kilpatrick, D. G., Resnick, H. S., Ruggiero, K. J., Conoscenti, L. M., & McCauley, J. (2007). *Drug-facilitated, incapacitated, and forcible rape: A national study*. Rockville, MD: National Criminal Justice Reference Service.

Krause, K. H., Miedema, S. S., Woofter, R., & Yount, K. M. (2017). Feminist research with student activists: Enhancing campus sexual assault research. *Family Relations, 66*(1), 211–223.

Krebs, C. P., Lindquist, C. H., & Barrick, K. (2010). *The historically Black college and university campus sexual assault (HBCU-CSA) study*. Retrieved from

www.nsvrc.org/publications/historically-black-college-and-university-campus
-sexualassault-hbcu-csa-study

Krebs, C., Lindquist, C., Berzofsky, M., Shooks-Sa, B., & Peterson, K. (2016). *Campus climate survey validation study, final technical report.* Retrieved from www
.bjs.gov/content/pub/pdf/ccsvsftr.pdf

Krebs, C. P., Lindquist, C. H., Warner, T. D., Fisher, B. S., & Martin, S. L. (2007). *The campus sexual assault (CSA) study: Final report.* Washington, DC: National Institute of Justice, US Department of Justice.

Krebs, C. P., Lindquist, C. H., Warner, T. D., Fisher, B. S., & Martin, S. L. (2009). College women's experiences with physically forced, alcohol- or other drug-enabled, and drug-facilitated sexual assault before and since entering college. *Journal of American College Health, 57*(6), 639–647. doi.org/10.3200/JACH
.57.6.639-649

Kress, G., & Van Leeuwen, T. (2001). *Multimodal discourse: The modes and media of contemporary communication.* London, England: Edward Arnold.

Lincoln, Y. S., & Guba, E. G. (1985). *Naturalistic inquiry.* Thousand Oaks, CA: Sage.

Littleton, H. L., Rhatigan, D. L., & Axsom, D. (2007). Unacknowledged rape: How much do we know about the hidden rape victim? *Journal of Aggression, Maltreatment & Trauma, 14*(4), 57–74.

McIntosh, P. (2005). Gender perspectives on educating for global citizenship. In N. Noddings (Ed.), *Educating citizens for global awareness* (pp. 22–39). New York, NY: Teachers College Press.

Meyer, R. E., Höllerer, M. A., Jancsary, D., & Van Leeuwen, T. (2013). The visual dimension in organizing, organization, and organization research: Core ideas, current developments, and promising avenues. *Academy of Management Annals, 7*(1), 489–555.

Polkinghorne, D. E. (1988). *Narrative knowing and the human sciences.* New York, NY: SUNY Press.

Pollock, D. (2006). Marking new directions in performance ethnography. *Text and Performance Quarterly, 26*(4), 325–329.

Riessman, C. K., & Quinney, L. (2005). Narrative in social work: A critical review. *Qualitative social work, 4*(4), 391–412.

Rose, G. (2007). Researching visual materials: Towards a critical visual methodology. *Dies., Hg., Visual Methodologies. An Introduction to Interpreting Visual Materials.* London, UK: Sage.

Schafran, L. H. (2015). *Barriers to credibility: Understanding and countering rape myths.* Retrieved from https://www.nationalguard.mil/Portals/31/Documents/
J1/SAPR/SARCVATraining/Barriers_to_Credibility.pdf

Schein, E. H. (1992). *How can organizations learn faster? The problem of entering the Green Room.* Cambridge, MA: Alfred P. Sloan School of Management, Massachusetts Institute of Technology.

Schwartz, M. D., & Leggett, M. S. (1999). Bad dates or emotional trauma? The aftermath of campus sexual assault. *Violence Against Women, 5*(3), 251–271.

Sinozich, S., & Langton, L. (2014). *Rape and sexual assault victimization among college-age females, 1995–2013.* Retrieved from www.bjs.gov/content/pub/pdf/rsavcaf9513.pdf

Smith, W. A. (2004). Black faculty coping with racial battle fatigue: The campus racial climate in a post-civil rights era. *A long way to go: Conversations about race by African American faculty and graduate students, 14,* 171–190.

Sturken, M., & Cartwright, L. (2001). Scientific looking, looking at science. *Practices of Looking: An Introduction to Visual Culture,* 279–314.

Suarez-Balcazar, Y., Orellana-Damacela, L., Portillo, N., Rowan, J. M., & Andrews-Guillen, C. (2003). Experiences of differential treatment among college students of color. *The Journal of Higher Education, 74*(4), 428–444.

Townes, E. M. (1993). *Womanist justice, womanist hope.* Atlanta, GA: American Academy of Religion.

Treiman, D. M. (1981). Recklessness and the Model Penal Code. *Am. J. Crim. L., 9,* 281.

Tutwiler, S. W. (2016). *Mixed-race youth and schooling: The fifth minority.* New York, NY: Routledge.

Vidu, A., Schubert, T., Muñoz, B., & Duque, E. (2014). What students say about gender violence within universities: Rising voices from the communicative methodology of research. *Qualitative Inquiry, 20*(7), 883–888.

Watson, V. T. (2013). *The souls of White folk: African American writers theorize Whiteness.* Jackson: University Press of Mississippi.

Weitz, A. J. (2002). *Communicative and perceptual factors contributing to date rape: Interviews with perpetrators* (Unpublished doctoral dissertation, Southern Illinois University at Carbondale, IL).

West, C. (1995). *Critical race theory: The key writings that formed the movement.* The New Press.

White House Task Force to Protect Students From Sexual Assault (US). (2014). *Not alone: The first report of the White House task force to protect students from sexual assault.* Retrieved from www.justice.gov/archives/ovw/page/file/905942/download

Wilson, L. C., & Miller, K. E. (2016). Meta-analysis of the prevalence of unacknowledged rape. *Trauma, Violence, & Abuse, 17*(2), 149–159.

Witherspoon, T. N. (2008). *Ordinary theologies: Spiritual narratives of Black female principals* (Unpublished doctoral dissertation). The University of Alabama.

Wooten, S. C. (2017). Revealing a hidden curriculum of Black women's erasure in sexual violence prevention policy. *Gender and Education, 29*(3), 405–417.

Wollen, P. (1972). *Signs and meaning in the cinema* (Vol. 9). Bloomington, IN: Indiana University Press.

Women of Color Network. (2006). Sexual violence, communities of color. Retrieved from womenofcolornetwork.org/docs/factsheets/fs_sexual-violence.pdf

Zimmerman, A. (2016). Transmedia testimonio: Examining undocumented youth's political activism in the digital age. *International Journal of Communication, 10,* 21.

Part III

RESISTANCE BY/FOR ADMINISTRATORS, FACULTY, STAFF, AND STUDENTS

Complexifying the Narrative

Campus Activism and the Impact on Professionals of Color

Jonathan A. McElderry and Stephanie Hernandez Rivera

COMPLEXIFYING THE NARRATIVE

Amid rising racial tensions throughout the United States, college campuses have seen an increase in student activism, specifically as it relates to racial issues (Berrett, 2015; Brown, 2015). Many grassroots student groups have issued demands intended to improve campus climate and ensure equity for communities of color (Brown, 2016; Brown & Mangan, 2015). The University of Missouri was the site of national attention when the culmination of continued campus activism, a student's hunger strike, and the University Division 1 SEC football team's refusal to play in a conference game resulted in the resignation of the University of Missouri system president and university chancellor.

As two administrators working directly with minoritized students on campus, we witnessed the escalation and explosion of campus racial tensions at the University of Missouri. However, mid-level administrator perspectives and stories have been largely absent from or misrepresented by mainstream media, which have often focused on students and their efforts (Fernandes, 2016; Mangan, 2015; Schmalz, 2016; Supiano, 2015) or visible campus leaders and senior administrators (Stripling, 2016a, 2016b; Thomason, 2016). In contrast, we provide an in-depth analysis to understand how administrators at varying levels engaged in race-related issues and worked with student activists. We believe it is important to share our own experiences as previous administrators because we can provide other practitioners in the field of student affairs and higher education with greater insight on what to consider during times of racial campus unrest.

Specifically, this chapter provides our narratives as two administrators in higher education who worked directly with marginalized student populations in times of increased campus tensions. We begin by providing an overview of the campus unrest at Mizzou and present a theoretical framework for the chapter. Then, we discuss the research findings of the chapter, situate our discussion in relation to the theories, and discuss the chapter's contribution to research, policy, and practice. Finally, we provide suggestions for future implications.

CAMPUS UNREST AT MIZZOU

The University of Missouri (Mizzou) is the first public university west of the Mississippi River. It is a land-grant, research university with very high scholarly productivity, and it is the flagship of the state's university system. Mizzou has 19 colleges and schools with more than 300 degree programs, and it is one of five universities throughout the country that offers law, medicine, veterinary medicine, and a nuclear research reactor. According to the Fall 2014 Enrollment Summary, at the time of this investigation there were 35,441 students enrolled at Mizzou, 27,654 of whom were undergraduates. Of the undergraduate enrollment, 2,268 students were listed as Black/African American.

The summary of events that follows is not exhaustive, but merely a contextual depiction of the events leading up to the fall of 2015 at the University of Missouri campus. The most recent wave of student activism began at the University of Missouri in August 2014, directly after the murder of Michael Brown in Ferguson, Missouri. Prior to the start of the fall semester, three queer Black women began organizing their peers under the name #MU4MikeBrown and led the first act of resistance in the form of a "Hands Up, Don't Shoot" photo shoot. These women along with a Black, Afro–Puerto Rican, and South Korean woman continued to coordinate various demonstrations and acts of resistance on campus. These students reached out to senior administrators to have a private meeting with other student groups on campus to present a "Call to Action" list. By April 2015, the university administrators held a "Call to Action Progress Report Town Hall" after students became frustrated by the lack of transparency and accountability from university administrators. By the fall of 2015, all of the central organizers in these efforts had graduated except for one.

In September 2015, the Missouri Student Association (MSA) president, who identifies as a Black queer man, was called racial and heterosexist slurs. Approximately a week later, while the Legion of Black Collegians

Homecoming Court was practicing for an upcoming performance on Traditions Plaza, they were called the N-word by a White man in a historically White fraternity. The following day, a #BlackLivesMatter study hall occurred in Jesse Hall (the administrative building). As the semester continued, various groups continued to mobilize. #ConcernedStudent1950 came to fruition through the homecoming demonstration on October 10 and halted the annual homecoming parade to address the university system president Tim Wolfe about his lack of acknowledgment and response to racial incidents on campus. On October 20, students issued a newly created list of demands that primarily focused on the Black student experience. After several weeks of protests and demonstrations, a graduate student, who at the time was a member of #ConcernedStudent1950 and a Mizzou undergraduate alum, announced that he would be embarking on a hunger strike until Tim Wolfe resigned from his position or was terminated. It is important to acknowledge that none of this student's friends or peers knew he would be embarking on this hunger strike. He announced it to fellow members of #ConcernedStudent1950 the day before he emailed the system president, Board of Curators, and blind-copied various individuals, including us.

Immediately, students began fiercely mobilizing and coordinating a "campout" on the quad. They stated they would be sleeping at the campsite until the resignation of the president to save their friend. By November 7, 2015, a meeting between the student on the hunger strike and Black players from the football team resulted in the Black football players refusing to play until the system president's resignation. However, based on some conversations, it is unclear if all of the Black football players were on board with the strike. The following day, the entire team participated in the strike with the support of the head coach. The refusal to play would have resulted in the university losing upwards of $5 million. The protests soon became national news covered by most major networks across the country. Protests began to occur across college campuses in support of Mizzou, demanding changes for the other institutions. On Monday, November 9, after nearly 7 days of the student's hunger strike, and less than 48 hours after the football team announced they would refuse to play, Tim Wolfe resigned as the president of the University of Missouri system. Shortly thereafter, the chancellor of the University of Missouri–Columbia campus resigned as well. However, this was also related in part to receiving a no-confidence vote from the deans of the various colleges on campus.

Although the aftermath of the resignations was a joyous moment for students in the movement, the backlash resulted in death threats against the protesters, Black students on campus, and harm done to the Black Culture

Center. Over the next year and a half, the institution would experience state legislators threatening to cut funding at the Mizzou campus, enrollment dropping significantly, layoffs, budget cuts, and residential hall closings, as well as a mass exodus of faculty and staff from the institution. Some of these issues were due to a lack of commitment and continued cuts to higher education, which are also happening in states across the country. Additionally, the racial tensions, institutionalized racism, campus demonstrations, increased negative portrayals in the media, as well as other factors continued to affect the institution.

CONTEXTUALIZING THE EXPERIENCES OF PEOPLE OF COLOR

We utilize two theoretical lenses to examine our experiences relating to campus unrest and crisis. Critical race theory (CRT) contextualizes the experiences of people of color in a way that centers our experiences and stories. CRT originally emerged out of legal scholarship and has been used in framing educational research, particularly after Daniel Solórzano (1997) worked to combine concepts of other theorists to create and identify the four basic tenets of CRT. These tenets are: (1) the centrality and intersectionality of race and racism, (2) challenge to dominant ideology and commitment to social justice, (3) centrality of experiential knowledge, and (4) interdisciplinary perspective (Solórzano, 1997). In using critical race theory, we are able to effectively analyze our own experiences as well as others' experiences to support the tenets.

Additionally, because the experiences of women of color are gendered and racialized, we also use critical race feminism (FemCrit) to examine how gender and ethnic identity are interconnected in their analyses and interpretation of experience. Critical race feminism fuses together the concepts of critical race theory and feminist theory to work to acknowledge women of color's experiences and the imposition of oppressive structures on their lives (Evans-Winters & Esposito, 2010; Verjee, 2012; Wing, 1997). In addressing the multiple marginalities that women of color experience, FemCrit is able to challenge traditional and conventional ways of theorizing, challenge dominant ideologies and structures, and place an emphasis on the experiences of women of color (Wing, 1997). In addition to the theoretical lenses, we acknowledge our own positionalities and identify who we are in relation to this analysis in the next section.

In understanding our experiences and positions through our theoretical lenses, we utilize a duoethnography format. Duoethnography is a collaborative process between two researchers in which their experiences are centered and analyzed in juxtaposition in order to form a potential new analysis and gain insights through critical reflection (Chappell, 2013; Monzó & SooHoo, 2014). Duoethnography centers our experiences and narratives (Chappell, 2013), and using it to work in conjunction with CRT and FemCrit allows for a detailed and richer analysis of the pláticas. Pláticas are understood as a collaborative process of dialogue (Guajardo & Guajardo, 2008). Additionally, this format was applied in order for us to make sense of the challenges we faced at the institution during a time of crisis, the ways our personal experiences were interconnected with these challenges, and the ways we use these insights in moving forward.

In order to utilize the duoethnography format, we recorded pláticas. Pláticas are about storytelling and gaining knowledge from these stories. We use this method because it allows us to learn "the nature of our realities" in a way that keeps our stories authentic (Guajardo & Guajardo, 2008). Other cultures also use storytelling and sharing to transmit knowledge, and so we found it appropriate to apply in this chapter. These pláticas provide narratives of our experiences as administrators during a time of crisis and racial unrest at the University of Missouri working directly with students. The pláticas recorded were dialogues during a presentation for a student affairs practitioners' conference that we were collaborating on. The topic of the presentation was the same as the topic of this chapter. The pláticas focused on the main points of the presentation: what led up to the events of the fall 2015 semester; our experiences, challenges, and struggles leading up to the fall of 2015; our roles in the movement; as well as the ways we reflected on that time.

UNDERSTANDING OUR EXPERIENCES

Through our analysis, we observed a trend in the language we used to describe the feelings we had experienced as we dialogued. We used the feelings that arose most often or the feelings that came out of an analysis of experience to contextualize and communicate our narratives. These feelings are isolation, exhaustion, silenced, taxation, and invisibility. Isolation represents the feeling of being disconnected from our colleagues and administrators on campus. It also refers to feelings of loneliness and abandonment that often emerged in our pláticas. Exhaustion represents the mental, physical, and emotional weariness we felt during these times of campus unrest, particularly as campus unrest efforts grew and administrators became less effective in addressing student needs. The feeling of being silenced was something we internalized because of messages from other colleagues, supervisors, the institutional culture, or simply our own fears of what would occur if we were to speak up. Feelings of being silenced also occurred when we were unsure of ourselves or felt a lack of trust with individuals depending on the situation, as well as silencing others we interacted with. We combined personal taxation and invisibility because, although we were heavily engaged in the times of campus unrest in different ways and to different extents, our voices and experiences remained largely invisible. Therefore, we found all these themes to be interconnected. In many ways, these emotions were interconnected and at times even a result of one another; for example, feelings of taxation and invisibility also led to potentially increased exhaustion. We present our narratives and the dynamics that arose most frequently within our pláticas.

Isolation

Stephanie. Analyzing the recordings assisted me in understanding the ways I began to isolate myself from those around me in my work life. Through my reflection with Jonathan, I recalled a time when I was explaining my frustration with White women crying and centering themselves in dialogues about race and racism and my attempt to communicate this in a meeting, where I was then held accountable by my supervisor. This supervisor explained that how we as people of color experienced these acts should have been addressed by their direct supervisor, also a White woman. Although the supervisor was aware of previous instances and the behaviors did not cease. Additionally, I had already explained to one woman in particular in a one-on-one meeting why her actions were inappropriate because she had come to discuss race relations and again began to cry.

With incidents such as these occurring, I began to withdraw from those who I did not trust and kept to myself. Later, when I had a conversation with another supervisor, I learned that taking on this self-protective coping strategy was also something that was frowned upon. I reflected with Jonathan, saying, "That was really isolating because it's like okay I am not going to deal with anybody and just keep to myself and be cordial and professional, but then when I did that, I'm told that I'm intimidating and unapproachable." Students even approached me at one point and asked if I made a White woman cry. It was frustrating for me that students were questioning me about fabricated stories they were told and the lack of respect from colleagues who told these tales; this made me withdraw even more.

Jonathan's experience was very different than mine, in that he was a point of contact for so many people. "I tried to listen a lot because we weren't really getting that elsewhere, at least not that much." I wanted to be a supportive colleague and friend to Jonathan and colleagues in the GOBCC and attempted to listen; however, I also relied on Jonathan for support because he was one of the only people I felt I could trust. In one of our pláticas, I communicated this to him:

> I felt like as a new professional, there wasn't enough support, and
> I think people knew that not only was I trying to support everything
> that was going on in my space as an office of one but I was also trying
> to support my colleagues because I saw that they didn't have enough
> support and I didn't feel like there was enough coaching for that
> and there was barely any check-in. . . . There were colleagues in the
> same building who were not checking in on me.

Navigating this environment became challenging because I wasn't sure what I could do or say, and additionally I felt I had very few people to rely on. Isolation was not something I experienced solely at work, but also in the surrounding area. In one recording, I commented about feeling "isolation being in a new place, isolation being a new professional." Because I didn't come from Columbia, Missouri, the Midwest was a new experience for me, so in addition to navigating my work environment, I was attempting to navigate a new geographic space and location. Isolation also came at a cost to my familial relationships; I often did not disclose the crisis I felt was occurring at work to my mother, who is a huge support system for me: "I didn't want to stress her out and that was really hard not to be able to communicate with her." I worried my mother would fear for my safety and having her daughter halfway across the country. I began to hold back in our conversations and avoided the subject of work entirely.

Exhaustion

Jonathan. My responsibility in my role was to serve as an advocate for the Black students on campus and to support them in their endeavors. This was shown through the many student organizations I advised and working beyond the 9-to-5 time frame. During a reflection I stated, "This job was beyond a 9-to-5 for me; it was a part of my everyday life." I would often process with Stephanie the exhaustion of having to be everything to everyone while simultaneously writing against a deadline to complete my dissertation. It was exhausting to sit in meetings and not have people take responsibility for the areas where students were impacted, particularly because during this time I was expected to attend various meetings about these issues.

I struggled with balancing my role as a campus administrator and as an advocate for the students. I recall one of the Mizzou GOBCC student employees broke out into tears during a meeting with campus administrators because to her and other students it was apparent that they weren't being transparent or forthcoming with how they were addressing the students' "Call to Action" list. She stated, "Why do they keep trying to play us? They don't even care." All I could do was hug her and tell her everything was going to be all right, even if I was unclear what senior administrators were doing and felt as though they had very little understanding that this was a serious problem.

Additionally, not all students agreed with the protests and hunger strike. There was a need for constant mediation and to develop spaces for students to dialogue. There were many group and individual conversations that went well into the night that I had with students about the state of the campus, whether the student participating in the hunger strike would live, and if we would be okay. As tired as I was, someone had to fill this role for the students, and I often found myself serving as a major support system for many students during this time, even though I was also experiencing feelings of fear, isolation, and lack of community. In the midst of it all, I had to balance my emotions and suppress them to not alarm the students. I recall a time talking with Stephanie, where I fell to my knees in the kitchen in the GOBCC in tears and cried out, "I'm not sure if I can make it through this." Almost immediately, I pulled myself together because I did not want to let the students see me in this manner. Physical, mental, and emotional exhaustion were prevalent during this time period.

Silenced

Jonathan. Navigating a national protest was unchartered territory for me, colleagues, and students. In reflecting on the experience, the perspective that was often lost in the narrative was ours, as administrators who had the institutional knowledge of the past 2 years on campus and had positive relationships with students on campus. I can recall processing with Stephanie my frustration of feeling silenced and how I felt that in order to maintain my position, I couldn't speak out. I would always think that the campus protests did not have to reach the level they did.

My identity as a Black man was salient because I had seen the institution's response to other faculty and staff who had publicly supported the students' efforts. Because of this, I would inquire about the protocols in place regarding speaking with the media and so forth. Repeatedly, I was told that this would be left up to our university spokesperson, but I observed other faculty and staff speaking out with their opinions and perspectives. I felt they were more protected by academic freedom than I was. Interview requests came from national news outlets and even Spike Lee, the movie producer who filmed a documentary regarding the events on campus. Although I wanted to speak out because my story needed to be heard, I didn't, out of fear of losing my job or retaliation from the institution. The lack of accountability and direction for my position left me feeling silenced and as though my voice didn't matter. As I later reflected on my experience during this time, "I became frustrated because my voice wasn't included in the narrative and offered a very unique and important perspective that provided full context to the campus unrest."

Because Blackness manifests itself in different ways, I constantly had to be mindful of my actions and how I navigated situations. Sadly, I quickly came to realize how true this would be. During a time when the department I was in attempted to create a diversity-related position, I was asked to review the job description and provide feedback. Upon providing feedback that the position seemed rushed, students needed to be involved, and there wasn't an infrastructure to sustain the person in this role, I quickly was villainized. Two days later, my supervisor at the time received a phone call that I was "protesting" on the steps of Jesse Hall. She responded, "That can't be true because we are both off campus working on a campus project." Despite the fact that Jonathan is a common name, when an administrator heard that "Jonathan" was protesting on the steps of Jesse Hall, a key administrator couldn't differentiate between a student and myself.

I became frustrated and hurt because I had worked at the institution for 5 years and felt I was a stellar employee and had always worked vigorously to make sure I followed all procedures, but the moment the administrator didn't like what I said, all my achievements, degrees, and hard work were erased, and I became just another Black person. This feeling caused me to feel further silenced by the institution and isolated because those I thought I could trust were no longer around. Although apologies ensued, this incident alone changed my ideology of how I navigated the world as a Black man, and particularly how I navigated Mizzou as an institution and in all my interactions with others. This experience brought me clarity that to the majority, Black people look and act the same, despite any degrees, job titles, and accomplishments we may have or the ways we are diverse. As disheartening as this reality was, it paralleled greater societal trends in which Black and Brown bodies are criminalized and dehumanized.

Taxation and Invisibility

Stephanie. Because of my passion for equity and inclusion work, I was often sought out for these purposes within the institution. Within the pláticas I discussed having to attend multiple meetings to assist administrators in understanding the frustrations of students. Even when I provided my perspective on what could be done, it didn't seem to be taken seriously because it was never acted on:

> You [Jonathan] and I met with certain senior administrators and it was more our thoughts about what was going on versus what we can do and I think we did try on various occasions to say this is what should be done, but that wasn't really happening, and then once the fall came, things really started to spiral out of control.

Additionally, Jonathan and I both felt administrators met with us solely to appease students and keep them quiet, and discussion assisted me in making a connection to feeling invisible even with being "at the table." As Jonathan discussed having to work on the ground with students and meet with senior administrators, I responded:

> But I think that the only reason there was a desire to stay connected to us was because they thought that by staying connected to us and like . . . I think a lot of it was about, like they thought that like, having us there would keep the students complacent.

To that, Jonathan replied:

> Yeah, I think we were used as a tool. . . . I think what they did not know was it's great to keep us, but these students had gone so far to the right already that our influence was no longer . . . we weren't stopping anyone.

The feeling of being used and exploited persisted while I was the coordinator of the Multicultural Center. I often felt taxed to do work that was outside of my job description and focus to benefit the institution:

> I felt really pulled in a million directions because people saw this person in the Multicultural Center role as the person who was supposed to go out and do all these inclusion and diversity presentations, and I found myself doing that at so many different levels . . . and there

was no understanding of the fact that I am a one-person area and I think at one point both of us [Jonathan and I] were asked to do some kind of training for the executive cabinet and that was so far out of our scope.

Although this form of exposure brought me great visibility as a "diversity expert," I still felt invisible. Jonathan assisted me in recognizing this by pointing out the lack of support I received as both a new professional and someone doing this work. I even recall having a colleague (a White woman) tell me that someone had communicated to her that she should have administered a presentation I created, instead of me. Today, I reflect on the ways I was often paid in public affirmations but was not equitably compensated.

DISCUSSION

As explained earlier, we worked to identify the areas that were the most common themes within our analysis. This analysis shaped from a CRT and FemCrit lens has allowed us to interpret our findings through a framework that centers our stories and experiences in order to challenge dominant structures and beliefs, to determine how these ideologies and institutions can work to become more equitable. A tenet of CRT is centrality of experiential knowledge. This tenet is woven throughout our discussion of the themes that emerged and how we interpreted them. Our previous experiences as practitioners of color during a time of racial tension and campus unrest provide an opportunity for our own growth and reflection, but also an understanding of our experience as insight into oppression and inequity. Additionally, through our analysis of our pláticas, we hope readers will understand our experiences through our analysis, as well as their own, and not misinterpret or misuse our stories for their own purposes.

Throughout the pláticas, we both discussed feelings of isolation and how the perceptions of colleagues often do not understand this as a response to a hostile environment, but rather as a personality trait or character flaw. This speaks to the centrality of race and racism in CRT and how our colleagues did not consider race when they were perpetuating racially coded assumptions against us. We also discussed feeling that colleagues and senior administration seemed unable or unwilling to challenge their own dominant ideologies. This type of isolation can occur as a response to racial battle fatigue from constantly feeling as though we had to be tokens, or advocate for ourselves and students through times of racial distress. We are both from the East Coast, so we discussed the ways social isolation often affected the ways we navigated a different environment. We were not only attempting to understand ourselves in relation to our work, but also in relation to a different spatial location. Stephanie specifically talked about having to navigate her relationship with her mother in a way that would not make her mother fearful and the impact this had on her ability to process and gain support.

Although Jonathan and Stephanie both discussed feeling isolated, we also found support in each other and discussed the ways this was beneficial throughout the pláticas. We found that our commitment to CRT helped us with the challenges that we face.

We both recognized the benefit of having the ability to process a hostile environment and observed our ability to use humor as a mechanism in coping and persisting. This allowed us to make sense of a difficult situation, without falling captive to feelings of helplessness and frustration. Additionally, this humor allowed us to feel comforted and as though we had a supportive confidant we could trust. Humor serves as one of our own forms of resistance in challenging dominant ideologies and structures that would rather perceive us as "angry people of color."

In engaging in this form of dialogue, Stephanie was able to distinguish how Jonathan's experience with fears of violence, both direct and through the form of threats, was much more pervasive. In the pláticas, this reinforced her need to attempt to be present for him and her other colleagues in that space as much as possible. She felt she had to overcompensate for the lack of support from colleagues and administrators, even when she felt taxed, exhausted, and drained from her own work. In reflection, she recognizes now that although part of this has to do with her understanding the isolation felt in doing inclusion and equity work, part of it was also recognizing the ways Blackness and Black people were treated at the university and in the larger society. Stephanie demonstrates a commitment to social justice and desire to advocate for an experience outside of her visible identity as seen as a light-skinned Puerto Rican. In this experience, there is also a connection to FemCrit as Stephanie believes the intersectional nature of her identities is connected to her desire to care and overcompensate, and in many ways, be self-sacrificial as a woman of color (Wing, 1997).

These behaviors also emerged when Stephanie discussed how Black women were overextended and their emotional and mental well-being was at a greater risk. Stephanie recognized feeling a certain level of guilt when she could not be at every event or support everyone. This also emerged as she at times addressed inappropriate behaviors from colleagues. Although her experiences as a woman of color dealing with White women's tears was draining, inappropriate, and hostile, she also felt the need to speak up and address these behaviors. This was in part due to her recognizing that there would be a difference between how she would be received versus her other Black colleagues, as she mentioned in one recording. She, like Jonathan, believed that White colleagues who believed themselves to be "allies" should have been more in tune with the racial battle fatigue this can cause by demonstrating a commitment to social justice work through addressing these behaviors themselves.

In processing exhaustion and the role it played, Jonathan realized that because he was the point of contact for many administrators on campus, there was a need to always be present with the students. Although he was exhausted from balancing work responsibilities while navigating the movement, he felt because of the connection he had with students that he had to be there. This was referenced as he discussed having to be at work constantly or feeling as though he was at work when he wasn't. This was particularly true during the time of campus turmoil, when fear and exhaustion over what could happen was a constant worry for him, even after he went home. In discussing being at work after hours, Jonathan acknowledged that this occurred because students needed an outlet to get their frustrations heard, and that would often occur in the late hours of the night. Had students felt a level of commitment to social justice from the institution or other colleagues and administrators, Jonathan may have not felt as much of this weight.

Jonathan spoke about the balance of being an administrator and advocate repeatedly throughout the pláticas. Within this section, he emotionally acknowledged what a major conflict that was and how this conflict in and of itself created a sense of exhaustion. Having to constantly consider the ways he could be held accountable was a common feeling for Jonathan as a Black man. His race was an extremely salient identity as he considered the ways he navigated the environment and interactions with others. Additionally, outside of having to deal with all this, he had to handle internal conflicts among student groups and protest organizers. Because students did not always agree or were sometimes in conflict with one another, Jonathan was required to become interdisciplinary in his approach when engaging students in dialogue and encouraging them to consider the issues and dynamics from multiple perspectives.

Fear of being targeted or held responsible led us to be cautious and intentional in how we engaged with students, particularly in the second year as students took the protests and demonstrations to "another level." Additionally, we both acknowledge how we perpetuated this form of silencing onto our students as we discussed how we would "prep" them for meetings with administrators. We encouraged students to be silent and potentially complacent toward disparaging acts, as opposed to engaging the perpetuator on how these behaviors were harmful and inappropriate.

We participated in very mainstream ideologies and had to recognize how our commitment to social justice fluctuated. In listening to the recording, Stephanie observed this same behavior when encouraging Jonathan to demonstrate he was not "bitter or resentful" about his experience at Mizzou and perhaps that it had not broken him or his spirit while she simultaneously protected the institution. Additionally, Jonathan recognized that he felt he had to "protect" the institution and demonstrate some form of allegiance to it. Listening to these recordings reinforced in us the ways we contribute to systems of dominance and the ways people of color often participate in respectability politics or unhealthy coping mechanisms in order to maintain a certain level of strength that would potentially remain undetected. We often also participated in our own silencing for fear of an increased hostile environment or job insecurity in addition to being at places in our careers that still felt very unfamiliar.

Stephanie reflected on her immense frustration with the movement in the second year and how the efforts of women of color the year before had been largely invisible and ignored. Although she communicated this to Jonathan on various occasions within and outside of the pláticas, she never addressed students in the movement. Much of Stephanie's analysis of her life experiences is through a FemCrit perspective; however, in reflecting on this, she seemed unsure if students at that time would have confused her critique with a lack of support, since she was unsure of how she would have been outwardly received, as the second year the movement was led and directed mainly by Black students. She admits it was a true failure on her part to engage students in a dialogue about how they perpetuated oppressive behaviors, particularly because the community that she is most interested in serving is very invisible—women of color. The use of FemCrit, as well as CRT, however, may have been helpful in her assisting students to understand their own critical consciousness, how they challenge their internalized dominant ideologies and behaviors, and how they demonstrate their commitment to social justice.

The stagnation of administrators is one of the factors that led to increased unrest at Mizzou, and in the second year, Black women in particular continued to lead efforts to mobilize the community, although they were often in the shadows of one man and a football team. This stagnation resulted in Black students in the movement being overextended and having to deal with difficult emotional and mental states as well as the overexertion of the professionals who worked to support them and one another. Stephanie was frequently called upon as a "diversity expert" in multiple university settings, especially during a time of crisis around race-related issues on campus. Jonathan was always the point of contact on how to deal with Black students and address their concerns or needs and the threats that Black students and the GOBCC received. Identity taxation, which expands on Amado Padilla's (1994) work of cultural taxation, is identified by Hirshfield and Joseph (2012) as the way faculty and, in our case, administrators of color are required to shoulder additional emotional, physical, and mental labor. We believe the addition of this labor is again connected to the institution's lack of commitment to social justice, as well as a refusal to centralize racism as an ongoing issue at the university.

Jonathan also addressed these same feelings as he talked about how difficult it was to say no to students. Feelings of guilt often emerged because he had to say yes to everyone, even administrators. He was always at a meeting upon request, supported students as much as he physically and mentally could, and served as a mediator in various contexts and scenarios. Although very different in scope, these feelings of being taxed to do the work that others did not seem willing to do was exploitative in nature for both Stephanie and Jonathan. This form of taxation is highlighted repeatedly within the pláticas, as well as throughout the other three emotions felt. Employing CRT, institutions could better support those who supervise individuals of color, particularly in diversity work, by considering the ways they overstretch employees. Although these roles provided increased visibility, the visibility was small in scope and did not provide Stephanie and Jonathan with extra support, compensation, or recognition from the institution. It felt as though their passion for social justice and serving students of marginalized identities was in some way interpreted as being only a passion, and not the rigorous work it actually was.

STUDENT ENGAGEMENT, CAMPUS POLICIES, AND PRACTICES

There are several implications that can be derived from this investigation of student engagement, campus policies and practices, and appropriate institutional response. When thinking about student engagement, it is important for universities to create resources and support to help guide students through activism so that students can successfully use their First Amendment rights. Also, it would be beneficial for institutions to fund educational programming that highlights student activism as a means to explore values, self-identity, and personal interests. Lastly, administrators should ensure that campus policies and their approach to responding to activism are well known among students so that their actions do not come off as reactive.

Administrators need to ensure that there are campus policies and practices in place for students as well as faculty and staff. Putting these policies in place ensures that everyone in the community is on the same page when it comes to what is and is not appropriate for faculty and staff. This ensures that faculty, and particularly staff who may not be as protected, can support and advocate for students without fear of being reprimanded. However, it was also learned from Mizzou that faculty are not always as protected as one might think: A nearly tenured professor was fired from the institution because of her role in the movement and some inappropriate comments she made. We have seen institutions across the country, including Mizzou, protect faculty for much worse. This challenged the power that faculty have. Institutions should also develop a campus or divisional philosophy regarding student activism that does not suppress students' rights. Additionally, parameters need to be set for student activism and guidelines established for when activism moves toward campus policy violations.

Senior administrators should be aware of the taxation and racial battle fatigue experienced by practitioners who do diversity and inclusion work, particularly when this work is closely aligned to the individual's own identity(ies) and requires that colleagues assist in campuswide crises. We believe that if institutions truly support unity and a collectivistic and community culture, colleagues should directly support communities in times of campus unrest to take some of the workload from those who may already be exhausted and overextended. Campus administrators need to assemble a team to address campus climate and produce actionable items. This interdisciplinary team should comprise individuals across campus, as well as students, and should be given some form of power that will allow their recommendations to be taken seriously. In other words, do not create a task force, another committee, or a team just to demonstrate an action taken, but rather support a true commitment to creating change agents. There should also be protocol in place for administrators to address student activism concerns so that students are clear about how changes can occur, and are provided with a realistic yet clear timeline and process.

For professionals of color, it is important to find community and refuge both within and outside of their institutions, which is a true challenge, particularly depending on the geographic location and whether there are familial support systems. Finding individuals one can trust can be difficult, but it can truly create an opportunity for support and healing from experiences as challenging as the ones presented in this chapter. Additionally, professionals of color need to be cognizant of the ways they are wielders of power over their students and potentially other colleagues, and the ways that they may internalize oppressive systems and structures and perpetuate them. Additionally, they should attempt to engage their colleagues at different levels of the institution to support communities of color. When student unrest does occur, knowing the exact protocols for their role will increase their ability to navigate the situation. Self-care is important throughout the entire process in order to effectively serve the needs of the students, as well as to advocate for oneself. Professionals of color doing equity work can feel as though they must choose between advocating for students and advocating for themselves, but open communication with supervisors is key. Boundaries are also necessary and supervisors should recognize that when professionals of color say no to opportunities or more work, it may be that they are setting up boundaries for themselves so that they are not taxed and exhausted. Under hostile and abusive conditions, it is important that professionals of color exercise the use of the human resources office or department.

Lastly, appropriate institutional response to campus activism is key in an effort to keep a campus issue from becoming a national headline. An administrative response team should be assembled to handle crisis situations and instances of campus unrest. Administrators should be equipped with mediation/conflict management skills and have knowledge of student development and social movements and protests on college campuses. Administrators across campus should understand what is happening on the ground, and communication with stakeholders and the media should happen honestly and openly. The media can be controlling when it comes to the narrative at the university, drawing assumptions and coming to their own conclusions about what has happened. None of this benefits the institution when it is not aware that naming where it could have done better can help prevent inaccurate stories. Additionally, campus administrators should have a high emotional intelligence, nonverbal communication skills, and relational and sincere self-awareness when engaging in these dialogues and attempting to address student needs.

Many outsiders have attempted to name what has happened at the University of Missouri in the past few years, and it is important for them to acknowledge that they have as limited a scope of what has happened at Mizzou as do we. Our stories represent who we are. These stories provide our lens for looking at these events, and while that provides more detail, it still does not provide a complete picture of what has transpired there in recent years or in the history of institutional racism, culture, and campus activism. Many of the senior leadership who were once at Mizzou, specifically during these 2 years, are no longer there. There has also been a restructuring that has resulted in a new division focused on inclusion work and bringing individuals to spearhead this work into this division. However, the lessons to be learned and the result of changes through these lessons will take time to witness. Our hope is that new individuals in leadership positions will take heed when students make requests, demands, or calls to action, and not allow it to erupt, but this hope is not only for the University of Missouri; it is for institutions across the country that are fostering and creating the same dynamics. The University of Missouri may have been the media's focus, but it surely isn't the only institution where there is work left to be done, dynamics left to challenge, or a culture that awaits transformative leaders and practices.

REFERENCES

Berrett, D. (2015, March 19). Stunned by a video, university of Oklahoma struggles to talk about race. *The Chronicle of Higher Education*. Retrieved from www.chronicle.com/article/Stunned-by-a-Video-U-of/228611

Brown, S. (2015, November 9). At Yale, painful rifts emerge over diversity and free speech. *The Chronicle of Higher Education*. Retrieved from www.chronicle.com/article/At-Yale-Painful-Rifts-Emerge/234112

Brown, S. (2016, January 6). Diversity courses are in high demand. Can they make a difference? *The Chronicle of Higher Education*. Retrieved from www.chronicle.com/article/Diversity-Courses-Are-in-High/234828

Brown, S., & Mangan, K. (2015, November 24). Turn over tactics: Activists refine their demands as protests over racism spread. *The Chronicle of Higher Education*. Retrieved from www.chronicle.com/article/Torn-Over-Tactics-Activists/234328

Chappell, D. (2013). In ethnographic research, might two heads be better than one? [Review of the book *Duoethnography: Dialogic methods for social, health, and educational research*.] *Youth Theatre Journal*, 27(1), 87–89. Retrieved from www.tandfonline.com/doi/abs/10.1080/08929092.2012.723460

Evans-Winters, V. E., & Esposito, J. (2010). Other people's daughters: Critical race feminism and Black girls' education. *The Journal of Educational Foundations*, 24, 11–24.

Fernandes, R. (2016, March 8). "We got to capture what you didn't get to see": Filming concerned student 1950. *The Chronicle of Higher Education*. Retrieved from www.chronicle.com/article/We-Got-to-Capture-What-You/235623

Guajardo, M., & Guajardo, F. (2008). Two brothers in higher education: Weaving a social fabric for service in academia. In K. P. Gonzalez & R. V. Padilla (Eds.), *Doing the public Good: Latina/o scholars engage civic participation* (pp. 61–81). Sterling, VA: Stylus.

Hirshfield, L. E., & Joseph, T. D. (2012). "We need a woman, we need a black woman": Gender, race, and identity taxation in the academy. *Gender and Education*, 24, 213–227.

Mangan, K. (2015, December 15). Silence breakers: Concerned student 1950. *The Chronicle of Higher Education*. Retrieved from www.chronicle.com/article/Silence-Breakers-Concerned/234588

Monzó, L. D., & SooHoo, S. (2014). Translating the academy: Learning the racialized languages of academia. *Journal of Diversity in Higher Education, 7*, 147–166.

Padilla, A. (1994). Ethnic minority scholars, research, and mentoring: Current and future issues. *Educational Researcher, 23*, 24–27.

Schmalz, J. (2016, January 3). "Man up" on racism. *The Chronicle of Higher Education.* Retrieved from www.chronicle.com/article/Video-Man-Up-on-Racism/234776?cid=cp15

Solórzano, D. G. (1997). Images and words that wound: Critical race theory, racial stereotyping, and teacher education. *Teacher Education Quarterly, 24*, 5–19.

Stripling, J. (2016a, February 2). Confronting a racial divide, Missouri's interim president finds anger and finger-pointing. *The Chronicle of Higher Education.* Retrieved from www.chronicle.com/article/Confronting-a-Racial-Divide/235137?cid=cp15

Stripling, J. (2016b, April 22). Inside how Missouri's leadership scrambled to quell a campus crisis. *The Chronicle of Higher Education.* Retrieved from www.chronicle.com/article/Inside-How-Missouri-s/236208

Supiano, B. (2015, November 10). Racial disparities in higher education: An overview. *The Chronicle of Higher Education.* Retrieved from www.chronicle.com/article/Racial-Disparities-in-Higher/234129

Thomason, A. (2016, January 22). Former Mizzou chief blames others for resignation in "confidential" letter. *The Chronicle of Higher Education.* Retrieved from www.chronicle.com/blogs/ticker/former-mizzou-chief-blames-others-for-resignation-in-confidential-letter/108151

Verjee, B. (2012). Critical race feminism: A transformative vision for service-learning engagement. *Journal of Community Engagement and Scholarship, 5*(1), 57–69.

Wing, A. (1997). *Critical race feminism: A reader.* New York, NY: New York University Press.

CHAPTER 7

Preparing for the Storm in Times of Peace

Strategies for Preparing Higher Education Presidents for Campus Racial Crises

Mahauganee Shaw Bonds and Sydney Freeman Jr.

In recent years, scholars and administrators alike have agreed that higher education leadership development should not be left to chance (Wright, 2007). There are many complex challenges facing higher education leaders today, including the changing public perception of the role of education, higher demands to secure external funding, campus racial tensions, increased regulation, and a litigious environment (Freeman, Carr-Chellman, & Kitchell, 2018). Although a burgeoning literature base is developing related to the preparation of student affairs leaders to address campus crisis (Molina & Shaw Bonds, forthcoming), this literature is rarely incorporated into educational and professional development opportunities (Shaw, 2018). Additionally, crisis management and crisis leadership preparation has been an underresearched academic topic in the higher education arena, specifically as it applies to the college and university presidency. The goal of this chapter is to discuss the skills and competencies that college and university presidents need to master in preparation for navigating the diverse types of campus emergencies they are certain to encounter as campus leaders, with a focus on navigating racial unrest on campus.

HIGHER EDUCATION PRESIDENCY

Investigations into the higher education presidency have been a topic of immense interest of those who study in the field of higher education (Bertrand Ricard & Brown, 2008; Bowen, 2013; Freeman, 2011; Trachtenberg,

Kauvar, & Gee, 2018). Higher education presidents have many roles and responsibilities. One of their chief duties is to serve as the primary representative for the institution (Thacker & Freeman, 2019). The role of college or university presidents is vested with great responsibility, both substantive and symbolic (Thacker & Freeman, 2019). Presidents are responsible for the entire institutional enterprise. In many cases, they are indirectly in charge of hundreds, if not thousands, of employees who are charged to serve students.

The higher education presidency has evolved over the past 4 centuries within the United States. Presidents do not enjoy the same deference and standing within and among various constituencies, both internal and external to their institutions, as they did in the past (Bornstein, 2003; Dennison, 2001). This reality can cause unique challenges in times of crisis if a president has not generated goodwill and trust among various constituencies. Though there is an active discussion regarding what background produces the best college presidents (Burton, 2003; de Vise, 2010; Farrington, 2008; Goodall, 2009; June, 2007; Keller, 2010; Lum, 2008; Stripling, 2011), neither the rigor of academic training nor the business savvy of corporate experience represents guaranteed preparation to lead in times of crisis.

HIGHER EDUCATION PROGRAMS

Higher education is a field of study that has developed over the past 120 years. In the past century, it has grown in size and influence, and now has its own professional societies, subfields, research and policy centers, and graduate and postgraduate training programs (Freeman, Hagedorn, Goodchild, & Wright, 2014; Rumbley et al., 2014). As a field that exists strictly at the graduate level, higher education master's and doctoral programs prepare their graduates to serve in administrative, faculty, student affairs, and policy analyst positions (Wright, 2007). Increasingly, people have sought degrees in this field to prepare for senior-level positions within the academy, including the college and university presidency (Freeman, 2012). Although this field derived from the scholarship of leaders in the United States, over the past 40 years, many new programs have sprung up internationally (Rumbley et al., 2014).

A variety of higher education programs exists to develop leaders to serve in different institutional types and contexts. Some of these programs include curricula that prepare leaders to work at minority-serving institutions, community colleges, or in international contexts. Additionally, some programs prepare leaders for specific subdivisions within an institution, such as academic or student affairs (Eddy & Roa, 2009; Hughey & Burke, 2010). As alternatives to these degree-granting programs, nonprofits, professional associations, and academic institutions offer certificate and degree programs targeted toward current or aspiring executive leaders seeking preparation and qualification for assuming a presidential post (Freeman & Kochan, 2012). Yet, Freeman (2016) suggests that higher education programs are best equipped to prepare future higher education presidents to address campus racial issues:

> Higher education graduate programs provide the best academic foundation for successful leadership in the field. We have seen in some instances that those who have other disciplinary training, without adequate preparation in academic governance and cultural competency, particularly in business, have been professionally unsuccessful. For example, Tim Wolfe, former president of the University of Missouri system, had a wealth of corporate experience; however, he was woefully unprepared to effectively lead his institution during a time of crisis. With little to no exposure to student development theories and cultural competencies, his leadership style and lack of knowledge of the sector proved to be a part of his presidency's demise although he was respected for his corporate experience.

Although there have been studies of the preparation and socialization of mid- to senior-level leaders in higher education programs (Freeman, 2012, Herdlein, 2004), few examine the preparation of these graduates to manage crisis (e.g., Shaw, 2018; Trahan, 2012). To date, no research has examined the graduate degree program preparation of college and university presidents related to crisis management. This chapter combines scholarship on the college presidency with that on emergency management to derive suggested practices for managing the racial unrest that has become commonplace in campus communities.

THE PRESIDENT'S ROLE IN CAMPUS CRISIS MANAGEMENT

Crisis management has become more central to the daily functions of higher education and has received more attention from researchers and scholars who have developed increasingly sophisticated methods of classifying and categorizing the types of crises that plague college campuses. Campus crises are defined as "low probability/high consequence events" (Weick, 1988, p. 305) that disrupt campus operations and threaten institutional resources—physical, human, or fiscal—or that pose a reputational or political threat to the institution (Zdziarski, 2006). By these broad strokes, there are many common incidents on college campuses that can and should be classified and approached as crises.

To lessen the overwhelming breadth of crises, emergency management scholars have provided typologies that help differentiate levels and types of crisis (Jaques, 2007; Pauchant & Mitroff, 1992; Zdziarski, Rollo, Dunkel, & Associates, 2007). These typologies are most useful for identifying which campus professionals should be included in the crisis response and prioritizing which aspects of a response process are most important to address immediately. Zdziarski and colleagues (2007) suggest a typology for campus leaders that includes three types of crises—environmental, physical, and human—and three levels of crisis: from least to most severe, critical incidents, campus emergencies, and disasters. In offering this typological scheme, Zdziarski and colleagues suggest that the crisis type should be based on where an event originates. Thus, a snowstorm that causes building pipes to freeze in an academic building includes both environmental and physical emergencies, but the primary threat that needs management is environmental. Until the institution has proper plans in place to manage the threat of the snowstorm, the physical impacts and threats of the storm should not be the focus.

Zdziarski and colleagues's (2007) classification scheme can help identify which campus units are implicated in the response process, yet it does not often identify the types of crises that rise to the level of presidential leadership. That is, though the president should be informed of pressing campus issues, representatives of the physical plant, registrar, and campus safety can likely coordinate an effective response to the impacts of a snowstorm on a physical facility and the people and course schedules associated with that facility.

Previous research on campus emergency response structures has confirmed that while various campus units are represented on official response teams, the campus president is rarely expected to serve in that capacity. Table 7.1 presents research findings from Mitroff, Diamond, and Alpaslan (2006) and Zdziarski (2001), assessing the level of participation of certain positions and functional areas on campus crisis management teams (CMTs). The Mitroff et al. study included survey responses from provosts at 117 U.S. institutions, and Zdziarski's (2001) included survey responses mostly from senior student affairs officers at 146 institutions who are members of the National Association of Student Personnel Administrators (NASPA). Findings from these studies have led researchers to suggest that legal counsel should be better represented across campus CMTs (Mitroff et al., 2006; Zdziarski, 2006). Interestingly, when conducting the same type

Table 7.1. Composition of Crisis Management Teams

Internal Stakeholder Role/Functional Area	Level of Participation on CMT	
	Mitroff, Diamond, & Alpaslan (2006)	Zdziarski (2001)
Chief Student Affairs Officer	1 (91%)	3
Facilities/Physical Plant	2 (88%)	8
Public Affairs/University Relations	3 (86%)	2
Chief Financial Officer	4 (79%)	—
Campus/University Police	5 (74%)	1
Information Technology	6 (73%)	—
Security	7 (69%)	—
Provost/Chief Academic Officer	8 (68%)	13
Legal Counsel	9 (66%)	11
President	10 (64%)	12
Risk Management/Environmental Health & Safety	11 (62%)	9
Operations/Administrative Affairs	12 (49%)	10
Athletics	13 (26%)	19
Residence Life	—	4
Counseling Services	—	5
Dean of Students	—	6
Student Health Services	—	7
Student Activities	—	14
Human Resources	—	15
Campus Ministers	—	16
Other	—	17
International Student Services	—	18
Students	—	20
Faculty	—	21
Employee Assistance	—	22
Dean of Faculties	—	23

Note: The numbers representing the level of participation on the CMT are rank ordered, with one indicating the most represented position. Mitroff, Diamond, and Alpaslan provided percentages representing the number of times a certain position or functional area was reported as being represented on the team; these percentages are provided in parentheses.

of assessment using the CMTs of Fortune 1000 companies, Pauchant and Mitroff (1992) found that the chief legal counsel was the most represented, present on the CMT roster 90% of the time. On this point, higher education institutions can take a lesson from the corporate world in the construction of well-rounded crisis management teams. More recently, many campuses have established an emergency management functional area within the institutional structure or developed positions that focus solely on coordinating and implementing crisis response (Farris & McFreight, 2014).

Although Table 7.1 shows that the university president is often not an active CMT member, Jablonski, McClellan, and Zdziarski (2008) point out that the crisis response "plan that is developed needs to carefully consider the expectations of the president and the roles and responsibilities he or she will assume in an actual crisis event" (p. 18). These authors go on to note that institutional size, institutional type, presidential personality, and the crisis itself will ultimately dictate how a president is involved in the crisis response process (Jablonski, McClellan, & Zdziarski, 2008). In a study of how community college presidents approached the turbulent moments of their positions, Murray and Kishur (2008) found that the incidents these campus presidents recalled as the most challenging fit four categories: financial, personnel, political, and public relations. These categories are very different from the types of crises outlined in crisis management schemas targeted at campus professionals; yet, they are the outgrowth of those crises. To return to the earlier example, a poorly managed snowstorm can have very real consequences related to institutional finances, personnel, political relationships, and public opinion. Thus, while others on campus are more likely to take center stage in responding to crises as they arise, presidents are often expected to manage any collateral damage arising from the crisis response process.

PREPARING FUTURE LEADERS TO ADDRESS CAMPUS CRISES

As is clear from Table 7.1, people holding senior-level executive positions tend to be most highly engaged in the response to major campus crisis incidents. Due to this fact, senior-level administrators often are the campus professionals who receive the most extensive and formal crisis management training. However, this is often not the case for graduate students who are being formally trained for leadership in the academy. In an interview with a president who earned a doctorate in higher education administration, Freeman (2011) asked if they had any training or preparation in the area of crisis management, and the response was, "Yeah, crisis management. I don't think that we talked for a single minute in my doctoral program about crisis management and you know you're going to have it" (p. 263). This president likely did not receive crisis management training in their doctoral program because graduate students are not often prioritized as members of the campus community who need to hone crisis management skills and competencies. Yet, graduate students who pursue an executive track postgraduation become the next leaders of businesses, institutions, and government entities—people who are consistently evaluated on their perceived ability to navigate and manage difficult circumstances (that is, crises) as they arise. Those who remain in the higher education and student affairs arenas for the duration of their careers are certain to encounter varying levels of campus crises on an annual, if not more frequent, basis. Thus, it is a major oversight for graduate preparation programs in higher education and student affairs to exclude crisis management units and courses from their curricula.

As a field of study, student affairs (which is a major subset of work in higher education) has agreed on the importance of crisis management skills within the professional competencies expected of those who work in the field (ACPA & NASPA, 2010, 2015; Shaw, 2018). While higher education programs prepare graduates to work in the field of student affairs, Trahan's (2012) study of crisis management's presence within the curriculum at the master's level found high variation across programs. Of the 150 existing student affairs programs identified, Trahan received responses from 59, only one of which noted a crisis management course. However, the faculty respondents in Trahan's study reported evidence of crisis management skills and concepts being taught inside courses without a strict crisis management focus.

Of these crisis management concepts, the one most often taught (38 programs, 84.4%) was making appropriate referrals. Compared to many of the other crisis management skills and concepts listed as response options, making referrals, though important, is one of the most passive ways a person might participate in campus crisis management; yet, it is the method most consistently covered in graduate programs preparing people to enter the field. In contrast, using the National Incident Management System (NIMS)—the standard crisis response structure and system recommended by the U.S government as a whole community approach to crises, which has been adapted into guides for educational entities (REMS TA Center, 2018)—was the least taught (2 programs, 4.4%) skill.

Within Trahan's (2012) study, there was a clear tension between what faculty believe is important for students to learn and what the curriculum will allow. Many crisis management skills and concepts rated as important by faculty were also noted as absent from the curriculum of their program.

As one nonrespondent noted in a message declining participation in Trahan's (2012) study, "all of these concepts are very important and they should all be taught during the first year. But there is no more room in the curriculum" (p. 112). What students learn during their graduate experiences is a function of the standards for their primary field of study, the expertise of the faculty who lead their program, and the institutional guidelines regarding the number of hours one must complete to earn a particular degree or certification. Unfortunately, for higher education and student affairs, crisis management is not highly revered and widely studied enough to register as a key topic for graduate students to master.

While crisis management is sparsely covered in higher education graduate programs, the executive leadership programs and trainings that exist for current and aspiring campus administrators often include units on crisis management. Because senior-level administrators are typically perceived as the first responders to institutional crises, they are the people often targeted for professional development opportunities on crisis management. Understanding that their graduates will one day be these senior leaders, faculty in graduate programs need to focus more energy on how to infuse crisis management into the curriculum. If there is no space for a course on the topic, then there should be efforts to identify where and how crisis management intersects with the topics covered in existing courses. Certain topics, such as diversity and inclusion, counseling, student development, campus environments, and the history of higher education, are standard courses in higher education programs; each of these course topics connects to crisis management. Given the current organization of the curriculum, alumni of higher education programs often graduate underprepared to confidently manage many of the campus emergencies they will encounter.

RACIAL UNREST ON CAMPUS

Campus racial unrest is not a new phenomenon in U.S. higher education. There are innumerable historical and contemporary examples, with many of the former stemming from the landmark struggles to admit and enroll Black students in predominantly White institutions. For example, in 1963, James H. Meredith, a Black male student, desegregated the University of Mississippi. This action took place among rioting that cost the lives of two people along with property damage and more than $4 million spent for Meredith's security. The following year, the University of Alabama was desegregated, even though the governor of the state, along with White students, faculty, staff, and community members tried to physically block the entry of Black students (Bradley, 2016). In modern times, there have been several major flashpoints related to racial unrest on U.S. campuses, spanning institutional sizes, types, and sectors (see Cole & Harper, 2016; Davis & Harris, 2015; Garcia, Johnston, Garibay, Herrera, & Giraldo, 2011; Garcia & Johnston-Guerrero, 2016). Below, we offer a few examples.

In spring 2017 at Evergreen State College, a series of email exchanges was sent between a Black staff member (Rashida Love) and a White faculty member (Bret Weinstein) who disagreed about the activities associated with school's annual Day of Absence/Day of Presence. Love had proposed that White students be asked to go off campus to discuss issues of race as a sign of solidarity with people of color (Fowler, 2017). Weinstein disagreed and expressed that he felt that approaching the issue in this manner was a form of oppression for Whites on campus. Once some students who supported Love learned of this exchange, they disrupted one of Weinstein's class sessions. The incident was recorded and went viral via social and mainstream media. Soon after, students protested on campus, calling on Weinstein to resign and labeling him a racist. Concerns for the safety of the campus became an issue as a death threat was made. George Bridges, the president of Evergreen, decided to close the institution for 3 days until they knew they could ensure the safety of the campus (Fowler, 2017).

The University of Michigan is another institution that has been plagued with racial unrest over the past few years. Incidents such as posters being found around campus that stated, "We must secure the existence of our race and a future for white children. Make America White Again," put the institution in the center of discussions regarding racial tensions on campus (Adams, 2017, para. 1). Other incidents include:

> Swastikas and phrases such as "Jews Die" were also spray-painted in a skate park in downtown Ann Arbor [University of Michigan's location]. . . . On the Rock, a landmark close to the campus, spray paint was used to scrawl "F—Latinos" and "MAGA," for Make America Great Again, a campaign slogan of President Trump. . . . In the West Quad Residence Hall, the doors to the rooms of three black students were vandalized with the N-word written on the students' name tags (Adams, 2017, para. 4–5).

In response to these incidents, students protested in various forms—a march, a street blockade/study-in that disrupted the campus bus route and traffic flow, and one graduate student who took a knee for 24 hours (Adams, 2017; Beresford & Harmon, 2017). President Mark Schlissel condemned the racialized aggressions and expressed support for student protesters, yet the university acknowledged the "tension between prohibiting offensive speech and not stifling free speech" (Adams, 2017, para. 18).

Howard University, a prestigious historically Black college and university (HBCU), found itself in the center of a potentially volatile racial situation when two White women, both wearing "Make America Great Again" hats and one also wearing a pro-Trump T-shirt, visited the campus. The two women said the reason they came to the campus was to get something to eat, and they accused Black students at the university of being hostile and harassing them (Rogo, 2017). Both Howard University students and the two visitors took to social media to share their displeasure at the situation, which was diffused when the visitors decided to leave campus. The university statement released after the incident boasted about the quality of their student body and reaffirmed the university's values.

One of the most well-publicized racial clashes came in the form of protest on the campus of the University of Virginia, where torch-bearing racists walked across the university lawn chanting, "You will not replace us," while carrying signs that included anti-Black and anti-Jewish rhetoric. After the group clashed with antiracist opposers, a White male, James Alex Fields Jr., who had displayed sympathy for White Nationalist, White supremacist, and neo-Nazi philosophies, ran his car into a crowd, killing Heather Heyer, a 32-year-old White woman who was among the antiracist protesters. This and other major racial incidents on U.S. campuses have caused higher education leaders to rethink the safety measures they have put in place to secure the well-being of all individuals on their campuses during protests (Schmidt, 2017).

In the African American Studies Department at the University of South Carolina in January 2018 near Martin Luther King Jr. Day, racial epithets such as "Dumb Black Asses" and "You Stupid Monkeys" were posted on the department's bulletin board display case (Bowers, 2018). Although President Harris Pastides described the occurrence as "an abhorrent and unacceptable display of hatred," using "despicable words of bigotry and racism," students still called for him to resign (Wilks, 2018, p.18).

A recent study of racially biased campus events analyzed 205 news-generating incidents on U.S. campuses from 2005 to 2010 (Garcia & Johnston-Guerrero, 2016). The six most common forms of racial bias across the events studied were graffiti or vandalism, the production and display of physical media with racially motivated messages, noose hangings, racially themed parties, verbal remarks, and assault or fighting. Many of these categories are represented among the example events described above. From releasing statements to completely closing the campus, presidents played a response role in each of these examples of recent racialized campus crises.

With these incidents in mind, one might question whether presidents are adequately prepared for such crises. Cole and Harper (2016) analyzed 18 statements issued by college presidents in response to racial campus incidents over a 3-year academic period from 2012 to 2015. They found that although presidents were comfortable talking about racial incidents in a broad sense and sometimes addressed the group or person who committed a racist act, few were willing or prepared to acknowledge systemic or institutional challenges that facilitated a culture that would allow for these situations to occur. In the remainder of this chapter, we offer frameworks and strategies that presidents can use to more effectively anticipate racial incidents and lead in their aftermath.

PRESIDENTIAL STEPS FOR MANAGING RACIAL UNREST

Crisis management frameworks offer useful approaches for managing the racial unrest that has cyclically plagued U.S. college campuses over the course of history. In this section, we offer two such frameworks, the crisis management cycle and the punctuated-equilibrium paradigm. The crisis management cycle is always displayed in a circular manner that progresses through five stages: planning, prevention/mitigation, response, recovery, and learning. Though we list planning as the first stage, people and organizations can enter the cycle at any appropriate point, given their current circumstances. Moreover, while learning is listed as a distinct phase, learning happens consistently throughout the crisis management process. Regardless of whether one is in the planning stage or the response stage, new information is always being received, filtered, and applied to the process.

Although we discuss the preparedness of graduate students and higher education leaders earlier in this chapter, it is important to note here that the preparation received in courses and trainings dedicated to crisis management is only a foundation (a necessary, yet ever-evolving, foundation) for the act of actual crisis management. This educational foundation provides a framework for approaching future crises and a sense of confidence in doing so, both of which are valuable in a time of crisis, and in responding to the questions and critics that are sure to surface afterward.

In the wake of any campus crisis, there is a common narrative that includes questions regarding what went wrong, what indicators were missed that allowed the situation to progress to the level of impact the crisis had, whether and how the situation could have been prevented, and what the institution and its leaders need to do to chart the path forward. Inherent within these questions are the various phases of the crisis management cycle.

Knowing these stages can help organize not only the crisis management process, but also what is communicated: what was our plan; what steps did we take to prevent or mitigate the impacts this incident; how did we respond; what is needed in order for us to claim recovery; what did we learn? Applying the crisis management cycle to instances of campus racial unrest typically helps highlight the missteps in campus administrative efforts that have created space for racial tension to fester. Before expounding more, we need to introduce a second framework, the punctuated-equilibrium paradigm (Gersick, 1991; Romanelli & Tushman, 1994).

The punctuated-equilibrium paradigm is helpful for understanding how events within the life cycle of an organization can disrupt operations and change the course of an organization's progress. Shaw (2017) overlaid punctuated-equilibrium with another theory, convergence/upheaval (Tushman, Newman, & Romanelli, 1986), in explaining how colleges and universities experience crises:

> Both theories suggest that organizations operate in a steady state (*equilibrium* or *convergence*) for long periods of time. This equilibrium period can be disrupted (*punctuated*) by a brief, yet necessary, period of revolutionary change (*upheaval*). The equilibrium or convergence states, in which organizations operate for long periods of time are considered stable, but are not absent of change. (p. 104)

Campus crises punctuate the steady operational state of postsecondary institutions, causing the institution and its constituents (most immediately, the administrators, students, faculty, and staff) to enter a stage of upheaval where changes must occur before the moment of crisis will subside. While these two theories overlap, for the sake of clarity, we use the language of punctuated-equilibrium throughout the remainder of this chapter. In this conceptualization of the utility of crisis management skills, campus presidents and their first responders play an invaluable role in bringing the campus community back to a state of normalcy where equilibrium can be achieved.

These two frameworks from the crisis management literature—the crisis management cycle and the punctuated-equilibrium paradigm—are helpful in evaluating examples of racial unrest that have temporarily crippled campus operations and leadership. Infusing these frameworks into how we discuss and approach racialized crises can decrease the number of media-grabbing incidents on college and university campuses and increase the success rate of mitigating and responding to such crises. As Zdziarski et al. (2007) write, "a good crisis management system needs to address not only the response phase but the pre- and postphases as well" (p. 46). Thus, the remaining subsections below highlight the three phases of the crisis management cycle that most immediately surround a crisis event—preparation and mitigation, which directly precedes a crisis event; response, which immediately follows the onset of a crisis event; and recovery, which is the long-term process of institutional equilibrating after a crisis.

Preparation and Mitigation

Different conceptualizations of the crisis management cycle may use the terms *preparation* and *mitigation* interchangeably with *prevention* to describe a phase in which there is a focus on either eliminating or moderating the potential impact of a forthcoming crisis. However, in order for campus leaders to invoke this stage of the crisis management process, they must first anticipate a forthcoming crisis. In times of racial unrest, campus administrators often express surprise at the idea of racialized events on their campus. Presidential statements following racial incidents often highlight the misalignment of the sentiments expressed by the perpetrators of the incident and the values and norms of the campus community (Cole & Harper, 2016). Inherent in these presidential statements is a belief that by establishing community norms—often through guiding philosophies such as an institutional mission or a code of conduct—incidents that are antithetical to the established norms should be effectively prevented. Establishing community norms of inclusivity and espousing an institutional value on diversity is but one step toward mitigating discriminatory events on campus; it is not a stand-alone preventative measure. Mitigating racial incidents on campus requires the same level of anticipation, monitoring, and attention as does enrollment management, course registration, fundraising, or any other operational procedure.

In their depiction of the crisis management cycle, Pauchant and Mitroff (1992) include a *signal detection* stage directly prior to preparation/prevention. They refer collectively to the activities that happen in their signal detection and preparation/prevention stages as "proactive crisis management" (p. 135), while referring collectively to the activities of the response and recovery phases as "reactive crisis management" (p. 135). In efforts to prepare for and mitigate racial incidents, campus presidents must practice proactive crisis management to lessen the need for reactive crisis management. Proactive crisis management begins with identifying signal detection mechanisms as related to identity. One such signal would include any data collected on campus climate. Campus climate data often reveal areas where (1) the campus community falls short of established norms and expectations of conduct and engagement with people holding historically marginalized identities; and (2) the campus environment is experienced as unwelcoming, marginalizing, or alienating. Harper and Hurtado (2007) outline nine common themes across colleges and universities that struggle with issues of race and racism; this list is a good place to begin for institutions without their own climate data to mine.

Another signal is information available from staff responsible for the diversity, inclusion, and equity function on campus. Several staff and faculty serve in these roles on college and university campuses: chief diversity officers; faculty in ethnic studies programs; and staff who oversee cultural centers, multicultural affairs offices, international or global affairs offices, or any other campus entity with a mission of serving the needs of underrepresented students and scholars. These campus professionals, whose work focuses on helping the campus community learn about, interact with, and integrate identity and identity-based issues into their daily routines, are uniquely positioned to know the pulse of a campus community. Presidents would be wise to receive regular reports from their colleagues in these positions, and to heed their warnings regarding racial tension brewing in the campus community. Small incidents that are overlooked can compile and intensify, growing into an incident that will have a larger impact and force the campus into reactive crisis management techniques (see, for example, Trachtenberg, forthcoming).

Response

Response is the phase of the crisis management cycle that happens immediately in the aftermath of a crisis to deescalate the threat posed to the safety of the campus community and the continuation of campus operations. By eliminating any ongoing, active threats to the campus, crisis response focuses on eliminating the "emotional bleeding" (Griffin, 2007, p. 158) that crisis invokes. Racial unrest on campus can be the result of either an active threat to the campus community or the news of a past racist incident or event. In the latter instances, the racist incident may be one that happened recently or one that happened long ago but only recently gained attention.

Regardless of whether there is a past event, a recent event, or an ongoing event that alarms the campus community, there is a general expectation that campus leaders will respond and offer direction in a manner that slows the momentum of the crisis. Often, this response has been seen in the form of a formal statement released to the campus community and public. Analyses of these statements (Cole & Harper, 2016; Davis & Harris, 2015) reveal that language denouncing racism or linking racist behavior and sentiments to the systemic and historical roots of racism is not included. Some presidential statements following racial incidents do not even make mention of the incident to which they are a response (Cole & Harper, 2016).

While campus presidents are rarely members of the coordinated team of first responders deployed to contain a crisis, they are one of the most likely spokespersons who may appear to the media and the campus community to deliver formal statements and updates about a crisis response process. A president in this situation should work closely with their public relations officer to develop their statement and their stance, as well as the target audiences and the schedule on which information should be communicated (Lawson, 2007). The worst thing a president can do in the aftermath of a racial incident is not to acknowledge the incident, its impacts, and the community's need for guidance.

Recovery

Often deemed the final stage in the crisis management cycle, recovery is a process that brings a campus community as near to an organizational equilibrium as possible following a crisis response. Recovery is a long-term process; depending on the severity of a racial incident on campus, recovery may last anywhere from several months to several years. The length of the recovery period will vary for universities, with each needing to identify its own recovery goals and milestones (Shaw, 2017). In the aftermath of racial unrest, recovery goals that extend beyond returning a sense of safety to the campus will likely include overarching goals such as helping the campus community process the events and heal from their negative impacts. Progressive recovery is the goal, with each step in the recovery process moving the campus closer to complete healing.

Campus crises often leave deep psychological impacts on the people who lived through the trauma of the moment (Griffin, 2007). Racialized incidents that result in unrest are certain to leave an impact on many within the targeted community and even those who empathize with the targeted community (e.g., Shaw & Karikari, 2017a). Actions taken or not taken by campus leaders in the response phase help dictate the needs of the recovery phase. An inadequate response to a racial incident on campus can push a college or university into a transformation process focused on improving the campus climate for people of color (e.g., Wong(Lau), 2017). Recovery and healing for a campus community can be quite an unwieldy process. The emotional bleeding triggered by a racial incident may appear stabilized by the crisis response, but often leaves an open wound that runs the risk of being reactivated by the smallest puncture in the campus racial dynamics. Although there is no set checklist, we offer suggestions for some potential steps along the pathway forward after a campus has been touched by racial unrest.

Provide space and resources for the campus to process and heal. In the wake of a racial campus crisis, many faculty and staff seek guidance and resources for working with students who have been negatively impacted and helping them navigate the lingering emotional turmoil while also maintaining a focus on their educational responsibilities. Student affairs and other administrative professionals often are on the front lines of tending to the emotional and social support needs of students as they react to and organize their own actions in response to racial incidents. Meanwhile, in the wake of a major campus incident that has sparked racial unrest and spilled into classrooms by way of weighing on students' hearts and minds, faculty may find their course policies governing classroom discussion to be "inauthentic, disconnected, and frankly ludicrous" (Wong(Lau), 2017, p. 34). Faculty who feel compelled to will create processing space by altering course sessions, topics, or materials; volunteering to create space for the larger campus community to process; or even developing new courses that provide students the opportunity for scholarly exploration connected to their recent experience (Conley, 2016; Dache-Gerbino et al., 2018; Huston & DiPietro, 2007; Shaw & Karikari, 2017b); yet, even these faculty may need support and guidance on how to facilitate these conversations (Wong(Lau), 2017). Relying on their cabinet members, presidents should work alongside their provost, chief diversity officer, chief student affairs officer, and campus safety officers to devise plans for a phased recovery process that will provide the physical and emotional space and resources needed to collectively heal.

Establish or intensify a focus on the campus climate. Crises present opportunities to make needed changes to campus structures and processes (Shaw, 2016). While each is unique in its manifestation and impact, all racialized incidents have one thing in common: They highlight negative aspects of the campus racial climate (Harper & Hurtado, 2007). The recovery period is a good time to revisit the latest campus climate results to identify any missed signals in the data that preceded the recent crisis, and to identify issues that will need to be addressed before the campus community can move closer to the desired equilibrium state. If there are no climate data to review, the recovery period is the time to develop a plan to regularly collect and monitor data on the campus racial climate.

Research on presidents' efforts to advance agendas related to increasing diversity and improving campus climate has found that role-modeling was one method that helped presidents demonstrate their personal commitment to the agenda and provide their campus constituents with an example of how to enact the agenda (Kezar, 2007; Kezar & Eckel, 2008). As presidents provide periodic updates to the campus community regarding their progress toward recovery goals, there is renewed opportunity to use their statements and actions to model the types of dialogue and interactions they hope to see increased on campus.

Take lessons from higher education history and institutional peers. Neither protests nor racist or racialized incidents are new to U.S. colleges and universities. Higher education history provides many lessons on how universities have responded to student unrest (e.g., Shaw, 2012; Williams & McGreevy, 2004; Wynkoop, 2002) and specifically to student unrest that results from racist or racialized incidents (e.g., Cole, 2015; Douglas & Shockley, 2017; Farrell & Jones, 1988; Trachtenberg, forthcoming; Wynkoop, 2002). Historical accounts of institutional responses and presidential responses provide valuable insight on the missteps, successes, and failures of past responses to racial unrest and its precipitating events. In addition to the historical accounts, contemporary research and news stories guide readers to recent and ongoing instances of the same. Current or aspiring campus presidents who want to test and build their capacity to respond quickly, authentically, and compassionately in times of racial tension can use these past and present examples as case studies to reflect on their own convictions and values and how that might play out if they were leading the campus at the center of a racial crisis.

Develop a sophisticated response plan for racial incidents. In attempts to eliminate complete reliance on the instincts of campus first responders, written crisis response plans exist to anticipate crisis scenarios, to note the resources required to enact a response should a certain scenario occur, and to guide how first responders coordinate their approach. While "no manual can anticipate every situation" (Paterson, 2006, p. 28) and unfolding crises do not typically leave time to read a detailed plan before taking action, basic plans give campus leaders a mental outline of the policies and procedures to follow. Establishing such a plan for racialized crises forces campus administrators to anticipate the possibility of such events within their campus community and to proactively account for the resources and complete any training required to respond appropriately. As Davis and Harris (2015) note, "the lack of a systematic approach to handling racial incidents is problematic because it results in treating these incidents as isolated and rare rather than pervasive and normal" (p. 65).

Understanding that "crises do not consist of a single, isolated event but instead involve a complex chain of crises that the originating catastrophe sets off" (Mitroff et al., 2006, p. 62) helps in identifying the true role of a written crisis response plan. Though it is good practice to have a written plan, the plan is "less important than the ability to improvise during an actual [crisis] event" (p. 66). The written plan is intended to provide guidance, but the reality of a "complex chain of crises" highlights the importance of decisionmaking, and thus, the preparation to make weighty decisions during a crisis response.

To create a plan for racial incidents, it is important to consider the types of events that could occur and identify the ones most likely to impact one's campus. Both Farrell and Jones (1988) and Garcia and Johnston-Guerrero (2016) categorized racial incidents in their research and listed the general types of racial incidents that impacted college and university campuses. Going a step further, Garcia and Johnston-Guerrero (2016) also offer a classification scheme for racial incidents, classifying microinvalidations and microinsults as *racial microaggressions* and classifying assaults and intimidation as *racialized aggressions*. It is possible that these differing types of incidents may inflict different levels of harm and disruption and thus require different responses and resources. In constructing a plan for racial incidents, the three previous suggestions should all be taken into account.

IT'S ABOUT CRISIS MANAGEMENT

This chapter explored challenges that college and university presidents face in preparing to effectively manage crises, and offered suggestions for effectively responding to racial unrest on campus. We maintain that presidents need to ensure proactive monitoring of their campus racial climate and develop their confidence and competence both to eliminate campus policies, environments, and cultures that may incubate racial tensions and to swiftly and authentically respond to racialized incidents. Presidents and their cabinets should routinely conduct tabletop drills in which they use recent events from other institutions to talk through their own response concerns and process. Taking steps to establish systems with the flexibility to respond to unique incidents and prepare themselves to lead in the midst of crisis will help college and university presidents keep their institution on a forward path.

REFERENCES

ACPA-College Students Educators International, & NASPA-Student Affairs Administrators in Higher Education. (2010). *ACPA and NASPA professional competency areas for student affairs practitioners.* Washington, DC: Authors.

ACPA-College Students Educators International, & NASPA-Student Affairs Administrators in Higher Education. (2015). *Professional competency areas for student affairs educators*. Washington, DC: Authors.

Adams, L. (2017, October 5). Racist incidents plague U. of Michigan, angering students and testing leaders. *The Chronicle of Higher Education*. Retrieved from www.chronicle.com/article/Racist-Incidents-Plague-U-of/241390

Beresford, C., & Harmon, M. (2017, September 25). Students protest last week's racist incidents, block bus routes. *The Michigan Daily*. Retrieved from www.michigandaily.com

Betrand Ricard, R., & Brown II, M. C. (2008). *Ebony towers in higher education: The evolution, mission, and presidency of historically Black colleges and universities*. Sterling, VA: Stylus Publishing.

Bornstein, R. (2003). *Legitimacy in the academic presidency: From entrance to exit*. Lanham, MD: Rowman & Littlefield Publishers.

Bowen, W. G. (2013). *Lessons learned: Reflections of a university president*. Princeton, NJ: Princeton University Press.

Bowers, P. (2018). Racist signs appear at African American Studies department at University of South Carolina. *The Post and Courier*. Retrieved from www.postandcourier.com/news/racist-signs-appear-at-african-american-studies-department-at-university/article_a784a31e-fadd-11e7-bb40-8f4edf3ca4fc.html

Bradley, S. M. (2016). Black activism on campus. *The New York Times*. Retrieved from www.nytimes.com/interactive/2016/02/07/education/edlife/Black-HIstory-Activism-on-Campus-Timeline.html#/#time393_11359

Burton Jr., V. S. (2003). *Structured pathways to the presidency: Becoming a research university president*. Doctoral dissertation, University of Pennsylvania, Pennsylvania.

Cole, E. R. (2015). Using rhetoric to manage campus crisis: An historical study of college presidents' speeches, 1960–1964. *International Journal of Leadership and Change, 3*(1), 11–18.

Cole, E. R., & Harper, S. R. (2016). Race and rhetoric: An analysis of college presidents' statements on campus racial incidents. *Journal of Diversity in Higher Education, 10*(4), 318–333.

Conley, J. (2016, October 7). Responding in the classroom to a racial incident on the campus (essay). *Inside Higher Ed*. Retrieved from https://www.insidehighered.com/views/2016/10/07/responding-classroom-racial-incident-campus-essay

Dache-Gerbino, A., Aguayo, D., Griffin, M., Hairston, S. L., Hamilton, C., Krause, C., Lane-Bonds, D., & Sweeney, H. (2018). Re-imagined post-colonial geographies: Graduate students explore spaces of resistance in the wake of Ferguson. *Research in Education, 0*(0), 1–21. Retrieved from journals.sagepub.com/toc/riea/0/0

Davis, S., & Harris, J. C. (2015). But we didn't mean it like that: A critical race analysis of campus responses to racial incidents. *Journal of Critical Scholarship on Higher Education and Student Affairs, 2*(1), 62–78.

Dennison, G. M. (2001). Small men on campus: Modern university presidents. *Innovative Higher Education, 25*(4), 269–284.

de Vise, D. (2010). Study: Most provosts don't want to be presidents. *The Washington Post.* Retrieved from voices.washingtonpost.com/college-inc/2010/07/study _provosts_dont_wantwant.html

Douglas, T. M. O., & Shockley, K. (2017). Truths, triumphs and testaments of hope when campus and community voices rise. *Journal of Negro Education, 86*(3): 199–203.

Eddy, P., & Roa, M. (2009). Leadership development in higher education programs. *Community College Enterprise, 15*(2), 1–20.

Farrell, W. C., & Jones, C. K. (1988). Recent racial incidents in higher education: A preliminary perspective. *The Urban Review, 20*(3), 211–226.

Farrington, E. L. (2008). Strategies to reach gender parity in college presidents. *Women in Higher Education.* Retrieved from www.whihe.com/printBlog.jsp?id=19251

Farris, D., & McFreight, R. (2014). The professionalization of emergency management in institutions of higher education. *Homeland Security & Emergency Management, 11*(1), 73–94.

Fowler, L. (2017). Another Evergreen professor resigns following racial protests. *Crosscut.* Retrieved from crosscut.com/2017/12/evergreen-state-college-racial -protests-professor-resigns-olympia

Freeman, S., Jr. (2011). *A presidential curriculum: An examination of the relationship between higher education administration programs and preparation towards the university presidency.* Unpublished Doctoral Dissertation, Auburn University, Alabama.

Freeman, S., Jr. (2012, Fall). The future of higher education programs: Implications for policy and practice. *The eJournal of Education Policy,* 1–8. Retrieved from www4.nau.edu/cee/jep/journals.aspx?id=542

Freeman, S., Jr. (2016). Higher education as a vocation: A commentary. *Teachers College Record.* Retrieved from www.tcrecord.org/content.asp?contentid =21655

Freeman, S., Jr., Carr-Chellman, A., & Kitchel, A. (2018). The Negentropic university: A commentary. *Teachers College Record.* Retrieved from www.tcrecord .org/content.asp?contentid=22389

Freeman, S., Jr., Hagedorn, L., Goodchild, L. & Wright, D. (Eds). (2014). *Advancing higher education as a field of study: In quest of doctoral degree guidelines— Commemorating 120 Years of Excellence.* Sterling, VA: Stylus Publishing.

Freeman, S., Jr., & Kochan, F. (2012). The academic pathways to university leadership: Presidents' descriptions of their doctoral education. *International Journal of Doctoral Studies, 7,* 93–124. Retrieved from ijds.org/Volume7/IJDSv7p093 -124Freeman353.pdf

Garcia, G. A., & Johnston-Guerrero, M. P. (2016). Challenging the utility of a racial microaggressions framework through a systematic review of racially biased incidents on campus. *Journal of Critical Scholarship on Higher Education and Student Affairs, 2*(1), 49–66.

Garcia, G. A., Johnston, M. P., Garibay, J. C., Herrera, F. A., & Giraldo, L. G. (2011). When parties become racialized: Deconstructing racially themed parties. *Journal of Student Affairs Research and Practice, 48*(1), 5–21.

Gersick, C. J. G. (1991). Revolutionary change theories: A multilevel exploration of the punctuated equilibrium paradigm. *The Academy of Management Review, 16*(1), 10–36.

Goodall, A. H. (2009). *Socrates in the boardroom: Why research universities should be led by top scholars.* Princeton, NJ, & Oxford, UK: Princeton University Press.

Griffin, W. (2007). Psychological first aid in the aftermath of crisis. In E. L. Zdziarski, N. W. Dunkel, & J. M. Rollo (Eds.), *Campus crisis management: A comprehensive guide to planning, prevention, response, and recovery* (pp. 145–181). San Francisco, CA: Jossey-Bass.

Haley, K., & Jaeger, A. (2012). "I didn't do it the right way": Women's careers as faculty in higher education administration. *Journal of the Professoriate, 6*(2), 1–26.

Harper, S. R., & Hurtado, S. (2007). Nine themes in campus racial climates and implications for institutional transformation. *New Directions for Student Services, 120,* 7–24.

Herdlein, R. J., III. (2004). Survey of chief student affairs officers regarding relevance of graduate preparation of new professionals. *NASPA Journal, 42*(1), 51–71.

Hughey, A. W., & Burke, M. G. (2010). External confirmation of adherence to standards: As applicable to academic programmes as to business and industry. *Industry & Higher Education, 24*(4), 257–262. Retrieved from dx.doi.org/10.5367/000000010792609754

Huston, T. A., & DiPietro, M. (2007). In the eye of the storm: Students perceptions of helpful faculty actions following a collective tragedy. *To Improve the Academy, 25,* 207–224.

Jablonski, M., McClellan, G., & Zdziarski, E. (Eds.). (2008). In search of safer communities: Emerging practices for student affairs in addressing campus violence. *New Directions for Student Services,* 1–38. doi:10.1002/ss.300

Jaques, T. (2007). Issue management and crisis management: An integrated, nonlinear, relational construct. *Public Relations Review, 33*(2), 147–157.

June, A. W. (2007) Why presidents are paid so much more than professors. *Chronicle of Higher Education, 54*(12), A12.

Keller, J. (2010). Typical college CFO: White, male, and not likely to seek a president's job. *Chronicle of Higher Education.* Retrieved from wiredcampus.chronicle.com/article/Typical-College-CFO-White/123697

Kezar, A. J. (2007). Learning from and with students: College presidents creating organizational learning to advance diversity agendas. *NASPA Journal, 44*(3), 578–609.

Kezar, A. J., & Eckel, P. (2008). Advancing diversity agendas on campus: Examining transactional and transformational presidential leadership styles. *International Journal of Leadership in Education, 11*(4), 379–405.

Lawson, C. J. (2007). Crisis communication. In E. L. Zdziarski, N. W. Dunkel, & J. M. Rollo (Eds.), *Campus crisis management: A comprehensive guide to planning, prevention, response, and recovery* (pp. 97–119). San Francisco, CA: Jossey-Bass.

Lum, L. (2008). Forming a pipeline to the presidency. *Diverse Issues in Higher Education, 25*(7).

Mitroff, I. I., Diamond, M. A., & Alpaslan, C. M. (2006, January/February). How prepared are America's college and universities for major crises?: Assessing the state of crisis management. *Change, 38*(1), 60–67.

Molina, D., K., & Shaw Bonds, M. D. (forthcoming). Emerging research on student affairs emergency management: Lessons learned and issues yet unexplored. *Developments.*

Murray, J. P., & Kishur, J. M. (2008). Crisis management in the community college. *Community College Journal of Research and Practice, 32*(7), 480–495.

Paterson, B. G. (2006). Establishing a crisis response team: Moving from institutional to personal response. In K. S. Harper, B. G. Paterson, & E. L. Zdziarski, II (Eds.). *Crisis management: Responding from the heart* (pp. 3–24). Washington, DC: National Association of Student Personnel Administrators.

Pauchant, T. C., & Mitroff, I. I. (1992). *Transforming the crisis-prone organization: Preventing individual, organizational, and environmental tragedies.* San Francisco, CA: Jossey-Bass.

Readiness and Emergency Management for Schools Technical Assistance (REMS TA) Center. (2018). *Comprehensive NIMS Implementation Activities for Schools and IHEs.* Retrieved from rems.ed.gov/docs/NIMS_ComprehensiveGuidance Activities_2009-2010.pdf

Rogo, P. (2017, August 21). Two White women showed up at Howard University wearing "Make America Great Again" Caps. *Essence Magazine.* Retrieved from www.essence.com/news/two-white-women-howard-university-make-america -great-again/

Romanelli, E., & Tushman, M. L. (1994). Organizational transformation as punctuated equilibrium: An empirical test. *Academy of Management Journal, 37*(5), 1141–1166.

Rumbley, L., Altbach, P., Stanfield, D., Shimmy, Y., de Gayardon, A., & Chan, R. (2014). *Higher education: A worldwide inventory of research centers, academic programs, and journals and publications.* Bonn, Germany: Lem-mens Media.

Schmidt, P. (2017). Charlottesville violence sparks new worries about safety during campus protests. *The Chronicle of Higher Education.* Retrieved from www .chronicle.com/article/Charlottesville-Violence/240927

Shaw, M. (2018). Teaching campus crisis management through case studies: Moving between theory and practice. *Journal of Student Affairs Research and Practice.* Retrieved from doi.org/10.1080/19496591.2018.1399894

Shaw, M. D. (2012). The influence of campus protest on student conduct policies: The case of Indiana University Bloomington. *Journal of the Indiana University Student Personnel Association,* 14–26.

Shaw, M. D. (2016). Organizational change as a function of disaster recovery: Lessons from Gulf Coast institutions. *College Student Affairs Journal, 34*(3), 62–75.

Shaw, M. D. (2017). Pathways to institutional equilibrium after a campus disaster. *Journal of Contingencies and Crisis Management, 25*(2), 103–113.

Shaw, M. D., & Karikari, S. N. (2017a). Mattering, healing, and sharing in the process: Working through the trauma of losing Black lives (Part I). *Developments, 15*(1–2). Retrieved from developments.myacpa.org/read-developments/

Shaw, M. D., & Karikari, S. N. (2017b). Mattering, healing, and sharing in the process: Working through the trauma of losing Black lives (Part II). *Developments, 15*(3). Retrieved from developments.myacpa.org/read-developments/

Stripling, J. (2011). The graying presidency. *The Chronicle of Higher Education.* Retrieved from https://www.chronicle.com/article/The-Graying-Presidency /129140

Thacker, R. & Freeman, S., Jr. (2019). Avoiding derailment: symbolic leadership and the university presidency. *International Journal of Leadership in Education*, 1–21. Retrieved from tandfonline.com/doi/abs/10.1080/13603124.2019 .1631388?journalCode=tedl20

Trachtenberg, B. (forthcoming). The 2015 University of Missouri protests and their lessons for higher education policy and administration. *Kentucky Law Journal,* 107.

Trachtenberg, S. J., Kauvar, G. B., & Gee, E. G. (2018). *Leading colleges and universities: Lessons from higher education leaders.* Baltimore, MD: Johns Hopkins University Press.

Trahan, L. L. (2012). *An exploratory study of crisis management and disaster mental health training in master's-level student affairs preparation programs* (Doctoral dissertation). University of Georgia, Athens, GA. Retrieved from getd.libs.uga .edu/pdfs/trahan_lori_l_201212_phd.pdf

Tushman, M. L., Newman, W. H., & Romanelli, E. (1986). Convergence and upheaval: Managing the unsteady pace of organizational evolution. *California Management Review, 29*(1), 29–44.

Weick, K. E. (1988). Enacted sensemaking in crisis situations. *Journal of Management Studies, 25*(4), 305–317.

Wilks, A. G. (2018). USC students vent at school officials after racist flyers posted on campus. *The State.* Retrieved from www.thestate.com/news/local/education /article195474764.html

Williams, P. R., & McGreevey, M. R. (2004). Student activism at Ithaca College: Reflections on management and leadership. *New Directions for Higher Education*, 61–72. doi: 10.1002/he.165

Wong(Lau), K. (2017, Summer/Fall). Diversity work in contentious times: The role of the chief diversity officer. *Liberal Education*, 34–37.

Wright, D. (2007). Progress in the development of higher education as a specialized field of study. In D. Wright & M. Miller (Eds.), *Training higher education policymakers and leaders: A graduate perspective* (pp. 19–34). Charlotte, NC: Information Age Publishing.

Wynkoop, M. A. (2002). *Dissent in the heartland: The sixties at Indiana University*. Bloomington, IN: Indiana University Press.

Zdziarski, E. L. II. (2001). Institutional preparedness to respond to campus crises as perceived by student affair administrators in selected NASPA member institutions. (Doctoral dissertation). Texas A&M University, College Station, TX. Available from ProQuest Dissertations and Theses database. (UMI No. 3033906).

Zdziarski, E. L. II. (2006). Crisis in the context of higher education. In K. S. Harper, B. G. Paterson, & E. L. Zdziarski (Eds.), *Crisis management: Responding from the heart* (pp. 3–24). Washington, DC: National Association of Student Personnel Administrators.

Zdziarski, E. L. II, Rollo, J. M., Dunkel, N. W., & Associates. (2007). *Campus crisis management: A comprehensive guide to planning, prevention, response, and recovery*. San Francisco, CA: Jossey-Bass.

Part IV

VOICES FROM THE FIELD

CHAPTER 8

Presidential Leadership in the Midst of a Storm

An Interview with Andrea Luxton, President of Andrews University, on Her Leadership in Response to the #ItIsTimeAU Uprising on Her Campus

Ty-Ron M. O. Douglas, Dena Lane-Bonds, Sydney Freeman Jr.,
Lucy Douglas, and Brittany Fatoma

What goes through the mind of a university president when Black and Brown students and staff members release a viral YouTube video about racism on their campus? This is what President Andrea Luxton faced in February 2017 as a segment of her students and staff declared #ItIsTimeAU to address racism at Andrews University. In addition to responding to historical injustices at Andrews University, the #ItIsTimeAU movement was ignited when the student and staff leaders became frustrated by the university administration's response to the message of an invited Black History Month campus celebration event speaker. The speaker presented a message grounded in social justice that critiqued the current U.S. presidential administration and racial discrimination in American history. . . . As Chaplain Michael Polite asserts in his interview in the subsequent chapter after President Luxton's interview below, "[m]any White families and donors were offended [by the speaker]. They pushed for the administration to release a formal apology for allowing the speaker to come in an attempt, we [the protestors] believe, to discredit the message. Our administration did yield to those requests."

Notably, Andrews University is a private, doctoral-granting, Protestant, nonprofit institution of higher learning that boasts a diverse student population, particularly in nationality. It is deemed the flagship university of the

Seventh-day Adventist (SDA) denomination, a denomination that also endorses a variety of K–12 and higher education institutions in the United States and globally, such as medical universities (Loma Linda University) and an HBCU (Oakwood University). Prior to serving as president of Andrews University, President Luxton served in senior leadership positions in ethnically and racially diverse universities in three different countries: the United Kingdom, Canada, and the United States. The interview below is a case study for how President Luxton responded to an uprising on her campus. View the #ItIsTimeAU Public Service Announcement video that was released to social media by a group of students and staff for context: www.youtube.com/watch?v=lpskBk0fp4o

> **Dr. Douglas:** If you could, just take us inside of the war room a little bit when you receive word about the video that has been released and the reality that it's going viral. What does a president think or do? What would you say to colleagues who find themselves in a similar leadership situation?
>
> **President Luxton:** Well, let me start by running you through how I thought and what we did. Unfortunately, I was in California at the time [of the release of the video] and so I saw the video from there, within a few hours of its release. My initial reaction was to think this part was not fair, that part was not true, and that bit is only partially right. So, my first reaction was honestly to be a little bit defensive. Then, within the first hour or 2 hours, I went through a lot of changes in my mind and I got to a point that said, "Wait, let's get behind the details here and to what is really happening and get some context." What is fair? What is right? Within those first few hours I also received a lot of calls, a lot of emails, and a lot of advice. Some of the most helpful were from people that said, "I know you'll look at this and it could have been done a different way, but I was at Andrews University in 1960 (say) and my experience was this and so please do not discount this too easily." Those kinds of comments really helped me frame my thinking and my conviction that we had to get to the root of the issue and not deal with the surface. On the surface you could say, for example, that a lot of the things they're demanding are things that were already in our plan. Some of them even already introduced. But that wasn't really the point. The point was the hurt, the feeling that was almost indescribable by the students themselves. Later they would say, "I can't give you any specific example that happened to me, but it did happen to

my father," or it happened to an uncle, or it happened to a friend. And there were even people who said they had never been willing to say anything before. "I've never told anyone about this before but . . ." and then out would come the story.

So with all of these voices, I would say it took us 24 hours of listening from the release of the first video to know how we were going to respond—what we felt was the right thing to do. And soon after that, we were clear about the best way to respond—a combination of my speaking in a general assembly, and the release of a video. Of course, it still took a while to put that together and then to decide how to frame the conversation in the assembly, recognizing how many different opinions and expectations were across the campus. I wanted to embrace as many individuals as I could with the response. Andrews University Official #ItIsTimeAU Response Video: www.youtube.com/watch?v=jr8f0IZJxUc

Dr. Douglas: If you were to give counsel to other presidential leaders in the first 24 hours of a crisis such as this, what would you say they should do?

President Luxton: I would say pause, find a quick, but open "let's talk" type of comment, give yourself time to frame where you want to go, then do a lot of listening, and try to get to the real issues that needs the response.

Dr. Douglas: Okay. You mentioned that maybe some would have wished that the students would have responded in a different way. I know that there were different perspectives on that. Some felt that there was an urgency or need to be explicit and public in the demands because there had been inertia or lack of urgency in the administration's responses in addressing some concerns. Then, and correct me if I'm wrong, there was the immediacy of the apology given in response to feedback or pushback in response to the sermon that was preached by an African American pastor during the campus chapel service. So, there were concerns related to that, and that a person of color offered the apology on behalf of the administration. And there was the frustration that there was the willingness to apologize so quickly in that context, but less urgency in apologizing for all that has taken place on campus historically?

President Luxton: I agree this is the difference between different perceptions and why I think you can't respond in this type of situation with just the facts. So, if you looked at the facts, I actually had offered a public verbal apology for historic and current racism 6 months before that was published in several church and university venues. However, it didn't have the immediacy of communication to the campus perhaps, and while some students were present, there were more alumni present probably than current students. Then there was the person that offered the apology to the chapel presentation. I was out of town and the apology was given by the provost and that was his job—it wasn't because he was a person of color. I would note that only a few months before that, we had a speaker who had been attacking Obama and attacking democratic positions. Once again, because this became a personal attack, we offered an apology then, too. This was in line with the stand we took at the beginning of the year that we need to be able to address critical issues, but we need to be able to do it with civility. And *civility*, the way we defined it, was not calling out names of people or attacking groups or individuals, but keeping to the issues.

So, in the case of the sermon, a range of students (not just from one cultural group) felt personally attacked because they were Republicans and they felt they were being called sexist, racist, xenophobic, etcetera, by the speaker in what they saw as a compulsory chapel service. So, the question that the university faced was, what do you do? We said we expect civility. We have offered an apology in the earlier setting. How could we now say to the people insulted this time that you don't matter? That was the logic of it. But as I mentioned earlier, you can't just look at facts or logic. The student reaction was a response of people feeling devalued. It triggered something that was way deeper and that's why we felt that we needed to respond directly to that situation and not say, but we did this, we did this, we did that. So we decided to just listen to the feelings that this group had and respond to them.

Dr. Douglas: Looking back, is there anything that you would have done differently in your presidency prior to the release of #ItIsTimeAU video?

President Luxton: Well, while it's easy to look back, I think once we had decided that we had a challenge with negative national political rhetoric and the polarization this was causing on campuses, and confirmed our plans to model civil discourse in another way, then we could have been more up front with any speaker that came to campus, and made sure they knew our expectations (especially from the pulpit). Or else we could have not made events

compulsory (or expected) for students. I say that because I think
the students that objected to both the language against Democrats
and then those against Republicans were most upset because they
felt they had no choice but to be there and listen.

Dr. Douglas: Okay. As it relates to the specific response to #ItIsTime,
is there anything that you would have done differently? Are you
pleased with the way things have gone post the climax of the
protest?

President Luxton: I'm pleased that we focused on what we really
felt was the right thing to do. If we had thought it all through
strategically, maybe we would have come to the same conclusion
but that is not what drove us. Also, I think that the response we
had was much better than we had anticipated, even though I don't
think we ever again acted with a specific result in mind. Some
people remain upset with us, but it is a minority.

Dr. Douglas: And by some people, would you say that includes people
on multiple sides of the proverbial fence, or would you say there is
a particular demographic that is more frustrated than the other?

President Luxton: I would say it's a group that feels that we sold out
their history.

Dr. Douglas: Sold out their history by . . . ?

President Luxton: Well some people would say, "I was here in the '60s
and let me tell you what happened to me," and so I would listen
and I conclude that's not okay. And then someone else would say,
"I was here in the '60s and none of this happened—it's just not
true." Right?

Dr. Douglas: And so it's a demographic that is frustrated?

President Luxton: It's a demographic that feels that somehow their
history has now been told in a different way that they do not
think is accurate or true. They feel sold out by us, I think, by our
response, and that's unfortunate.

Dr. Douglas: Right. And I would think that most of those individuals
are White, correct?

President Luxton: I would say that it's folks who just experience
situations totally differently and they just do not understand.
I think that's the way I'll put it: They just do not understand.

Dr. Douglas: I would contend that one of the complexities of the
Seventh-day Adventist Church is race and racism, and this has
implications for SDA higher education contexts.

President Luxton: The connection to the realities of society and the
world is a challenge. It's particularly difficult when you are in a

university setting, as you have a change of students every year. So, every new person that comes to campus comes with their history, their experience, their understanding of the norms of relating and working with diverse groups. You're constantly reflecting the community and the church that you are a part of. You can't escape that to some degree. So you're constantly trying to create models that are better than those in the community around and maybe what the church has been able to achieve. I think one of the most interesting and potentially rewarding parts of this whole journey has been a number of comments that I've had from people that have said the church will not be the same again now because of the #ItIsTime situation. Andrews will not be the same again; the (SDA) church will not be the same again. There may be a long journey ahead, but if this view is right, the path forward can be potentially transforming.

Dr. Douglas: Absolutely!

President Luxton: That's exciting and really rewarding, especially since it was not something that was in our heads.

Dr. Douglas: Sure.

President Luxton: As I said, our heads were very much in, "Okay, what's the right thing here?"

Dr. Douglas: I guess some would argue that this wouldn't have happened if there wasn't a significant rupture or if the mechanisms of this information age weren't used. Do you agree that the mechanism had a role to play in it, especially as it was very public?

President Luxton: Those questions are like double-edged swords. What would we have preferred? I know my own heart and the heart of my team, and I honestly can say that if the students had come in and given us a statement of concerns, even if it was a video, we would have responded positively. . . . But would it have had the impact beyond ourselves? Probably it wouldn't have. However, I don't like the concept of, "Let's all go to social media now and put stuff out there because that's the only way we can get a response." It's sad to me that we made a public apology 6 months before and it did not get any traction. Now we respond to something in the social media in a different medium, maybe being a little bit more in your face, a little bit more explicit, a little bit more directed, and it travels around the world and gets so much response.

One of those dangers are the people who do not understand social media. So, in our case a number of people said, "Wow, that must be a terrible place to be." And parents called their students asking if they were safe and should they take them out of school. And they would say, "Yeah, oh, everything is fine here; what's the problem?" So I think there's a disjuncture between what social media can do to highlight and push things forward and the reality of it being misinterpreted by those who don't understand it.

    . . . [S]pecifically on [responses related to] race, I have had emails from those that liked what we did and those that did not . . . some parents saying they wouldn't think of sending their children here after this and others who said they had never thought of [Andrews as an option for their child] but now were seriously looking at us. So I think you get a mix of reactions. I think [there was] the feeling by some that we just gave into pressure and we just were weak.

Dr. Douglas: How do you attempt to navigate communication and perspectives of vastly different demographics?

President Luxton: Well, I think the whole concept of diversity and inclusion is about the importance of every individual valuing every individual. As we move on with having a vice president now in place, I think it's very important that every group feels that they're listened to. I think if someone feels their voice is heard, even if people more distant may look on and think you make the wrong decision, the chances are most individuals will feel they have a place and that they are part of the community. One of the things that struck me most during our experience was the difficulty that people had that if you speak to one group or one demographic and you express your value of them, it's somehow seen by others as devaluing them. That was a hard one for me to comprehend.

Dr. Douglas: I think part of that is the language component as well. Right? So, when you think of movements like Black Lives Matter, there are some for whom it mobilizes and resonates positively and others who see it as divisive. How do you navigate those conversations? As a leader, how do you approach language like Whiteness, or White supremacy, or systematic oppression . . . terms and realities that may not be considered easy conversations? . . .

President Luxton: I think that goes back to the other issue we had when we had the speaker here: Some students felt very affirmed because of the language that he used and others felt very assaulted by the language he used. So what do you do? I think we have to be able to have difficult conversations, and we have to be able to do it in the context of mutual respect.

Dr. Douglas: As we transition to a close, is there anything else you believe is important to mention?

President Luxton: As I think over the 5 or 6 days between when the student video came out and we responded and I had to lead out in chapel, there's no question in my mind that this was a God moment. I don't know if you saw the chapel part of our response?

Dr. Douglas: I did. I saw the service as well. (See the chapel service and President Luxton's remarks beginning at 5:30: www.youtube.com /watch?v=QKkXUHvEbEY)

President Luxton: The most amazing thing to me . . . was when I stood up in the chapel and everyone started applauding and didn't stop. I hadn't said a word. That was a sign to me that the whole community was saying, "Yes, we're going to find a solution here." I started out with the words "We are going to be Okay," which seems to have been taken up as a kind of a mantra on the campus by some of the students. . . .

Dr. Douglas: Do you think that your gender played a role there as well?

President Luxton: You know, a lot of people have suggested that. Maybe. I do think that there's some leadership approaches that women often do differently from men and maybe that did play a part in it as well. But how all of that came together . . . ? Maybe in 20 years I'll understand.

Dr. Douglas: I'm sure you engaged in a lot of prayer.

President Luxton: Yeah, absolutely.

CONTEXTUAL CONSIDERATIONS FOR REFLECTION FROM THE EDITORS

There isn't a universally accepted manual for how a university president responds during a campus uprising. President Luxton's approach provides an exemplar of how one president responded. Specifically, Luxton drew on her faith, her team, and her belief that listening to the various voices on her campus was key to guiding her university at this critical time. Still, it is clear that navigating the divergent values and views across individual and institutional stakeholders is difficult. For example, President Luxton's suggestion that diversity and inclusion is about "every individual valuing every individual" is well meaning, but certainly not a comprehensive description. There are always larger systematic and systemic realities and histories that must be considered (and challenged) regarding how individuals within and across people groups have been/are included and excluded. Not all individuals are heard with the same amplification, as exacerbated by the combined realities of privilege and pressures like from donors. Questions like "Whose values prevail when every individual does not value or listen to every other individual?" are important considerations. In the faith-based context in which Luxton leads, many on her campus and across the denominational community that her campus serves would assert that biblical principles could (and should) be the standard and stabilizer. Yet, history reveals complexity as to how religion has been mobilized and (mis)used to both oppress and liberate. For example, according to Dr. Meredith Jones-Gray, a historian at Andrews University, the institution had two cross burnings in 1969 and 1974, which remains a part of the institution's collective history. These histories, along with the perpetuation of contemporary wrongs by these same religious institutions (affiliated denominational leaders, for instance), complicate and inhibit healing processes. Similarly, Dr. King's frustration with the inaction and indifference of White evangelical clergy and parishioners during the civil rights movement—as expressed in his "Letter from a Birmingham Jail"—is a relevant historical example. The inaction and indifference of far too many White Christians remains a frustration today for those committed to social justice. Ironically, even on Andrew's campus, there are divergent religious interpretations of the protest and approach of the students and leaders on this parochial campus. The chapter that follows exemplifies this divergence of opinion, by elucidating the beliefs and activism of a university chaplain who walked the same campus as President Luxton and read the same Bible as President Luxton, yet experienced and responded to the campus climate differently.

CHAPTER 9

#ItIsTimeAU

A Conversation with Chaplain Michael A. Polite About Advocacy, America, and Engaging Activism with Andrews University Students

Ty-Ron M. O. Douglas, Ransford Pinto, Noelle W. Arnold,
Evan Willis, and Christine Woods

Michael A. Polite formerly served as the associate chaplain for Faith Development at Andrews University, a Seventh-day Adventist Christian predominantly White institution. Andrews houses a denominational seminary and immerses ecclesiastical theological positions in its colleges' curriculums.

On February 18, 2017, Michael A. Polite organized nine Black student leaders at Andrews to protest what he describes as the unchecked, systemic racism that was being perpetuated by the institution. This protest was facilitated on social media through the #ItIsTimeAU campaign. In under 72 hours, the campaign reached more than 175,000 views on Facebook alone. The campaign lasted 5 days and led to an official apology being released by the president and the creation of a new cabinet-level position for diversity and inclusion.

The following interview provides an insider's perspective on the organization of this uprising, as well as outlines strategies Polite used to successfully lead a group of students in a nonviolent protest.

Dr. Douglas: What was the context of "It Is Time Andrews University"?
Chaplain Polite: Andrews University has a story/history of racial
   discrimination. It was founded as a missionary school primarily,
   so that focus was to take the gospel of Jesus Christ into all
   the world. Sadly, many conservative Christian denominations'
   missions are clouded by a colonizing worldview. They look to

colonize all people and assimilate all people. This is the history that frames Andrews as well. Andrews began to grapple with this history during the time [recent] a guest speaker [pastor] came to campus [to speak for a Black History Month celebration event]. He came on campus with a social justice push and calling attention to our current [U.S.] presidential administration, and calling out the American history of [racial] discrimination. . . . Many White families and donors were offended. They pushed for the administration to release a formal apology for allowing the speaker to come in an attempt, we believe, to discredit the message. Our administration did yield to those requests.

That incident was a catalyst. I began meeting Black students (or others who were troubled about the events) to talk about how they felt. And as I listened to how they felt, it was clear to me it wasn't about the speaker or even the university apologizing. Their sentiments were based on a well-documented history of racism. We have Black alumni who have refused to hang their degrees, to post their degrees at their place of business and employment. . . . This racist history has never been addressed on an institutional level. The students were really articulating their desire to put together a protest that would motivate our administrators to finally speak to this. That's how the #ItIsTime campaign was kicked off, and it outlined action steps that we desired to see our administration take to secure a safe environment for all students, not just some students.

Dr. Douglas: What were your key requests or expectations of administration?

Chaplain Polite: First was that all faculty and staff would have mandated diversity training. The second was that the faculty and staff of our institution would more accurately reflect the diverse population of its students. The third was that courses be generated within the departments that provide educational training outside of the lens of Eurocentric values. And the fourth was that the demonization of Black worship [expression] be disbanded on campus. Because we even have tenured professors who were continuing with that rhetoric in their courses.

Dr. Douglas: What was your strategy after that?

Chaplain Polite: The first was a social media protest. Within 48 hours, our video [https://www.youtube.com/watch?v=lpskBk0fp4o] had over a hundred thousand views. . . .

Secondly, we needed to address that within conservative Christianity there is this belief that any type of protest is ungodly. A goal is to pacify the population with the gospel of Jesus, instead of truly liberate them. We found that prospect very sad. Then we saw this other groundswell happen from individuals who are supporters. We saw this major tug of war, this polarization of our campus and its alumni, and supporters.

I was receiving a plethora of responses from staff and faculty on campus. Some faculty and staff members were praising me for courageously standing with students and others did not agree. My wife and I held periodic meetings with students of color throughout that week, trying to encourage them, trying to coach them as well as prepare them for their official meetings with administration. We did role-playing on how to sit down with administrators and negotiate. We also discussed how to recognize rhetorical traps and how to circumvent and navigate those.

Dr. Douglas: What were some of the rhetorical traps you were referring to?

Chaplain Polite: The first trap is a question-and-answer session based on validating the protest. I wanted the students not to get into a listing of examples because they can't control the narratives . . . [or whether people would be] honest about what happened. . . . We coached also on handling emotions. We talked about the art of speaking from the heart without allowing those emotions to overwhelm you and the conversation.

We coached on respect and how to approach negotiations from a place of strength but also from a place of giving due respect to those on the other side of the table. . . . We coach them on being great listeners and not coming to the table looking just to talk. The final thing that we coached them on was never to engage administrators, faculty, staff, or students with giving a rationale for what they did unless it was a formal venue, a formal meeting, and unless it was more than one of them there. We made a commitment as a team to not release information on our next stages until they were needed.

Dr. Douglas: You mentioned having them pay attention to empty language. Can you give us an example?

Chaplain Polite: One is flattery. You may be in the midst of administrators who continuously speak to flatter you by talking about how great of a person you are, how much they value you, how much they are excited that you are on their campus and a part of the institution, how they are excited to see how you are growing and progressing, and how they can't wait to see what you will achieve in the world. A student might feel validated when in actuality none of the action steps have been met.

Dr. Douglas: Was there literature and language you encouraged them to read in order to engage in productive conversation with administration?

Chaplain Polite: The first thing that we used during the campaign were recorded speeches or sermons from civil rights activists. I found that to be an awesome tool to foster a sense of pride, courage, and fortitude in our students as they heard the eloquence in which our Black leaders have always used to advocate as well as the strength that they used not backing down from institutional forces.

Dr. Douglas: What prepared you to do this work?

Chaplain Polite: It's funny because, ironically, Seventh-day Adventism grabs most of its values from the desire to be countercultural. There were these young folks in the United States looking at the religious terrain of Americans, saying there needs to be something different. You know, we need something different. There needs to be a different type of Christianity. Adventism at its inception was a denomination of activism. We've kind of lost that, as most institutions do. We have lost some of the undergirding of our denomination just by way of time and becoming institutionalized.

I consider the work of protest as prophecy. It is about truth telling at times when it's very uncomfortable and even at times when you don't have the power.

Dr. Douglas: You have mentioned how spirituality informs your protest. But how do you respond to another viewpoint that uses spirituality to question the approach of you and your team?

Chaplain Polite: I think all protest tends to be a battleground of interpretation.

Dr. Douglas: What would you want others to know and remember about the movement?

Chaplain Polite: I would want them to know that privilege is a dangerous thing. And that the goal of all change agents, all humanitarians especially, is to dismantle privilege. Andrews is all about raising up that clarion call once again. [We are saying] that privilege is a dangerous thing if the privileged do not see their number-one responsibility as making sure that privilege does not exist in their environment. For if a privileged individual affords their privilege to everyone in their environment, then it just becomes a corporate blessing.

Dr. Douglas: What was your approach to protecting and caring for your family during this difficult time?

Chaplain Polite: To be honest, my wife probably took care of me more. She was my coach. She was my voice of encouragement. In the aftermath, she now starts to talk about the toll that it took on her, which she was less likely to share during it because she didn't want to discourage me further. But as she saw my encouragement rebound, that was when I was able to be there to listen to her, to listen to the conversation that she had. She was the project manager for the provost's office on campus [during this time]. She work[ed] in the same presidential suite and [was] one of the ones that [was] hearing certain comments. She [was] the one getting the evil look and the harsh words from individuals on our administrative floor on campus. And so, it was my job afterwards to support her, to be a listening ear and then offer encouragement to her as she was to me.

Dr. Douglas: Did you ever feel unsafe?

Chaplain Polite: From a physical standpoint, no. From a job security standpoint, most definitely.

Dr. Douglas: What was the response of the entire student body and the community at large when you put the video out?

Chaplain Polite: It polarized our campus greatly, and I do want to point out the fact that it even polarized our Black community as well. Anyone who is a student of the civil rights movement, or any Black suffrage movement in American history, even dating back to the abolitionist movements of the early 19th century, knows that the Black community has never been able to gain complete solidarity on the topic of protesting. For 2 weeks afterwards, there seemed to be a polarizing paralysis over the campus. There were multiple forums convened for faculty, staff, and students to come and share their thoughts. It now seems as if individuals are focused on moving forward and creating positive change—not only here at Andrews but throughout the world.

Dr. Douglas: What is the process of leading such a movement? What would you share with other leaders who are engaged in this type of leadership?

Chaplain Polite: The first thing that I saw is that as administrators, we must recognize that adults desire validation. I've been asked, why did you decide to participate in such a public way? Why not coach them behind the scenes instead of being a part of the video? These questions have obviously come due to my position as an employee of the institution. And this brings me to my second point: Adults desire authenticity. They're not just looking for validation; they want to be validated by authentic individuals. A leader cannot be a "coach on the sidelines" in issues such as this. I felt that in this scenario they needed a person that was in the trenches with them in order to effectively validate their claims while authentically leading them. That leads me to my third point: Adults need comradery. They are looking for validation, authenticity, and comradery. I could not provide that authentic comradery unless they saw me as a person that was going through the struggles with them. In a way, sacrificial care was paramount to me being able to gain the leadership capital necessary for them to have trust in me. Understanding the importance of validation, authenticity, comradery, and trust.

You know, I was going to stop at trust, but I want to highlight one other thing—*courage*. As many of you know, if you've read Brené Brown's (2012) work, she brings us back to the original definition of *courage* coming from the word *cor*, which is the Latin word for "heart." So, courage wasn't attributed to anyone based on acts of valor. It was attributed to someone who had the courage to express, publicly, their true heart. And I wanted the students to know that I'm not just leading them as a function of my role as chaplain. [But I wanted them to know] I believe in this, I believe in your struggle, and I was willing to stand and let them know you're not alone in this.

All of that compelled me to see this as an opportunity to reclaim true education. *Education*, which comes from the Latin word *educare*, means "to bring to the surface." And I think a lot of our adult learning environments are based upon principles of training—which is the practice of "pouring something into someone" versus "pulling out of someone." I believe true education occurs when you look at an individual and invite them to have their natural potential brought to the surface.

Dr. Douglas: Was there a time during the #ItIsTimeAU movement when you were discouraged?

Chaplain Polite: Yeah. The discouragement comes not really from the voices that you would expect to be against you, but the discouragement comes from the people that you'd thought will be for you. Those who all of a sudden vehemently are opposing you and even taking shots at your character. Trying to discredit you, you know, pretty much trying to slander you based on your desire to advocate for students. So that was the hardest part.

I took hope from other cases such as [the University of] Missouri. It showed me a type of protest that does not require vandalism or even harsh aggression. But these students [Mizzou students] really came forward with an intellectual approach that was very successful at winning the support of others on campus including the football team. I think they saw themselves as standing in solidarity with the movement that is trying to raise awareness, and pretty much let America know we are tired of standing idly by while the system of oppression runs amuck in our communities and the entire country.

Q: How did you ensure that all voices were heard?

Chaplain Polite: I think it helped us that all the students in the video had positive relationships with each other. It takes both genders to transform community. . . .

The title for the campaign actually came from the students. I remember through a real random conversation that was brought up, right after we were finishing the recording of the PSA. And someone turned and said we need a hashtag. And we said, wow! We haven't thought about hashtag. So, I remember the students caucusing and one of them looked at the final line of our PSA and said you have 1 week. They voted and it was a unanimous vote to accept "#ItIsTime" as their official hashtag.

CONTEXTUAL, CONCLUDING THOUGHTS FROM THE INTERVIEWERS

The student protest led by Chaplain Polite is connected to a larger history of student activism in higher education that has resulted in structural change. For instance, in the 1930s, Oakwood Junior College, a historical Black school, led an organized protest that resulted in the appointment of the first Black president, J. L. Moran (Fisher, 2003). Under Moran's leadership, Oakwood changed from a junior college into a senior college (Williams, 1985). Thus, this student protest resulted in more than just a Black president; it also transformed the trajectory of the college to the point that it is now a university. Similarly, through the #ItIsTimeAU student protest, Andrews University was compelled to create a new cabinet position for diversity and inclusion, toward the development of a more equitable educational environment for students of color.

The #ItIsTimeAU campaign reveals that while religion can and has been used by some to oppress, religion and protest can go hand in hand as modeled across generations by civil rights leaders like Dr. King (Smith, 1996), and contemporarily, in the context of the #ItIsTimeAU movement at Andrews University and this interview by Chaplain Polite and the Andrews students.

REFERENCES

Brown, B. (2012). *The power of vulnerability: Teachings on authenticity, connection, and courage.* Boulder, CO: Sounds True.

Fisher, H. (2003). Oakwood college students' quest for social justice before and during the civil rights era. *The Journal of African American History, 88*(2), 110–125.

Smith, C. (Ed.). (1996). *Disruptive religion: The force of faith in social-movement activism.* New York, NY: Routledge.

Williams, D. S. (1985). *She fulfilled the impossible dream: The story of Eva B. Dykes.* Washington, DC: Review and Herald Publishing.

Afterword

The Bad and Ugly of Colleges for Black People

In the United States, images of college life are romanticized with beautiful buildings, the excitement of game days, rolling green grass, student quads, and classrooms filled with students. Concurrently, most college aspirants upon completion envision career opportunities, enhanced life outcomes, financial stability, and lifelong friendships. These attributes represent the "good" of college life, a word that was intentionally omitted from this chapter's title. In contrast, this Afterword is focused on the "bad" and the "ugly"—the experiences that clarify the troubled relationship that Black people continue to have with colleges. Frankly, far too many of the lived experiences of Black people at colleges conjure feelings of acrimony and stories that outline the challenges of fitting in, mistreatment, regret, and many other descriptors that do not align with utopian depictions used to describe college life.

The architects of *Campus Uprisings* are to be applauded for their vision and courage to confront the entrenched "bad" and "ugly" issues that plague Black people in colleges. Douglas, Shockley, and Toldson rightly assembled scholars who have committed research agendas focused on improving the experiences for Black people on college campuses. Equally impressive, the book is designed to be a resource for key players, including parents. The chapters creatively and directly address new and long-term challenges, such as discrimination in hiring and admissions policies, the digital nature of student activism, the contemporary role of HBCUs, racist monuments and buildings, Trump-fueled campus climate, campus protests, and sexual assault.

Without the direct discussions contained in these chapters, the uninformed have the luxury of ignoring the traumatic experiences of Black people in college. These traumatic experiences largely define the relationships that

Blacks in America have with colleges and universities, including HBCUs. Some wonder why Black people and their White counterparts have different relationships with their shared alma maters. Since "Ole Mother" treats them differently, the "stepchildren" elect not to come home for holidays or take care of "Ole Mother" when she needs it. Though it is true that life outcomes improve for Black students who survive college, the experiences are riddled with pain and long-term psychological damage.

Institutions of higher education should receive this book and this Afterword as a call to action: a call to think carefully about how to include the values and interests of those who were once barred from attending, but are now active members. In doing so, a serious examination of the rules by which it is decided who gets to be members, and whether these members will have equal status with existing members, is warranted. In what ways does existing organizational culture ignore or recognize the existence of new members and their differences? What does the climate study say about the experiences and treatment of all members? Lastly, would an analysis of the workforce show that all members have equal access to senior leadership roles, or are opportunities reserved for members with specific characteristics? The thought-provoking chapters in this book lay the groundwork for both institutions and leaders who want to answer the call to action.

—Jerlando F. L. Jackson

About the Contributors

James E. Alford, Jr. is an assistant professor of educational leadership and professional studies at William Paterson University.

Noelle W. Arnold is the associate dean for Diversity, Inclusion, and Community Engagement in the College of Education and Human Ecology and director of the Educational Doctorate Program in Educational Administration at The Ohio State University.

Lisa Bass is an associate professor of educational leadership, policy, and human development at North Carolina State University. The editor of *Black Mask-ulinity: A Framework for Black Masculine Caring*, her work focuses on education reform with an emphasis on equity and ethics, particularly the ethics of caring.

Barbara Boakye is a doctoral candidate at Howard University in the Department of Educational Leadership and Policy Studies.

Travis D. Boyce is an associate professor of Africana studies in the College of Humanities and Social Sciences at the University of Northern Colorado.

Mahauganee Shaw Bonds is an experienced higher education professional, having served as both a student affairs administrator and graduate faculty member.

Winsome C. Brayda is the strategic director for diversity and inclusion and multicultural programs and initiatives at Ohio University.

Lucy Douglas is a mental health expert and doctoral student at the University of Missouri who studies resilience and multigenerational family trauma and health.

Ty-Ron M. O. Douglas is an associate professor in the Department of Educational Leadership and Policy Analysis at the University of Missouri. The author of the award-winning book *Border Crossing Brothas*, Dr. Douglas engages in research that explores the intersections between identity, community space, and the social and cultural foundations of leadership and education—with an emphasis on Black masculinities, Black families, and athletics.

Brittany Fatoma is an early childhood educator and doctoral student at the University of Missouri, studying and working to improve the educational opportunities of marginalized students.

Sydney Freeman Jr. is an associate professor of adult, organizational learning and leadership at the University of Idaho. His research investigates the challenges facing higher education administration programs, specifically higher education as a field of study and the university presidency.

Brian Heilmeier is the associate dean of students for campus activities at Bowling Green State University.

Stephanie Hernandez Rivera is a doctoral student in the Educational Leadership and Policy Analysis Program at the University of Missouri. Her work experience in higher education has focused on creating equitable environments for marginalized student populations.

Jerlando F. L. Jackson is the Vilas Distinguished Professor of Higher Education and the director and chief research scientist of Wisconsin's Equity and Inclusion Laboratory (Wei LAB) at the University of Wisconsin–Madison.

Dena Lane-Bonds is a higher education professional and doctoral candidate at the University of Missouri in the Department of Educational Leadership and Policy Analysis.

Kofi LeNiles is a doctoral candidate in the Department of Educational Leadership and Policy at Howard University.

Andrea Luxton is president of Andrews University in Berrien Springs, Michigan.

Jonathan A. McElderry is the assistant dean of students and the director of the Intercultural Center at Wake Forest University.

Kelsey Morris is an assistant teaching professor in the Department of Learning, Teaching and Curriculum at the University of Missouri. His research interest include the implementation of multi-tiered systems of support in educational settings and universal systems of behavior support.

Ransford Pinto is a doctoral candidate in the educational leadership and policy analysis department at the University of Missouri.

Kmt G. Shockley is an associate professor at Howard University in the School of Education. His research interests include transformative African-centered education, educational transformation, and educational leadership. He conducts workshops; is a keynote speaker; has written numerous publications; and has appeared on various television, radio, and other media outlets, where he is known for his commonsense approach to true education and personal transformation.

Stephanie Shonekan is professor and chair of the W.E.B. Du Bois Department of Afro-American Studies at the University of Massachusetts–Amherst.

Ivory Toldson is the president and CEO of Quality Education for Minorities Network, an organization committed to improving minority students' access to high-quality education. He is a professor in counseling psychology in the School of Education at Howard University, where he also serves as the editor in chief for *The Journal of Negro Education*.

Evan Willis is a Seventh-day Adventist (SDA) pastor, a doctoral student in the curriculum and instruction program at the University of North Carolina at Charlotte, and a doctoral fellow in the Urban Education Collaborative.

Christine Woods is a clinical instructor in the Department of Social Work and a doctoral candidate in educational leadership and policy analysis at the University of Missouri.

Index

Academic-activists, 18–20
Academic Council, Howard University,
    22
Activism and protest at HBCUs, 14–35
    academic-activists, 18–20
    administrative issues, 16
    context, 14–15
    education for freedom *vs.* education
        for manual labor, 27–33
    forces preventing/impeding, 33–35
    Jones on, 16–17
    racism *vs.* equalitarianism, 22–23
    significance and result, 35
    student control, 25–27
    student self-determination, 23–25
    student unrest during 1920s and
        1930s, 15–17
    support and inspiration, 18–20
Adams, L., 124–125
African American Policy Forum
    (AAPF), 86
African American Studies Department
    at the University of South
    Carolina, 125
The Afro American, 19, 32
Agricultural and Technical (A&T)
    College, 60
Alexander, Sadie Tanner Mossell, 18
Allen, Aaron, 30
Alpaslan, C. M., 119, 120
Alpha Kappa Alpha, 24
Alpha Phi Alpha, 24
Altbach, P. G., 59, 61, 62
Alt-right movement, xviii
Alumni Bulletins, 26
"Alumni, Students Take Sides as Howard
    University Protest Draws on," 43

American Baptist Home Mission
    Society, 20
American Civil Confederate, 64
American Civil War, 66
American Missionary Association, 20
Anderson, E., 22
Anderson, J., 17, 18, 20, 21
Anderson, N., 81
Andrews-Guillen, C., 88
Andrews University, 152–159
Angen, M. J., 83
Antiwar movement, 61
Apathy, 61–62
Aptheker, H., 15, 19, 20, 24, 34
Armstrong, G., 83
Arnold, N. W., 85
Ashmun Institute (Lincoln University),
    20
Assault criticism approach to CSA,
    90
Association of American Universities,
    80
Association of Artists for Change, 70
Astin, A., xvii
Axsom, D., 85

Backes, B. L., 85, 87
Bad Butter Rebellion, 58
Barnett, R., 68
Barrick, K., 87
Bash, D., 56
Bauman, R., 84
Beadle, A., 69
Beals, Jesse F., 31
Bennett, Howard, 31
*Ben Tillman: Memories of an Agrarian
    Racist* (Cary), 56, 67

Berea College, 79
Beresford, C., 124
Berrett, D., 97
Berzofsky, M., 80
Bethune, Mary McCleod, 18
Betrand Ricard, R., 116
Bever, M., 56
Black academic-activists, 18–20
Black Greek letter organizations, 24
Black History Month, 6, 143, 153
"Black Life: Transdisciplinary
    and Intergenerational
    Conversations," 6
Black Lives Matter Movement, 3, 4, 63
Black magazines and newspapers, 19
Black "Mother" Emmanuel African
    Methodist Episcopal (AME)
    Church, 56
Black Reconstruction in America
    (Du Bois), 18
Black Seventh-day Adventist school, 21
Black Southerners, 20–22
Black studies at University of Missouri,
    3–12
  characteristics, 5
  classes, 4
  courses, 5
  interdisciplinary nature, 5
  Karenga on, 12
  Reid-Merritt on, 12
  Stewart on, 5
  systemic racism, 4
"Black Women in Music," 4
Bland, S., 5, 86
Boggs, Grace Lee, 7
Bornstein, R., 117
Bowen, W. G., 116
Bowers, P., 125
Boyce, T., 56
Boyd, Debra, 71
Boyd, Rekia, 86
Boyz n the Hood (film), 11
Bradley, S. M., 124
Brake, D. L., 84–85
Bread and Butter Rebellion, 58
A Brief Historical Contextualization of
    the Confederate Monument at the
    University of Mississippi, 73

Briggs, C., 84
Brinkley, A., 15
Broadhurst, C. J., 58, 59, 61, 62
Brooks, R., 56
Brown, Brené, 157
Brown, Mike, xviii, 4, 63, 98
Brown, S., 97
Brown II, M. C., 116
Brown University, 39
Brown v. Board of Education, 42
Bruner, J. S., 82
Bryan-Wilson, J., 84
Burke, M.G., 118
Burnett, A., 85, 86
Burns, M., 58
Burton Jr., V. S., 117
Butler, J., 6

Calhoun College, 55
Campbell, J. L., 70
Campus crisis management, 118–133
  focusing on campus climate, 131–132
  lessons from higher education history
      and institutional peers, 132
  preparation and mitigation, 128–129
  recovery, 130–133
  response, 129–130
  sophisticated response plan, 132–133
  space and resources, 131
Campus sexual assault (CSA)
  AAPF page on, 86
  assault criticism approach to, 90
  classifications, 87
  hashtag, 85–87
  overview, 79–80
  pervasiveness, 80–81
  racial frame, 87–89
Campus unrest
  critical race theory (CRT), 100–101
  experiences, 101–111
  student engagement and policies,
      111–114
  University of Missouri (Mizzou,
      98–100
Cantor, D., 80
Carmody, D. C., 85
"Carry That Weight," 81
Carson, A. D., 68, 69, 70

Cartwright, L., 83
Cary, N., 56, 57, 68
Castellanos, J., 88
Chalabi, D., 90
Chappell, D., 101
The Chicago Defender, 19
Christian, A., 5
The Chronicle of Higher Education,
    xviii
Chunnu Brayda, W., 56
CIRP (Cooperative Institutional
    Research Program), 62
Civil rights movement, 5, 60–61
Clark, Dustin, 69
Clemson University, 67–70
Click, M., 9, 10–11
Coffin, C., 43
Cohen, R., 62
Cole, D., 88
Cole, E. R., 124, 126, 128, 129, 132
Collegiate idea, 65–66
Collins, J., 70
Collins, P. H., 70, 79
Columbia University, 81
Comey, James, 39
Concerned Student 1950, 6
Confederate Park, 64
Conley, J., 131
The Crisis (magazine), 18, 19, 33, 34
Crisis management. *See* Campus crisis
    management
Critical race theory (CRT),
    100–101
Cullen, Countee, 19
Cullen, F., 87
Cullors, Patrisse, 4
Custodial deaths of Black women, 5

Dache-Gerbino, A., 131
Davis, Jefferson, 64
Davis, Richard, 70
Davis, S., 86, 124, 129, 132
Delgado, R., 72
Delta Sigma Theta, 24
Dennison, G. M., 117
Department of Black Studies at the
    University of Missouri, 4
De Vise, D., 117

Diamond, J., 56
Diamond, M. A., 119, 120
Dickey, J., 58
DiPietro, M., 131
Doermann, H., 19, 20, 22
Donovan, A. R., 85
Douglas, A., 70
Douglas, T. M. O., 45, 132
Drake University, xvii
Drewry, H., 19, 20, 22
Du Bois, W. E. B., 4, 18–19, 25–27, 34
Dunkel, N. W., 119
Duque, E., 81
Durkee, J. Stanley, 22
Dyson, W., 22

Eagan, K., 62
Early campus activism, 57–58
Eastern Michigan University, 62
Eckel, P., 131
Eddy, P., 118
Education, 157
Education for freedom *vs.* education for
    manual labor, 27–33
Ellsworth, F., 58
Emberton, C., 64, 67, 71
End Rape on Campus, 81
Equalitarianism *vs.* racism, 22–23
Esposito, J., 100
Evans-Winters, V. E., 100
Evergreen State College, 124
Evropa, xviii
Exhaustion, 103–104

Facebook, 8, 39, 69
    #ItIsTimeAU campaign, 152
Farrell, W. C., 132, 133
Farrington, E. L., 117
Farris, D., 121
Fass, P., 16
Feagin, J. R., 86
Fedina, L., 85, 87
Feenstra, A. E., 81
Fellman, M., 79
Fernandes, R., 97
Field, J. B., 69
Fields, James Alex, Jr., 125
Fisher, B., 87

Fisher, H., 27–29, 158
Fisher, M., 46
The Fisk Herald, 25
Fisk News, 33
Fisk University, 21, 25–27, 29, 31, 33
Fleming, J., xvii
Flory, I. P., 29–33
Flory, Ishmael, 29–33
Floyd-Thomas, S. M., 89, 90
Fluker, W. E., 89
Folsom, B., 62
Ford, D. R., 88
Fortune, Michael, 70
Fowler, L., 124
Fox News, 43
Franklin, V. P., 18, 19, 29, 34
Frazier, E. Franklin, 19–20
Freedmen's Aid Society, 20
Freeman, S., Jr., 116–118, 121
Free speech movement (FSM), 61
Fries-Britt, S., xvii
FSM. *See* Free speech movement (FSM)
Fyfe, G., 83

Garcia, G. A., 124, 125, 133
Garibay, J. C., 124
Garner, Eric, 4
Garza, Alicia, 4
Gasman, M., 21, 35
Gee, E. G., 116–117
Geiger, R., 16, 58
Gersick, C. J. G., 127
Giraldo, L. G., 124
González, J., 84
Goodall, A. H., 117
Graham, D., 72
Greek and social club life, 65–66
Griffin, W., 129, 130
Grinberg, E., 81
Guajardo, F., 101
Guajardo, M., 101
Guba, E. G., 83

Habermas, J., 38
Haitian revolution, 4
Haley, Nikki, 56

Hamburg massacre, 66–67
Hamill, A., 82
Hampton Institute, 21, 23
"Hands Up, Don't Shoot" protests, 63
Harmon, M., 124
Harper, S. R., 124, 126, 128, 129, 131
Harris, J. C., 124, 129, 132
Harris, R. M., 64
Harvard "Harassment/Assault Legal Team," 88
Head, Payton, 6
Herdlein III, R. J., 118
Herrera, F. A., 124
Heyer, Heather, 125
Higher education
   presidency/presidents, 116–117
   programs, 117–118
Hip-hop, 3
Hirshfield, L. E., 111
Historically Black colleges and universities (HBCU), 14–35
   foundation/establishment, 20–22
   missionary societies and, 20
Historical stones, 55–57
Hockaday, M., 5
Hofmann, S., 56
Holiday, B., 4
Holmes, J. L., 85, 87
Hopper, Grace Murray, 55
Hopper College, 55
Howard University, 21–23, 27
   Board of Trustees bylaws, 45–46
   HUResist, 39–43, 44, 45, 46, 48–49
   overview, 42–43
   plantation behavior, 22
   racial unrest, 125
   student occupation/protests at, 39–50
Hughey, A.W., 118
Hunger strike, 6, 97, 99, 104
HUResist, 39–43, 44, 45, 46, 48–49
Hurtado, S., xvii, 129, 131
Huston, T. A., 131

Ice Cube, 11
Inside Higher Education, 63
Institute for Colored Youth, 20

Intercollegiate Socialist Society (ISS), 59
Ireland, C., 58
Isolation, 102–103
Ithaca University, 45
#ItIsTimeAU campaign, 152–159
Iverson, S. V., 86

Jablonski, M., 121
Jackson, Shanita, 79
Jackson, Thomas "Stonewall," 64
James, A., 65
Jaques, T., 119
Jaschik, S., 62, 63
Jim Crow, 15, 18, 23, 29, 30–31, 32
Johnson, Charles S., 30
Johnson, James Weldon, 29
Johnston, M. P., 124
Johnston-Guerrero, M. P., 124, 125,
    133
Jones, C. K., 132, 133
Jones, L., 88
Jones, M. D., 16
Jones, T. E., 30–33
Jones-Gray, Meredith, 151
Joseph, T. D., 111
The Journal of Negro History
    (Woodson), 18
Jubilee Singers, 31
June, A. W., 117

Kaepernick, Colin, xviii
Kantrowitz, S., 66, 67
Karenga, M., 5, 12
Karikari, S. N., 130, 131
Katz, J., 89
Kauvar, G. B., 116–117
Keats, P., 84
Keller, J., 117
Kessler, F., 82
Kezar, A. J., 131
Khan-Ibarra, S., 63
Kilpatrick, D. G., 87
Kimball, T., 66
Kishur, J. M., 121
Know Your Title IX, 81
Krause, K. H., 82
Krebs, C., 80, 87
Kress, G., 79

Langton, L., 80
Law, J., 83
Lawson, C. J., 130
Lee, Robert E., 64
Leggett, M. S., 86
Legion of Black Collegians
    Homecoming Court, 98–99
"Letter from a Birmingham Jail"
    (King), 151
Levinson, S., 64, 71
Lincoln, Y. S., 83
Lindquist, C., 80, 87
Littleton, H. L., 85
Locke, A., 18, 23
Loewen, J., 64
Logan, R. W., 22
Logue, J., 70
Lost Cause ideology, 57, 63–74
Lum, L., 117
Luxton, Andrea, 143–151

The Maneater, 7–9
Mangan, K., 97
Martin, S. L., 87
Martin, Trayvon, 4
Martinez, J. M., 64
Mayfield, C., 3, 7, 12
McClellan, G., 121
McFreight, R., 121
McGreevey, M. R., 132
McIntosh, P., 88
McKenzie, F., 25–27, 32, 33
Meloni, B., 58
Meserve Charles Francis, 29
Mexican-American War, 66
Meyer, R. E., 80
Miedema, S. S., 82
Miller, K. E., 85
Mills, C., 64
The Mis-Education of the Negro
    (Woodson), 18
Missionary societies and HBCUs, 20
Missouri Student Association (MSA), 98
Mitroff, I. I., 119, 120, 121, 128, 132
Mizzou. See University of Missouri
    (Mizzou)
Molina, D., K., 116
Monument Avenue, 64

Monuments to the Lost Cause: Women, Art, and the Landscapes of the Southern Memory (Mills), 64
Monzó, L. D., 101
Moore, J., 89
Moran, J. L., 158
Moss, A. A., 22
Mule's Ear, 24
Muñoz, B., 81
Murray, J. P., 121

Narratives and dynamics, 102–111
National Football League (NFL), xviii
National Incident Management System (NIMS), 122
Neff, J., 73
"Negro University, for Negroes, by Negroes," 19–20
Nehls, C. C., 65
Nelson, Alice Dunbar, 18
Newman, W. H., 127
New Negro Movement, 17, 23
Nigger, xvii

Oakwood College, 21, 27–29
Oakwood Junior College, 158
Oakwood University, 144
Obama, Barack, 81
Omega Psi Phi, 24
Oppenheimer, M., 60
Orellana-Damacela, L., 88

Padilla, A., 111
Pastides, Harris, 125
Paterson, B. G., 132
Pauchant, T. C., 119, 121, 128
Peace movements against Vietnam War, 61
Peacock, Joseph Leishan, 29
Pearl Harbor, 59
Perez, C., 69
Peters, Elder George E., 28
Peters, M., 55
Peterson, K., 80
Photography, 82
Plantation behavior, 22
Player, Willa Beatrice, 18
Polite, Michael A., 143, 152–158

Political activism, 58–59
Polkinghorne, D. E., 82
Portillo, N., 88
Predominantly White institutions (PWIs), 38, 65–66, 123
Presidency/presidents, 116–117
    campus crisis management, 118–133
    higher education programs and, 117–118
Purdue University, xviii

Quinney, L., 89

Racialized aggressions, 133
Racial microaggressions, 133
Racial unrest, 123–126. *See also* Campus crisis management
    presidential steps for, 126–133
    University of Missouri (Mizzou, 98–100
Racism *vs.* equalitarianism, 22–23
Rebellions on early campuses, 58
Recovery, campus crisis management, 130–133
Reid-Merritt, P., 12
The Report of the President's Commission on Campus Unrest, 60–61
Reserve Officer Training Corps (ROTC) programs, 59
Response, campus crisis management, 129–130
Rhatigan, D. L., 85
Rice, Tamir, 4
Richardson, J., 23, 24
Riessman, C. K., 89
Roa, M., 118
Roach, R., 56
Rogo, P., 125
Roll, J., 73
Roll, N., 44
Rollo, J. M., 119
Romanelli, E., 127
Romo, V., 49
Roof, Dylann, 56
Rose, G., 83
Rotten Cabbage Rebellion, 58
Rowan, J. M., 88

Rubin, L., 73
Rudolph, F., 16
Ruff, C., 56
Rumbley, L., 117

Salovey, Peter, 55
San Francisco State University, 5
Savage, K., 55
Schäfer, M. T., 82
Schafran, L. H., 87
Schein, E. H., 87
Schlissel, Mark, 124–125
Schmalz, J., 97
Schmidt, P., 125
Schubert, T., 81
Schwartz, M. D., 86
Seltzer, N., 45
Seventh-day Adventism (SDA), 27, 144, 147–148, 152, 155
Sex-based discrimination, 89
Sexual Assault Awareness Month, 81
Sexual violence, pervasiveness of, 80–81
Shaw, M. D., 116, 118, 122, 127, 130, 131, 132
Shaw Bonds, M. D., 116
Shockley, K., 45, 132
Shonekan, S., 8
Shooks-Sa, B., 80
Singleton, John, 11
Sinozich, S., 80
Slattery, P., 73
"Slavery and Freedom," 4
Sliwinski, M., 63
Slowe, Lucy Diggs, 18
Smith, C., 159
Smith, W. A., 88
Socialism, 58–59
Social media, 63–74
Solórzano, D. G., 50, 100
SooHoo, S., 101
The Souls of Black Folk (Du Bois), 4
Southern Illinois University–Edwardsville (SIUE), xvii
Spiegel, J., 38
Stefancic, J., 72
Stewart, J. B., 5, 6–7
Stockton University, xviii

"Strange Fruit," 4
Streator, George, 33
Stripling, J., 97, 117
Stuart, J. E. B., 64
Student Congress Against War, 59–60
Student engagement and policies, 111–114
Student Nonviolent Coordinating Committee (SNCC), 60
Student occupation/protests at Howard University, 39–50
   administration building floors, 47–48
   Board of Trustees bylaws, 45–46
   collective voice, 44–46
   demands, 39–41, 43, 44–45, 48–49
   HUResist, 39–43, 44, 45, 46, 48–49
   LGBTQ+ students, 48
   strategies, 43
   #TakeBackHU campaign, 43
Student self-determination, 23–25
Students for a Democratic Society (SDS), 60
Student unrest during 1920s and 1930s, 15–17
Sturken, M., 83
Suarez-Balcazar, Y., 88
Sulkowicz, Emma, 81
Supiano, B., 97
Survivors Eradicating Rape Culture, 81
Svrluga, S., 45, 81

#TakeBackHU campaign, 43
Talladega College, 21, 23–24
Taxation and invisibility, 106–107
Taylor, J., xvii
Teatime Tiff, 58
Terrell, Mary Church, 18
Thacker, R., 117
Thackham, D., 71
Thelin, J., 16
Thomas, Alesia, 86
Thomason, A., 97
The Tiger, 70
Tillman, Benjamin "Pitchfork," 56, 66–67
Tillman Hall, 56–57, 66–71
Tinto, V., xvii
Title IX, 89

Toma, J. Douglas, 64
Tometi, Opal, 4
Tougaloo College, 60
Townes, E. M., 89
Trachtenberg, B., 129, 132
Trachtenberg, S. J., 116–117
Trahan, L. L., 118, 122–123
Treiman, D. M., 87
Troy, Elder Owen A., 28
Turner, M., 87
Tushman, M. L., 127
Twitty, A., 73

United Church of Christ and Oakwood,
    21
University of California–Berkeley,
    60–61
University of Chicago, 62–63
University of Florida (UFL), 65
University of Hartford, xviii
University of Louisville, xvii–xviii
University of Michigan, xvii, 62, 124–125
University of Mississippi, 62, 65, 68, 73
University of Missouri (Mizzou)
    Black studies at, 3–12
    racially driven protests at, 44–45
    racial unrest, 97, 98–100, 101
    student engagement, policies and
        practices, 113–114
University of North Carolina, 65
University of Virginia, 125
U.S. Copyright Act, 83

Van Leeuwen, T, 79
Verjee, B., 100
Vidu, A., 81
Vietnam War, peace movements against,
    61
Villalpando, O., 50
Visualities, protests and, 79–90
Visual memes, 82

Walker, D., 6
Wallenstein, P., 60
Warner, T. D., 87
Washington, L. M., 85
Watson, V. T., 86
Weick, K. E., 118

Weitz, A. J., 86
"We People Who Are Darker Than
    Blue" (song), 3
West, C., 85
Westfield State University, xvii
White, D., 65
White colleges and universities, 16
    administrators and faculty, 16
White racial frame (WRF), 86
"White Supremacist Groups Are
    Targeting College Campuses Like
    Never Before," xviii
Wilberforce University, 20
Wilkins, D., 56–57
Wilks, A. G., 125
Williams, D. S., 158
Williams, P. R., 132
Willingham, Kamilah, 88
Willsdon, D., 84
Wilson, L. C., 85
Wilson, R. G., 64
Wing, A., 100, 108
Winthrop University, 70–71
Wolfe, Tim, 6, 7, 99, 118
Wollen, P., 83
Wolters, R., 17, 19, 23, 26, 29
Wong, A., 62–63
Wong(Lau), K., 130, 131
Woodson, C. G., 18–19, 20
Woofter, R., 82
Wooten, S. C., 88
Worland, J., 70
World Trade Organization (WTO), 63
World War I, 15, 17, 59
World War II, 17, 59, 65, 72
Wright, D., 116, 117
Wynkoop, M. A., 132

Yosso, T. J., 50
Yount, K. M., 82
YouTube
    #ItIsTimeAU campaign, 143, 144,
        145
    "See the Stripes," 68

Zdziarski, E. L., II, 119, 120, 121, 127
Zimmerman, A., 81
Zimmerman, G., 63